THE FORGOTTEN ONES

By the same author

THE FATED SKY: AN AUTOBIOGRAPHY
ROCKET
THE THIRD SERVICE
BIRDS AND FISHES: THE STORY OF COASTAL COMMAND

The Regiment

The Forgotten Ones

THE STORY OF THE GROUND CREWS

AIR CHIEF MARSHAL

SIR PHILIP JOUBERT
DE LA FERTÉ

K.C.B., C.M.G., D.S.O.

HUTCHINSON OF LONDON

HUTCHINSON & CO. (*Publishers*) LTD
178–202 Great Portland Street, London, W.1

London Melbourne Sydney
Auckland Bombay Toronto
Johannesburg New York

First published 1961

*This book has been set in Fournier type face. It has
been printed in Great Britain by The Anchor Press
Ltd., in Tiptree, Essex, on Antique Wove paper
and bound by Taylor Garnett Evans & Co., Ltd., in
Watford, Herts*

Contents

Illustrations

Preface

For over fifty years I have been associated with private soldiers, airmen, naval ratings and non-commissioned officers of the three services.

I have met characters varying from the excellent to the near criminal. For the latter I have had considerable sympathy. They were the misfits in an environment which they neither understood nor were prepared to tolerate without revolt. In the end, of course, they found the system too powerful for them and either fell into a sullen obedience or found themselves back in Civvy Street with a bad discharge paper. The great mass of the others, once the strangeness of service life wore off, either determined to make a reasonable career or, in their dull moments, chanted the slogan 'Roll on my three!'—the three years of their regular engagement in peace-time.

When war broke out their differences disappeared and others appeared. The toughest defaulters often became the best soldiers, while some of the good boys failed the test of danger. During my long association with these varying types, in peace and war, I have gained some knowledge of them and have formed an affection and admiration for them which I hope adequately to express in the pages of this book.

I have been emboldened to put my hand to this task by the fact that nobody yet has attempted it. There is, to my knowledge, no book yet written that takes as its theme the 'other ranks' of the three services. Ships have been the heroines of many novels, regiments have been glorified collectively and aircrew have been accorded a magnificent publicity. But the ratings that fought in the ships, the private soldiers that carried their regimental colours to success, and, above all, the airmen and airwomen who served the aircraft that helped to crush Germany, have had scant notice accorded to them.

This book has been written in an attempt to correct this grave omission.

P.B.J.

The Forgotten Ones

THIS is the record of the regular soldiers, sailors and airmen who serviced British military aircraft, of the war-time enlistments, both voluntary and conscript, and of the women, who did so much to help in tasks both strange and difficult.

It should be none of my business to write about soldiers and sailors. But in the early days of flying there was no separate air service, and so the airmen were drawn from the Army and Navy.

As I propose to begin my story in these early days I have to write of the soldiers of the balloon and aeroplane battalions, and of the ratings of the Royal Naval Air Service. This is because of their connection with flying, and so I do not feel that I am trespassing on other writers' ground.

The history of British Army Ballooning starts in the middle of the nineteenth century when a School of Ballooning was formed at Chatham and placed in the hands of the Royal Engineers. At the beginning of the twentieth century the employment of man-lifting kites was given them as an additional responsibility. By 1908 airships were added, but the whole organization remained in the hands of the Sappers. It follows then that the Air Battalion, formed in 1911, and its successor, the Royal Flying Corps (Military Wing), in 1912, were largely manned by the R.E.s.

At this time the rates of pay for officers and men of the Sappers were slightly in excess of those for the rest of the Army. Consequently, recruiting could be selective, and so a higher standard of intelligence and education was built up than that which prevailed in other regiments.

I had hoped to become a Sapper myself, but did not show a sufficiency of learning and so had to be satisfied with joining the Royal Regiment of Artillery. This was in July 1907, and then began my acquaintance with the private soldier.

No. 148 Battery Royal Field Artillery was the junior battery of the 49th Brigade stationed at Aldershot. For some inscrutable reason the Record Office had manned it with about 50 per cent of Glasgow and Liverpool Irishmen. The balance came from all over the country and were more or less law-abiding. But our Irishmen were a race apart. On Saturday nights the cells of the guardroom were filled with them, and on Monday mornings they paraded before the Major to take their punishment. The Major was short-tempered and the 'medicine' was drastic. One sportsman, however, got his own back for a few glorious minutes. Standing in front of the table, '6 foot G.S.' covered with a grey army blanket that formed the C.O.'s desk, he was asked if he had anything to say in extenuation of the charge of 'Drunk and disorderly'. Using an extremely bad word he replied, 'If you say so and so and I say so and so then we're quits.' With that he seized the edge of the table and tipped the whole lot, inks red and blue, pens, blotting pad and stationery, into the Major's lap. The little man jerked backwards, upset his chair, snatched at the blanket and dragged everything on top of himself. It was a wonderful moment, and I, disliking the C.O. very cordially, was highly delighted. Poor Gunner Murphy spent the next few months in the 'Glasshouse', where there is no beer and a very restricted diet!

But when on manœuvres, away from the canteen, the same type of man became a most useful soldier. No longer in trouble for minor misbehaviour, he would be reliable, hardworking and conscientious in the care of his horses and equipment.

It was most rare to have any crime either at practice camp or on field exercise. The answer was, of course, that the men had plenty to do and no time left to loaf over a can of beer. One of my best wheel-drivers was a man who would not go into the canteen unless he had the price of a quart in his pocket. It just wasn't worth while. In barracks he was sleepy and idle—too sodden with drink to do his job properly. But get him away from Woolwich, where the battery had moved, and he was a first-class soldier.

It is probable that the very uncomfortable conditions under which the men lived were responsible for a good deal of the drunkenness and misbehaviour. There was no proper heating in the barrack rooms, the washing arrangements were most primitive, with only a cupful of hot water per man, and the bedding was just one degree better than that provided in the civil prisons. Understandably, bodily hygiene was not of the best. I heard of one man who kept his boots on for three weeks because it was too much trouble to take them off!

Venereal disease was a curse. A brother subaltern, attending the Herbert Hospital at Woolwich for an injury sustained out hunting, met in a corridor one of the best of our young gunners. 'Hallo, Wade, what are you doing here?' 'Attending for V.D., sir.' 'What have you been doing, you young fool? Sleeping with one of these local girls?' 'Well, sir, I knew she'd give me clap but I didn't think she'd give me syphilis as well.' It was this attitude of indifference to the consequences of promiscuity which struck me very forcibly at the time. Salvarsan was still in the laboratory stage, and no quick and certain cure existed for gonorrhoea. So one took one's chance and hoped for the best.

One most interesting aspect of barrack life at this time was the almost complete freedom from theft. In spite of the fact that there were no adequate facilities for the safeguarding of valuables I do not remember a single case where a theft by a comrade was brought to light. Admitted that the penalties on conviction were very severe, but there was a great sense of comradeship between the long-service men and they kept a sharp eye on any of the younger soldiers whom they suspected of having sticky fingers. In addition, they had a way of applying their own discipline to the anti-social types.

The family background of these men must be taken into account. Their homes were small and overcrowded. A bath once a week with the help of the kitchen copper was a luxury. Otherwise cold water in a tin basin and an all-over wash by sections. Food, except for the 'submerged tenth', was good and plentiful. Wages of £3 a week brought contentment. There was no hire purchase to put a load of debt round a man's neck, the 'electric theatres'—our present cinemas —were only just starting up and Saturday night in the local music-hall was the height of enjoyment. On Sunday mornings a high proportion of the population attended church and chapel, or listened to the Salvation Army bands at the street corners. In the afternoon maybe a ride on the top of a bus, to Kew or the river—'Chalk Farm to Camberwell Green All On A Summer's Day' was a popular song of the time.

But when unemployment came there was no help but the hated Poor Law—or enlistment. The young and the healthy usually chose the latter, and there is no doubt that a fair proportion of the recruits at this date were men who could not find work in civil life. The balance were from families whose sons had always joined some particular regiment, or the adventurers who wanted to see the world and have a fight.

In this short account I have tried to give a picture of the type of men that officers had under their command in the larger part of the Army. In the specialist corps, like the Royal Engineers, there was, as I have already said, a higher standard. It was from this better-educated and perhaps more intelligent body of men that the fitters and riggers of the Air Battalion were drawn.

As an example of the type of man that followed such a career I have drawn upon the experiences of Mr. E. F. Palmer, a retired veteran of the early flying services. In September 1909, after training as a Sapper at the Royal Engineers Training Battalion, Chatham, he was drafted to the Balloon School at Farnborough. Here he was quartered in the Blenheim Barracks, North Camp. Those barracks were normally occupied by the Brigade of Guards, but as they were close to the balloon sheds three of the blocks were allotted to the Balloon School.

A period in these barracks enabled the R.E.s to see and understand something of the Guards discipline. They even came to the point where they could interpret an order such as 'Stove pipes!' This of course meant 'Slope arms' in Guardee language. In the Balloon School balloons of 10,000 to 13,000 cubic feet were employed. In addition there was a section of Cody's man-lifting kites. The balloons would lift one or two men and the kites just one intrepid aviator! The kites were used when there was too much wind for the balloons. The kite section worked by flights of ten kites. By various ingenious devices nine of these were made to fly in a string and so produce a considerable lift in windy weather. To the carrier kite, the biggest of the flight, was attached the observer's basket. The observer took his seat, the guide was clipped to the taut cable and, filling his kite with wind as a yachtsman bears away in full sail, the observer shot up the cable to the required height, sometimes as much as 1500 feet above the ground. These man-lifting kites were in regular use until the advent of the aeroplane and the kite balloon brought their existence to an end.

The first airship with which Palmer was concerned was the 'Baby'. Built at the Royal Aircraft Factory this little ship was powered by a 30 h.p. water-cooled Green engine. Two out-board propellers were chain-driven from this power plant, which also drove the ballonet air pump. 'Baby' could carry two people—a pilot and an engineer—and her top speed was something in the order of 25 m.p.h. Later it was decided to increase her lift, so another section was built into her middle and various other improvements carried out. In this new form she became His Majesty's Airship *Beta*, capable of carrying a pilot, a pupil pilot and an engineer. The two pilots sat in hammock-like seats, but so little room had the engineer that he was forced at all times to stand. As the guard rail only came as high as his knees, any sudden turn or bump put him in immediate danger of death.

One of the earliest of a long series of propeller accidents occurred while *Beta*'s engines were being run up in her shed. A mechanic named Cowdrey noticed that one of the ballast bags was touching the exhaust pipe and beginning to smoulder. He rushed to pull it away and ran straight into one of the revolving propellers. He was very badly hurt, and though he recovered was disfigured for life.

Although airships were now in use, free balloons were employed for training and in carrying out the tests necessary to the granting of an aeronautic licence. A sergeant, a very skilled free balloonist, had a nasty experience.

Starting on a cross-country flight, with a 20 m.p.h. wind at ground level, he soon found that the wind at height was almost gale force. He decided he must land in spite of the danger of being dragged before he could get out of the basket. Nearing the ground, he dropped his grapnel, which proceeded to plough its way through hedges, haystacks and telegraph wires. Suddenly he was almost thrown out of the basket. The grapnel had caught in a farmhouse window! All seemed well except for the damage done, when a terrific gust snapped the cable and away went the balloon. Ahead loomed the Bristol Channel. Even if he got down now, he was going to suffer a long and painful drag along the ground. However, he did not wish to go swimming, so pulled firmly on the valve rope which promptly snapped. As a last resort he climbed up between the netting and the envelope and, reaching as high as he could, slashed a big hole, thus releasing the gas. The drag was as bad as he had foreseen, and only ended when the remains of the balloon caught in a woodland.

On a lighter note: *Beta* once went for a before-breakfast flight, an army captain in charge, and with Palmer as engineer. After some time Palmer got the order to slow the engine and prepared to land.

He looked down and saw that *Beta* was over a lovely park in which stood a big house. On the grass a white arrow pointed in the direction of the wind. At the sound of the engine from the house came a number of men led by a very dignified figure. Turning into wind and dropping the tow-rope *Beta* flew to where the landing party had assembled. The ship was hauled down, the guy-ropes manned and the car caught and held as well as by any service crew. These men must have had a first-class lesson, which they could not have learned in the servants' hall from which they had come. Even the gardener was on hand with ballast bags in a barrow!

After all was made fast the airmen went up to the house. Palmer was taken in charge by the butler—the dignified figure—and given a wash in hot water, something never available in barracks at that time. A footman stood by and handed him a towel, after which he was given a breakfast he has always remembered. When ready the scratch landing party turned out again and with never a hitch *Beta* was airborne and safely on its way home. The entry in *Beta*'s log-book about that flight did not contain a great deal of detail.

A short time before the Air Battalion was transformed into the Military Wing of the Royal Flying Corps a strange Guards officer came into the airship shed and started a general 'look round'. Palmer was working on *Beta* at the time and presently the officer came up to speak to him. He asked a number of questions that showed clearly his lack of technical knowledge. Finally he came to the point—'You know, Corporal, with the knowledge of the Royal Engineers and the discipline of the Guards we will make the new corps the best in the world!' 'You will find this very difficult, sir,' was Palmer's tactless answer. How was he to know that this was Lieutenant Barrington-Kennet, the first adjutant of the R.F.C., who most faithfully and with some success carried out his intention to make the new service a *corps d'élite?*

Flight Lieutenant S. R. Pegg, M.B.E., one of the first boy members of the R.F.C., has told the story of his training at Farnborough. He enlisted in October 1913, and after recruit drills and training the boys were sent to Jersey Brow to learn sailmaking, the only trade open to them. They did fabric work for all types of aircraft and airships. None of them liked the job very much as all wanted to be pilots or engineers. However, at the outbreak of World War I nearly all the trained men were sent to the B.E.F., which gave the boys an opportunity to apply for a different and more interesting trade. Pegg applied for engine fitting and was accepted.

At that time the boys were still in Blenheim Barracks, North Camp, Aldershot, and living accommodation was pretty rough. They lived, slept and ate in one room and meals were carried by two 'orderly men' from the kitchen, about 200 yards away, in open tins and tea buckets. What the food was like on arrival can well be imagined! The floor and tables were bare boards and had to be wet-scrubbed by hand each week, and woe betide anybody who made a mark on either during that week. Beds had no sheets and the boys slept in shirts and long pants in between rather coarse blankets. Pyjamas were considered somewhat sissy, anyway.

The pay was 4s. 8d. per week, of which they actually received 6d. After various mysterious deductions, the remainder was put by for the annual furlough. Pegg went on his first furlough of twenty-eight days with 30s.

There was no organized entertainment within the camp, or in fact any real attempt at organized games, so in leisure time the boys were left to amuse themselves as best they could. In any case the pay(?) would allow of no visits to cinemas or canteen. A lot of spare time was spent in the Garrison swimming baths which were free.

Technical training as known today was almost non-existent. The boys simply moved around from flights to workshops and engine repair shops learning the job whilst working at the job. Who said 'on the job' training was a new thing!

Most afternoons meant drill and school. At school no technical subjects were taught but only those which would qualify for the Army First-Class Certificate of Education.

Pegg told me he could honestly say that once accustomed to the austere and disciplined conditions as compared with home life—it did not take long—the boys never seriously complained, were fit, and really enjoyed their service life.

One amusing incident—the boys used to wear their Field Service caps as far on the side of the head as possible. This did not suit one of the officers, who through baldness wore his at 'top dead centre' and objected to the balancing act, as he called it. He gave a lecture one day on the correct position of wearing the cap. On the next parade this officer attended, all the boys turned out with their caps square upon their heads. The officer took one look and roared, 'All right, for heaven's sake put them back again, and walk alongside them as before.'

A. Turner, a slightly older man than Pegg, enlisted as an airman in February 1913. Like Pegg, he did most of his training 'on the job'. After his recruits drill at Farnborough he was posted to No. 3 Squadron R.F.C., which at that time was still at Lark Hill, Salisbury Plain. His commanding officer was Major Brooke-Popham and it is obvious that he had considerable respect and affection for 'Brookham'. Like Pegg, he had to 'make do and mend'. He learned to splice wire cable the hard way—by picking old splices to pieces. But in spite of the lack of skilled instruction he became proficient at his trade of fitter, as well as being a useful part-time rigger.

So, at first, the R.F.C. was hardly the ideal efficient service that Barrington-Kennet had hoped to build.

On the other hand the Royal Naval Air Service had its pick from the Navy, already a highly technical service. Its creation followed the lines of the normal commissioning of a ship. When the Admiralty decided to order a rigid airship—the unlucky *Mayfly*—from Messrs. Vickers, a commander and a rating were posted to supervise her construction. As other units were formed, the normal naval drafting procedure was followed and so a number of engine-room artificers, accustomed only to steam, suddenly found themselves handling highly temperamental and very explosive petrol engines. Since their basic training was thoroughly sound it was not long before they had mastered the mysteries of their new profession. The officers, nine times out of ten in possession of some cantankerous motor-car, had already learned about petrol engines in the hard way. I am bold enough to say that it was not the petrol engine that provided the big problem for the two flying services, but the contraptions that these engines were asked to push through the air. By 1908 Otto Benz's invention, the four-stroke petrol motor, had became an established and useful propellant. But the science of aerodynamics, in spite of centuries of study, from Icarus to Sir George Cayley, from Hiram Maxim to Lanchester and others, was still a mystery the fringe of which had only been touched. Empiricists like the Wright Brothers had built aerodynes which, under the most favourable circumstances, could be persuaded to leave the ground for a few minutes. But when I joined the R.F.C. in 1912 the pilots were still worried about reversed controls, stalling, spinning and nose-diving.

Judge, then, the problem facing the mechanics who, after a short course at a civilian aircraft factory and with a few printed instructions in hand, had to prepare the aeroplanes for flight. Their only background of experience was in carpentry and in handling fabrics that were used in the construction of balloons, and they had fairly vague ideas about the strength of the metals employed in the wings and fuselages of the machines they were called upon to service. The success they achieved throughout the years was in the nature of a miracle.

2

R.F.C. Personalities

W HO, then, were these men? Of what pattern were they made? They could not have burst forth on an astonished world complete in every attribute required by an air mechanic. Let the files of the Air Battalion tell their story.

But first it is necessary to give a short description of the battalion itself. The War Office established it with a Headquarters and three companies, each of which was to be 270 strong. But at the beginning only about one company strength could be mustered, and the rate of increase was extremely slow. In February 1912, nearly a year after its formation, the battalion possessed one company only, about 280 strong. This unit had two wings, one mounted and one dis-mounted. A battalion order laid it down that, in addition to maintaining a nominal roll of officers and men, the C.O. of the mounted wing 'would keep a similar list of horses showing marks as well as other details and should note any infirmities of temper or disposition and the general character of each horse'! Were similar details shown against each officer and man? The files do not say. It is clear, however, that more than half of the personnel were horse soldiers either mounted or drivers of the General Service wagons that carried the equipment.

Names of men who were to gain distinction appear on the rolls: Ramsey, Vagg, Goodchild, Ridd, Talbot, McCudden, Webb. They were all direct transfers from the main body of the Corps of Royal Engineers, and as such were skilled tradesmen.

Even the names of the horses are recorded—Cora, Clara, Christine—all in series of the letters of the alphabet, each entitled to four pounds of oats and three armfuls of hay a day! Nevertheless, the problems to be faced by military aviation in war-time were closely studied. Transportation ('in G.S. wagons') of the necessary equipment was regarded as a vital factor. Repair parks should be well forward—

but caution showed itself—not too far forward. 'To train the rank and file as aeroplane drivers without calling upon them to act as pilots is not a complete solution of the problem of reserves.' Here is some obscurity. Apparently an aeroplane could be driven by someone who was not a pilot! Such subtleties were beyond the young men of the day. Either you flew an aeroplane, in which case you were a pilot, or you stayed on the ground and remained a penguin—a flightless bird.

But the minds of the high-ups were groping towards a scheme which, in the end, created a reserve of non-commissioned officer pilots. Some years were to pass, however, before these men were regarded as adequate substitutes for officer aviators.

In spite of these hesitations some of the men made rapid advances to success. Let me take the case of a friend of mine. To me he was the exemplar of the best type of other rank that manned the Air Battalion and then rode to triumph in the R.F.C. and R.A.F.

Alfred Fletcher was born in 1881 and eighteen years later he joined the R.E. as a driver. He worked his way up the promotion ladder and in the spring of 1911 he was promoted to be Company Quarter-Master Sergeant in the Air Battalion. This unit was on a strictly peace-time basis, and so peaceful were its intentions that the Director of Military Aeronautics stated that he must give up all thought of preparing it for war. This in spite of the fact that Germany was already showing her teeth at the port of Agadir, where one of her gunboats, the *Panther*, had behaved most aggressively.

In this somnolent atmosphere Alf showed considerable dash and enthusiasm. In his spare time he learned to fly and qualified as a second-class pilot—an aeroplane driver, in fact. Let us face facts: he was not a good pilot. It is not given to everyone to have the sensitive hands, the sense of anticipation and the ability to judge the best way out of a difficulty that made—and continue to make—the skilled aviator.

So Alf's career was along the lines that had brought him promotion in the equipment branch of the flying service. He had good prospects, however. The Army generally had become interested in military aviation and the files give the dates of the very large number of visits paid by corps and regiments to the Air Battalion.

These same files contain a number of very human details. On 14th November 1911 the Commanding Officer opened a Christmas fund for the entertainment of the married families. Captains subscribed

10*s.* and subalterns 5*s.* Obviously the C.O. was prepared to make up any deficit after the party! The young guests numbered sixteen under five years of age, and eleven over that age. On the nominal role of supporters and parents appear the names of C.Q.M.S. Fletcher, Corporal Vagg, Sergeant Unwin and Corporal Goodchild. To the officers of the early R.F.C. these men were our friends and helpers. Let me add that £15 was collected and at Christmas a good time was had by young and old.

In the autumn of 1909, while the first British rigid airship was being built by Messrs. Vickers at Barrow-in-Furness, a naval officer, Captain Murray Sueter, and a chief petty officer named Rowe were appointed to watch the construction of the ill-fated *Mayfly*. This was the embryo of the R.N.A.S. When the *Mayfly* was destroyed in an accident the interest in naval flying was transferred to Eastchurch in Kent. Here a small body of civilian pilots, aircraft constructors and young naval officers had gathered to continue the development of the naval air service. A number of the mechanics who looked after the few aeroplanes available were civilians. Gradually, as the Board of Admiralty became more interested in naval aviation, these were supplemented by engine-room artificers, seamen, marines and wireless operators. By the beginning of 1912 a sizable force had been built up.

Some time before this the Government had been studying the whole problem of military aviation, sea and land, and had decided to combine the two services. On 1st April 1912 the Royal Flying Corps, Naval and Military Wings, was formed. Alf got his commission in the Military Wing and I met him for the first time at the end of 1912. He was a cock-sparrow of a man, about five feet nine inches tall, fairhaired and with a pair of sparkling blue eyes betokening the energy that lay in him. He was a wonderful friend to the young officer who might be in trouble with his stores accounts or some other problem of military administration. To use a modern expression, Alf could achieve the difficult at once—the impossible took a little longer. Throughout the Kaiser War he was one of the best of our administrative officers. During the period of uneasy peace he helped to build the Royal Air Force. In the Hitler War he was a tower of strength to those who leant on him. He died a few years ago, loved and admired by all who had worked with him. Dear Alf! Hail and farewell.

There were, of course, a thousand others like him, but since I knew him personally it was necessary that I should 'personalize' him.

There are many others to whom later in this book I shall hope to pay tribute.

When the Royal Flying Corps was born the Naval Wing was already distributed in a number of coastal stations, Eastchurch, Grain and Kingsnorth, for example. The Military Wing had its Headquarters at Farnborough, with detachments on Salisbury Plain. On the whole the sailors were well looked after. They were accommodated in billets or in hutted camps. The soldiery, under the austere rule of the War Office, spent a good deal of their service under canvas. Only those at Farnborough, the men of No. 1 (Airship) Company, Air Battalion, saw the inside of brick buildings. On Salisbury Plain the officers were accommodated in a very primitive inn known as the 'Bustard'. The men were under canvas at Lark Hill.

In the first volume of *War in the Air*, the official history of British Military Aviation during the Kaiser War, there is a prelude that covers the early days of flying generally and also the work of the pioneer aviators before war broke out. In this prelude is to be found some interesting comment on the treatment of the other ranks of the Air Battalion. In a memorandum sent by the Commanding Officer to the Chief Engineer Aldershot Command it is suggested that No. 2 (Aeroplane) Company should return to Aldershot from Lark Hill 'in order that the men may live in barracks, do a little drill and be generally smartened up. But as some new machines would need testing during the winter a detachment should be kept on Salisbury Plain and its numbers changed from time to time so as to prevent the discipline of the company becoming too lax.' The men of this detachment, as well as the officers, were housed at the Artillery Camp, Bulford, some miles from the aeroplane sheds. Transport was by horsed wagon—up to the sheds in the morning; back to Bulford for lunch; back again for afternoon work and then back to camp for the night. The amount of useful work carried out must have been almost negligible.

Gradually, permanent accommodation was constructed, but it was well on into 1913 before the Lark Hill detachment, now named No. 3 Squadron, moved to Netheravon, and had a sound roof over its head.

The Central Flying School at Upavon, designed to serve both Naval and Military Wings as a centre of instruction, was better treated.

Here the permanent buildings were ready by June 1912, although the School had opened earlier under canvas.

It is fair to say that in 1912 for one naval rating living under canvas there were twenty soldiers similarly accommodated. Their Lordships of the Admiralty, whether by habit or for reasons of sympathy with the ratings' lot, have generally seen to their comfort with rather more care than the War Office has used when dealing with soldiers.

Hardly had the new Royal Flying Corps begun to settle down when it was disrupted. The Admiralty never really accepted the Government's decision to amalgamate the two air arms and very soon the title 'R.F.C. Naval Wing' disappeared. It was replaced by 'The Royal Naval Air Service' and the separation which had always existed came to be recognized officially. Mr. Haldane, the parent of the original scheme, must have been seriously annoyed. The idea was splendid, but as events were to prove it was six years ahead of its time. Frankly, I was unable to visualize the appearance of, say, Commander Samson, wearing the buttonless, pocketless maternity jacket that was uniform for the Military Wing. Nor, if the boot had been on the other foot, would some of the army officers been very comfortable in a cocked hat and navy full dress. The transition to uniformity of dress—one of the biggest problems of amalgamation—that occurred during 1918 presented no particular difficulties. The maternity jacket had almost disappeared, full dress had for the moment gone by the board, and khaki was worn extensively by the R.N.A.S.

From the point of view of tradition, by 1918 the R.F.C. and R.N.A.S. had been so diluted by direct recruitment from the body of the nation that the 'True Blue' and 'Khaki for Ever' elements were too small to carry much weight.

On its formation the Royal Flying Corps was given a fairly ambitious target to reach. For the Military Wing there was to be an establishment of some 160 officers and over 1000 men. For the Naval Wing no more than fifty officers and some 500 men were to be raised. The Navy's problem was not serious. From the great fleet that existed, based on a two-power standard, it was not difficult to draft the necessary personnel.

But it was quite beyond the power of the Air Battalion, and indeed of the Royal Engineers, to provide a thousand skilled and semi-skilled men. Industry had to be called upon. So an appeal went out for blacksmiths, carpenters and joiners, clerks, coppersmiths, draughts-men, electricians, fitters, harness-makers, instrument repairers, metal turners, painters, pattern-makers, photographers and many other allied trades. Britain in 1912 was very different from what it is today. While there were plenty of carpenters, blacksmiths and fitters, the number of tradesmen that knew anything about petrol motors was strictly limited. There were ship's riggers but none that knew how to rig an aeroplane. Even chauffeurs were in short supply as cars were still almost a rarity on British roads. Electricity was regarded as some-thing of a mystery and wireless telegraphy savoured of black magic.

Somehow the recruits were collected, housed in spare barrack rooms in Aldershot North Camp, and, under the instruction of the Air Battalion mechanics, were knocked into some sort of shape. But, above all, they were disciplined! At the outset the Brigade of Guards took a hand. The first Adjutant, Lieutenant B. H. Barrington-Kennet, Grenadier Guards, was determined that the new service should have the technical skill of the Royal Engineers and the smartness of the 'Brigade'. With the agreement of his Commanding Officer, Captain F. H. Sykes, he arranged for the transfer of a number of Guards drill instructors to the R.F.C. Soon Farnborough Common was echoing to the roars of these redoubtable persons, and pallid recruits wilted under the flow of invective that minutely particularized their ancestry, their upbringing and their present state of uselessness. In the end the R.F.C. became an extremely smart and highly efficient corps, worthy to be on the 'Right of the Line' with their cavalry colleagues.

There is no doubt at all in my mind that the meticulous disciplinary training to which our mechanics were subjected made them more thorough and more reliable in their technical duties.

Names pass in review—Jillings, the first war casualty, shot in the bottom when acting as an observer during the Battle of Mons. Ridd, my flight sergeant, a little slow and rather too gentle. Street, my sergeant-major in No. 1 Reserve Squadron. Now Street, who had come to the R.F.C. from the Coldstream Guards, had a remarkably fine black moustache of which he was very proud. Amongst the sergeants was one Ted Smalley, an excellent fitter and a transfer from the Merchant Navy. He also had a heavy black moustache composed of hair as tough as barbed wire. His razor 'pinged' as he drove it through his day-old beard. One morning Smalley appeared with only two small tufts showing above his mouth—he had apparently committed the army crime of shaving his moustache. Sergeant-Major Street was furious. 'You've shaved your upper lip,' he shouted. 'No, I haven't,' said Smalley. 'I've still got a moustache and I bet you won't walk across it in your bare feet!' Childish, perhaps, but very funny at the time. Street had other troubles. . . . One day early in 1915 I was sitting in my office (made out of an aeroplane case) when outside an uproar started. Through the flimsy door burst Street, white with fury and every hair of his moustache bristling. Propelled in front of him was a civilian mechanic who I had already reason to know was a tiresome type. Street was holding the man's bowler hat which, in accordance with custom, he had snatched from the man's head when presenting him as a defaulter before me.

Rather startled, I asked for an explanation. 'Sir,' said Sergeant-Major Street, 'I gave this man an order and he spat in my face!' Here was a problem! I had no authority over the man, who was an employee of the Aircraft Factory. Street had committed a whole series of offences. He had no right to give the man an order. He had placed him under arrest without having the right to do so. Finally he had assaulted him by removing his hat and had used violence in bringing him before me!

Most fortunately, in the early days of the war civilians were very frightened of the military and did not know that, under the civil law, they still possessed considerable rights. I read the man a lecture on the impropriety of using his spittle as a weapon of contempt, and then, much to Street's fury, already at boiling-point, I dismissed him. Street is one of the men I shall never forget!

Of the less flamboyant types, the Squadron Sergeant-Major of No. 3—Ramsey—and his technical colleague Sergeant-Major Unwin, were two of the old-timers that I remember very well. They were too old to fly on active service, but their heart and soul were in the 'business'. Trustworthy and conscientious, they were part of the solid foundation on which the R.F.C. was built.

In spite of the high quality of its personnel within the R.F.C. itself there were numerous stresses and strains. The Corps was, in fact, a mixed bag of Sappers, Guardsmen and civilians. All had a different outlook on service life and the way to the development of a real *esprit de corps* was not clearly marked.

H. M. Hudson, who lived through this early period of difficulty, remembers what it meant to the individual airman:

'The Royal Flying Corps personnel largely derived from the Royal Engineers (maybe a kite and balloon section) and a number of Guardsmen, no doubt also some civilian technicians. There was little in common between R.E.s and Guards. Not much love or respect one for the other. I did not come directly from the Guards but I had that background. In the Depot it helped O.K. I was regarded benignly, especially by Sergeant-Major "Woof Woof" Brown. If I wasn't very sharp I was both spick and span and accurate. A good end man and a good pace setter, the stately tread of the Guards was (and is) just natural to me.'

After Farnborough, Hudson was posted to No. 6 Squadron and was sent to H.Q. Workshops. At this time R.F.C. squadrons were largely self-supporting and capable of operating in a detached role. It was assumed by the Technical Sergeant-Major—and for no good reason—that Hudson was not only a skilled blacksmith, but a coppersmith and welder as well. Hudson's helper, 'Batchy' Turner, was even less skilled and the pair of them were very soon in trouble of a minor sort. Worse was to follow when Hudson tried to persuade the Sergeant-Major that it was wise to introduce certain commonsense modifications on the copper pipes that fed oil and petrol to the engines. These pipes often came to his hand cracked. Now a cracked oil-pipe is bad medicine but a fractured petrol-pipe can (and did) result in premature cremation. The reason was clear—metal fatigue set up by vibration, and the cure equally obvious—periodical annealing. Hudson said as much to Sergeant-Major Wilkinson, who went clear off the deep end. Relations became worse than ever after that, but Hudson was to be justified. In any case these copper pipes got annealed whenever he had a chance to handle them.

Later the pipes were cut and joined together with rubber hose. That did something towards neutralizing the effect of vibration, but not completely. Trouble arose through the action of the petrol on the rubber. Bits became detached and blocked the jets in the carburettor.

Often Hudson found that infantrymen posted to the R.F.C. as sergeant-majors (disciplinarian) had a hard time of it—they just were not accepted. More so as often they were third air mechanics (substantive) and so junior or only just equal to those they were drilling.

So far as R.E.s were concerned, Hudson was neither flesh, fowl nor red herring, and a similar non-acceptance was met by him in purely Canadian squadrons. He would have done better to hide any reference to Guards.

What annoyed him was that he had little use for the 'Bull' of Guards either, but there it was, the label was well and truly round his neck. It was largely this feeling of being odd man out which caused him to return to Civvy Street in 1919.

No. 11015 Sergeant A. H. Smith served in two wars. At the outbreak of the First World War he was working as a clerk in a London factory, having previously been a wood-worker. In early 1915 he went to Farnborough as a clerk in the Royal Aircraft Factory, later known as the Royal Aircraft Establishment. When the Ordnance Aircraft Stores Department was formed he transferred to that as the pay was slightly more than at the Factory. The establishment of the O.A.S.D. was not more than ten, a Mr. Lang from Woolwich being in charge. The big balloon shed was taken over for storage. Very soon Smith transferred to this as a foreman storekeeper. And then on 27th October 1915 he joined the R.F.C. as a storeman. After some two or three weeks of 'square-bashing' he was sent to No. 1 Southern Aircraft Repair Depot. Here he worked throughout the war, not getting his discharge until August 1919. He considers the reason why he was never posted, though his medical category was A1, was probably due to his knowledge of stores procedures.

His chief recollections concern discipline and long working hours. The discipline—the continual parades, roll-calls and marching—was much resented, especially when N.C.O.s from the Army were brought in to supervise these activities. On one occasion all the senior N.C.O.s of the Depot were ordered to assemble in the cinema to hear a lecture on discipline by an uneducated army officer. 'I divide the subject into two parts,' he said—'The hinterior and the houtside'!

Working hours for the stores staff were seven days a week, till 8 p.m., with perhaps some relaxation on Saturdays and Sundays.

The main function of S.A.R.D. was to take in crashed aircraft, repair them and despatch them overseas. There was a big salvage department to take in the aircraft and dismantle them.

In the early days all pilots going overseas had to collect a pistol and lifebelt from the stores. Smith must have issued hundreds of these. The pistols and indeed the Lewis and Vickers guns which came a bit later were all dismantled, cleaned, assembled and tested by the stores staff. They worked from the instruction books, without expert aid of any kind. The chief 'armourer' was A. C. Conway, in civil life a grocer's assistant. Another was A. C. Browning, a civilian watchmaker. When a Lewis-gun was to be fitted, it was taken out to the aircraft, fitted on the circular gun-ring, and a burst was fired into the ground as a test. Smith recalls the last time this was done, as he was the firer. The C.O. at the time happened to be quite near the aircraft. When the burst was fired he jumped a foot into the air and subsequently gave orders that no further testing was to be done on the airfield.

When the S.E.5a, a biplane fighter, came into service the Lewis-gun had to be fitted to the top wing. Smith remembers the storemen going out to the aircraft and with blow-lamp and soldering-iron making the necessary connections to link up for firing. How they avoided setting fire to the aircraft or the shed packed tight with planes was just a miracle.

Some time in 1916, for the first time he saw girls worked in the stores and in the sheds—especially amongst the sailmakers—doping and sewing up the fabrics. They were the W.A.A.C.s, mobile and immobile. The former were in uniform and the latter were civilians and lived locally.

In the depot was Sergeant 'Johnny' Walker, an engine fitter. He was an untidy boy of about twenty-one, but a real genius with engines. If an engine defied all efforts to make it go, then Johnny was sent for and he alone could spot the trouble. Sometimes a pilot would refuse to take an aircraft up, on the plea that the engine was not functioning properly. Then Johnny would tinker with it and go up with the pilot to demonstrate that the engine was now O.K.

Smith served in the Reserve for four years from July 1924; and then joined again in January 1939 at the invitation of the Air Ministry. He was called up in August of the same year and went to France in September with No. 5 A.S.P. (Air Stores Park) and returned via Cherbourg at the end of May.

He was then posted to No. 16 Maintenance Unit where he was made Warrant Officer, Inventory Holder of all equipment, Security and Fire Officer and was Orderly Officer two or three times a week, as there was only one commissioned officer available. Later on as a result of an illness he was posted to the warmer south, finishing up at Ternhill in 1945.

Smith says he enjoyed every minute of his service in both wars and has no complaints. In his opinion on the whole the Air Force seems to recruit a good type of man and woman, keen to give of their best. His experience was that one got the best out of a man when the barrack-square type of discipline was at a minimum. His own proud boast is that he never once put a man or woman on a charge throughout his service career of some nine or ten years, yet always got willing service and obedience and was never on a charge himself.

Not every airman resented discipline and the drill standards of the Guards. C. R. King was one of those who appreciated what a Guards drill instructor could do for him, not only as a teacher but as a friend:

'When I first joined the recruit depot at Aldershot we had a Lance-Sergeant Stone from the Coldstream Guards as our Drill Instructor. He was exactly the man to take over young men from civilian life. He was tall and smart and his voice held you to instant obedience to his commands. After Parade he would talk to us in an informal way, and make us understand that discipline was a thing to make service life run smoothly. Many of us owed our happiness in the service to "Ginger" Stone's advice and example.'

A. V. Collett, now retired and living at Blackpool, was also one of the R.F.C. entries, as indeed was his brother whose regimental number was 413.

Collett's experience as a recruit at Farnborough followed the usual pattern, but he has surprised me very much with his story about the R.F.C. walking-out dress. I was quite unaware that this type of uniform had been designed or that it had been issued. Collett states that he would like to settle once and for all a question that has created a lot of argument—the existence of this walking-out dress. Apparently it consisted of half-Wellington boots, tight dark-blue overalls down which ran a broad red stripe, a light-blue buttoned-up-to-the-neck tunic with crossed silver cords, and a dark-blue peaked cap with a red band carrying the R.F.C. crest. Collett's brother was one of the few issued with this uniform and there is a photograph in his

son's possession to prove the fact. What a wonderful kit! No cavalry-
man in his full dress could have looked more beautiful in the eyes of
the local ladies.

Only about a dozen sets were issued by the time the Kaiser War
started, and when that happened it was the end of any attempt to make
the airmen look attractive when walking out!

3

The R.N.A.S. and its Personalities

MEMBERS of the Royal Navy may consider it wrong to put the story of the early naval fliers into so late a chapter. The Senior Service should hold its position—established in the pages of British history.

It is true, however, that the 'Brown Jobs'—the Army—were slightly quicker off the mark in matters of aviation and certainly produced a more substantial force. The R.N.A.S., inheritor of the Royal Flying Corps (Naval Wing), reached a total of some 60,000 officers, men and women, by the end of 1918. The R.A.F., successor of the R.F.C. (Military Wing), at the same date numbered 330,000 all ranks.

And so, grateful as I am to the Royal Navy for all its works, I feel the need to balance judgement in this story and that the third chapter is the right place for the R.N.A.S.

As is well known, naval aviation began at Eastchurch, where the Short Brothers had their flying school, and at Barrow-in-Furness where the first naval airship was built and died—prematurely. At first the officers who volunteered to fly at Eastchurch and the civilian instructors and designers were the only personalities. Not until Winston Churchill became First Lord of the Admiralty in 1911, and learned to fly under the care of Lieutenant Jack Seddon, did a trickle and then a stream of naval ratings join this new force that was being created.

One who followed this course was a young man called Teasdale. He entered the Royal Navy as an apprentice engine-room artificer at the age of sixteen in 1906, and transferred from the sea service to the Royal Flying Corps, Naval Wing, in 1913, when he was drafted to H.M. Air Station, Isle of Grain. At that time seaplanes were stationed round the coast at Calshot, Isle of Grain, Felixstowe, Yarmouth and Dundee, at which bases there were also landing grounds for aeroplanes.

Bristol box-kite

Army Airship *Beta*

Cody's unique monoplane

Beta's gondola

Cody's biplane

Sergeant Street and airmen in the early type of 'maternity' jacket

Most of the land aircraft 'lived' at Eastchurch and at the Central Flying School.

The maintenance personnel consisted of engine-room artificers and electricians for the maintenance of the airframes, and seamen, stokers and Marines, who assisted the artisan ratings, and also handled the aircraft. All these ratings were volunteers from the sea service and were, generally speaking, the younger men from the various branches of the Navy.

The engine maintenance ratings also undertook flying duties as air mechanics, and invariably accompanied the pilots when the aircraft were required to operate outside the immediate vicinity of the base. Engine failures occurred frequently! Such failures were usually of a minor nature which could be rectified by the air mechanic, provided a good landing had been made. When preparing for flight duties the mechanic's repair outfit consisted of an adjustable spanner, a pair of pliers, a screwdriver, a roll of adhesive tape, a piece of copper wire and a piece of string, all of which were carried in the jacket pockets! It was surprising what could be done with this simple equipment.

Sometimes Teasdale's duties involved carrying more elaborate utensils. In January 1914 the Admiralty were concerned about the failure of Submarine A7 to surface when exercising off Plymouth, and a question was raised in the House of Commons as to why the submarine had not been located and why aircraft had not been used for the search. As Calshot, the nearest R.N.A.S. station to Plymouth, had no serviceable seaplanes available, instructions were issued for the Isle of Grain to despatch a seaplane immediately, with a relief crew to proceed by train to Plymouth. As the chance of a seaplane being able to accomplish the flight successfully at this time of year was doubtful, a second seaplane was to be dismantled and despatched by train, with the necessary personnel to reassemble it at Plymouth.

Teasdale was instructed to prepare Maurice Farman (70 h.p. Renault engine) No. 73 for flight to Plymouth and to accompany the Commanding Officer, Lieutenant J. W. Seddon, R.N. In addition to his pocket repair kit he had to take an anchor and a coil of rope, and, since the engine required special mineral oil, a gallon tin of oil. As there was no storage accommodation in a Maurice Farman, the anchor and rope were stowed on one side of the pilot's seat and the can of oil on the other. When he had started the engine and clambered to his seat on the petrol tank behind the pilot, Teasdale found he had no

place to put his legs owing to the equipment stowed at the sides of
the pilot's seat. So he sat cross-legged on the petrol tank and held on
to a wing strut for security. This was a most uncomfortable posture,
which could only be relieved by keeping his head as low as possible
and holding on to the wing strut with one hand at a time.

The aircraft duly arrived at Calshot at midday. No difficulty was
experienced in refuelling, but it was so cold that Teasdale had to heat
the oil on the blacksmith's forge to top up the sump. The flight was
resumed as soon as possible in an attempt to get to Plymouth before
dark. This was successfully accomplished, the aircraft landing outside
the breakwater at about 4.30 p.m. (after spending six-and-a-half hours
in the air). Here it was met by a destroyer which had on board the
Admiral of the Port and the relief crew, the relief pilot being Lieutenant F. W. Bowhill, R.N. (later Air Chief Marshal). The relief crew
took over the seaplane while Lieutenant Seddon and Teasdale sought
the comfort of the wardroom in the destroyer.

The A7 was located by surface craft due to oil leakage, but the
whole crew had perished by the time No. 73 had landed.

Lieutenant Seddon was awarded the Britannia Trophy for 1914
for this flight.

Teasdale recalls that in preparation for the Naval Review in July
1914 four new Short seaplanes (160 h.p. Gnome engines) were received
at the Isle of Grain. These large rotary engines had fourteen cylinders,
mounted on a two-throw crankshaft, the cylinders being staggered in
two sets of seven. Difficulty was soon experienced with the rear sets
of cylinders which did not get sufficient cooling air, resulting in the
cylinder-head exhaust valves gumming up. To overcome this defect
streamline funnels were built on top of the engine cowling, and as
the flight was preparing to join the Fleet for the Review, where ships
of each class would be distinguished by an arrangement of white
bands painted on the funnels, the same method of distinction was
adopted by painting one, two, three and four white bands on the seaplane funnels. The four-banded seaplane was the Commanding
Officer's aircraft, which was numbered 122.

The flight of these four seaplanes duly left the Isle of Grain for
Calshot. One carried a wireless operator, and two carried spare pilots.
Teasdale acted as air mechanic for the flight. The weather was perfect
for flying and there was only a slightly choppy sea running in the
Channel.

When off Beachy Head the engine of No. 122 began spluttering and cut out due to a failure in the petrol system. In making an emergency landing she bumped rather badly, breaking the two front engine-bearer struts. This caused the undercarriage to fold up and the propeller to cut through the front of the undercarriage floats. One of the other seaplanes, in landing to ascertain the trouble, broke its starboard engine-bearer strut, so two out of four were in the ditch.

The wireless operator in one of the airborne seaplanes reported the position to a destroyer in harbour and in addition the attention of a coasting vessel steaming up the Channel was attracted. This ship reached the aircraft before being joined by the destroyer. As No. 122 was unseaworthy for towing the coaster undertook the salvage work, and picked the machine up with its derrick, dumping it inboard on the hatch covers. Teasdale was then taken over to the other disabled seaplane and, with the aid of a boiler tube and some spun yarn from the destroyer, mended the damaged undercarriage and sent the aircraft on its way to Calshot.

The coaster then proceeded to Dover, where the 'ship-wrecked' crew was transferred to H.M.S. *Shannon*. The following day a party arrived from Eastchurch with a propeller and new engine-bearer struts, which were fitted while the ship's carpenters repaired the under-carriage floats with tea chests, canvas and tar, and then the flight to Calshot was resumed. There new floats replaced the patched-up ones, so No. 122 flew at the Review after all.

Though the manning of the early R.N.A.S. was carried out successfully by transfers of technical personnel, engineers, carpenters, shipwrights and wireless operators, from the Royal Navy, with a complement of seamen for boat duties connected with the operation of seaplanes, it was not until war became imminent that the Admiralty turned its thoughts towards the recruitment of civilians to swell the ranks. The Crystal Palace—of all places—was selected by Their Lordships as the main training centre for these recruits.

J. H. Connelly, serving today as a civilian instructor at the Halton, Royal Air Force, School of Apprentice Training, gave me a lively description of his experiences at the Crystal Palace.

Connelly had served an apprenticeship in engineering with a firm making laundry machines at Keighley in Yorkshire, and when he reported to the 'Palace' he was already in a fair way towards promotion from 'improver' to expert.

The trade test for engineers on joining the R.N.A.S. was in three parts—practical, oral and interview. The practical test was simply a matter of making a neat job on a piece of steel with files and drills. The oral was designed to discover if the recruit knew anything about internal combustion engines. It did not matter if he knew nothing of this subject provided that he had a basic knowledge of engineering. Then came the interview with a fatherly type of Engineer Commander who really made him talk. The result of these three tests decided the rank in the R.N.A.S. At that time an Air Mechanic Second Class received 2s. per day and Air Mechanic First Class got 4s.

The first day on being kitted out with R.N.A.S. uniform Connelly and some others were sent into the grounds to walk about smartly and get used to their uniforms. A terrible shouting from the terrace above attracted their attention. To Connelly's horror he realized he was the cause of this disturbance. The Commander was purple with rage. Connelly, in his greenness, had actually walked across the 'quarter-deck' on the wrong side and failed to salute the flag. Result—three days IOA, which meant cleaning some of the many windows of the 'Palace'!

The recruits slept in hammocks in the galleries high up in the building and were not allowed into their dormitories until fifteen minutes before lights out. Each night for three nights Connelly found the lashing of his hammock undone and had to lash up again before he could retire. He thought his messmates were playing a joke on him but soon learned it was the naval patrol's method of teaching him to tie his knots correctly.

Connelly was far from being the only one who suffered from hammock trouble. In the second number of the *Bat*, the organ of the R.N.A.S. at Great Yarmouth, there is a moving story of a recruit's struggle to accustom himself to sleeping in this fiendish contrivance. If the name Reggie made for himself in the service does not go down to posterity for anything else, it assuredly will for the admirable manner in which he mastered the intricacies of the hammock. This success was not a walk-over. It took many weary hours to learn how to sling it, how to enter it, and how to descend gracefully from it. Summing up his labours, Reggie expressed the opinion that a man should serve at least seven years' apprenticeship in the art. He had been told that the hammock came from the Caribbean, and he often wondered why the Caribs had not confined themselves to simpler pursuits such as murder and other forms of violence rather than the foisting of the original hanging bed on many generations of unfortunate seamen.

The thousands of civilians who have served in the R.N.A.S. and in Coastal Area in its early days will remember the hammock with mixed feelings. It had its advantages but it was altogether too easy to cut the lashing at one end and dump an unsuspecting comrade on to an ice-cold deck.

Three weeks' intensive drill on the then Crystal Palace football ground soon licked the recruits into shape. Connelly's posting was to H.M.S. *Daedalus*—now known as Cranwell.

The first sod was turned at Cranwell on 28th December 1915, and this notable training centre was a very small affair when, in the spring of 1916, Connelly arrived, complete with kitbag and hammock. It consisted of some twenty huts, four hangars and a mess deck. Water was obtained from an old farm pump, and lighting was by paraffin lamps. The mess deck was later to become the main part of No. 1 College before the present college was thought of.

The engineer ratings were first introduced to the mysteries of the aero engine in a hangar which is now the Church of England church. These 'Gnome' engines of 70 h.p. were the latest power units. Connelly's lot, however, was soon to be changed for camp maintenance —the result of his early training on laundry machines.

The first life to be lost in a flying accident while he was at Cranwell was that of the Chief Flying Instructor. He was flying just under cloud-base when one of his pupils, flying solo, dived out of the cloud on to him.

At this time Lieutenant-Colonel Waterlow, ex-R.E., was posted to Cranwell to be O.C. Lighter-than-Air Section. He was well known for his preaching to landing parties to hang on to landing ropes, even if they were lifted off the ground by the wind. One day, glancing out of his office window, he saw the landing party having difficulty with a S.S. airship. He dashed out to give a hand on the landing ropes when the accident happened. All let go except three, who hung on as the ship soared up, and when their strength was exhausted fell to their death, the Colonel being the last to fall.

One of the most spectacular sights Connelly witnessed was on the south aerodrome. He says:

'Every flying hour was precious, and so aircraft were left standing just as they were after the morning flying, whilst officers and ratings went to lunch, with one rating as guard. Without warning the wind sprang up in a frolic. About sixty machines started to dance, prancing, bowing, hopping, skipping, leap-frogging, staggering, even standing on their heads, whilst all hands rushed out to curb their high spirits. Surprisingly enough, little damage was done.'

Returning to Teasdale's experiences at Eastchurch when he was an engine-room artificer, the early attempts at arming our primitive aircraft make instructive reading. He expresses the opinion that prior to the outbreak of the 1914–18 War the principal object of the R.N.A.S. had been to develop aeroplanes and seaplanes capable of flying in all conditions for reasonable periods. In trying to attain this objective little consideration could be given to the development of these aircraft as instruments of war. They could be used for scouting and spotting under war conditions, as they had been employed in the Balkan War, but design had not reached the stage where they could be considered as combat units.

When war did break out supplies of bombs, steel darts and Lewis machine-guns were received, but how these weapons were to be made use of was a matter of individual taste, requiring a display of ingenuity by the technical personnel.

There was much anxiety as to the possibility of serious damage and loss of life being caused by Zeppelins, for there was little that could be done at first in defence against such possible attacks. As the Isle of Grain was in a geographical position to intercept any raiders attacking London, instructions were issued to the effect that they should be rammed—this being in accordance with naval strategy. However, what appeared to be a more suitable method of attack presented itself. A German aeroplane had been commandeered in this country and this machine was fitted with a ground brake, which consisted of a boom rod hinged to the underside of the fuselage, on the end of which was fashioned an anchor-shaped hook to dig into the ground when operated by the pilot. This hook was replaced by a scythe-shaped blade, forged by the blacksmith, the idea being to skim over the top of the Zeppelin and rip it open. Fortunately neither of these methods of attack was put into action, but they indicate one of the early war problems and how it was intended to deal with it.

In September 1914 Teasdale proceeded in a cattle transport vessel to Scapa Flow, with two seaplanes for the air base established for the protection of the Grand Fleet against submarine attack when leaving and entering the harbour. When the Fleet was at anchor the principal duty of the base was to carry out patrols at dusk and dawn, to see if any hostile submarines were in the vicinity of the harbour. The armament available for attacking any enemy who might be encountered consisted of two sixteen-pound bombs which lay or rolled about on the floor of the cockpit. These it was hoped to drop by hand on any enemy craft. In addition to his technical ground duties Teasdale took part in the dusk patrols, which were the most important and also the most risky. It was clear that in case of a forced landing away from the vicinity of the base no rescue search would be possible after dark owing to the closing of the harbour entrance boom defence, and the necessity for the Fleet to be screened by a total black-out. On one of the evening patrols Teasdale's place as mechanic/observer was taken by an officer pilot who had joined the station, in order that he might become acquainted with the course of the patrol. This flight resulted in the first casualty, for the crew was never seen again. The remains of the wrecked seaplane was picked up in the North Sea some weeks later, when the engine was found to have a broken connecting rod.

During a gale in October all seaplanes and the Bessoneau hangars in which they were housed were wrecked, and the base closed down until more permanent accommodation could be provided.

The make-do-and-mend principles of the mechanics of the R.N.A.S. are well illustrated in the story that follows. After the closing of the Scapa base, Teasdale was posted to Fort George, Cromarty. Here he took over the maintenance of a White (?Wight) seaplane that was fitted with a water-cooled engine.

This seaplane was in service on anti-submarine duty and developed a slight water leak on the underside of the starboard radiator. Owing to the position of the defect, it could not be repaired with the radiator in position, so the seaplane was kept in operation with the water leakage reduced by the application of soap before each flight, until such time as it could be taken out of service. When the opportunity did occur for a permanent repair to be carried out, it was found that in order to be able to remove the radiator the petrol tank had to be removed, in order to remove the petrol tank the engine had to be removed, and in order to remove the engine the top wing had to be removed, so the whole job took about a week, although the actual

repair to the radiator after removal took about ten minutes. This
indicated how the designers of our aircraft had failed to take into
consideration the maintenance requirements!

Teasdale has one more story that seems worth recording. This
episode occurred on board H.M.S. *Ark Royal*—the first aircraft-carrier
of this name—when she was co-operating with the Navy during the
Dardanelles operation.

The first task in preparing the seaplanes for service on arrival
at the war station was to fit the armament to the aircraft. Teasdale
had made up his mind that it was unsound to have the bombs rolling
about in the cockpit and considered that their place should be somewhere outside the fuselage. So he constructed a bomb-rack. This was
made by suspending a length of light angle iron under the fuselage,
the angle iron having six slots to take eyed set-screws, which it was
intended to fit to the bombs. These would then be held in position
on the bomb-rack by a split pin on the end of a length of cable, the
other end of the cable being passed through to the cockpit and fitted
with a handle. A tug on the handle would remove the securing split
pin and release the bomb. The problem was how to fix the eyed set-
screw to the sixteen-pound bombs. Teasdale had no knowledge of
explosives, and no one else appeared to have either, but he knew that
a bomb was filled with T.N.T. and that a detonator was inserted when
it was required for use. He decided to drill a hole in the bomb casing
so that it could be threaded to take the eyed set-screw. Clearing everyone out of the workshop, the bomb was placed under the drilling
machine, and when the drill had penetrated about an eighth of an
inch, white powder (T.N.T.) came up the flutes of the drill. He made
a hasty retreat from the workshop, but nothing happened, and so
discovered that 'unarmed' bombs could be drilled with safety, provided the drill was not allowed to get warm. Thus the problem of
arming the *Ark Royal* seaplanes with bombs was solved.

The Lewis-guns had their cooling barrels removed and were
mounted in position to fire forward through the track of the propeller.
As a number of bullets passed through the propeller, in the interest of
safety only one tray of ammunition could be fired. As a precaution
against splintering adhesive tape was wrapped round the part where
the bullets would pass through. Not surprisingly the propellers were
rendered unserviceable after each tray of ammunition had been fired,
but such expenditure was seldom necessary. Commander Samson's

aeroplanes, based on the island of Tenedos, were usually available to deal with any hostile aircraft and prevent their interference with the seaplanes engaged in spotting for the Fleet.

From the regular R.N. tradesman back to the civilian entry. Mr. Goodman, who had been trained as an engineer, was one of those who joined the R.N.A.S. from civil life. He arrived at Sheerness to undergo his basic training in plain clothes but carrying his naval cap and hammock. His first problem was to learn how to get into his hammock without falling out on the far side.

After a few weeks' training he was fitted out with uniform and posted to Dundee Seaplane Station. There he found a mixed bag of regular naval men and a big batch of 'Hostilities Only' recruits. There was a good deal of friction between the two types of 'airmen'!

Goodman describes the aircraft as a pretty poor lot, as they were landplanes to which had been added floats and so were overloaded. One day a signal was received asking for an anti-submarine patrol. A seaplane took the water and taxied furiously up and down the River Tay. It never became airborne!

On moving to East Fortune he took part in an anti-Zeppelin operation. One of the Avros on the station had been fitted out with a box of Rankin darts for use against enemy airships, but none of the pilots had ever flown at night, and the station possessed no night-flying equipment. So, when a signal was received that a Zepp was approaching, first a brave young man, Sub-Lieutenant Cox, volunteered to carry out his first night flight, and then a makeshift flare-path had to be established with buckets filled with petrol. A man was stationed at each bucket, holding a box of matches. The orders were that as the aircraft approached the landing ground the matches would be struck and the petrol lighted. The business of throwing a lighted match from a safe distance into the petrol was found to present certain difficulties. With the aircraft overhead and looking for 'home' the match-men became desperate and approached nearer and nearer as each match fell short. Finally the flare-path went up with a roar, taking with it a number of eyebrows and quiffs, not to mention quite a lot of skin! The Avro landed and stood on its nose, but Cox was unhurt.

From East Fortune, Goodman was posted to No. 3 Wing R.N.A.S. in France. The airfield at Luxeuil was some distance away from the town and could only be reached by a bridge over a small stream. This bridge was guarded by French sentries and no one was supposed to cross it after 9 p.m. Two hearty drinkers, neither of them speaking French, found themselves the wrong side of the bridge an hour late. After prolonged argument and much misunderstanding the two ratings were allowed to carry on after giving their names. Needless to say, when the complaint came in from the French military authorities it was found that the culprits were called George Robey and Harry Tate!

Moving back to England, E. W. Hancock, now a distinguished engineer living in Coventry, had some interesting experiences as an airship rating.

He joined the R.N.A.S. in 1915 and was drafted to Mullion in Cornwall, which at that time was just a barren piece of land, with one hut for the ratings, of which he was one of the first sixteen.

Here they carried out a certain amount of 'labouring' and helping the contractors who were building the airship sheds (and of course enjoyed the hospitality of the mothers and daughters of the adjacent village of Helston). After a while the first airship arrived in bits and pieces. This was Airship C.9. The Captain was called Struthers and the station commander was Brabazon. The ship had been rushed down to Mullion to take part in the anti-submarine operations in the South-Western approaches. Her first operational flight was on 1st July 1916.

The second ship was C.P.22, which is the one Hancock had the most to do with. By this time he was a leading air mechanic and was responsible for the maintenance of engines, which at that time were V.8 cylinder Sunbeam engines, both forward and aft, with the air scoop behind the forward propeller.

There was considerable trouble with these engines due to oiling up, and sparking plugs had to be changed in the air. It could hardly have been comfortable, standing on a steel tube, hanging on with one hand with the sea a thousand feet below, and operating a spanner on a hot plug. In fact the Sunbeam Arab was a most unpopular engine.

Later a 220 h.p. Renault engine was fitted aft and a 100 h.p. six-cylinder Green engine forward. The air scoop was moved behind the rear propeller.

These changes prevented the buckling of the balloon, due to loss of air if the forward engine stopped (and the Sunbeams frequently did), and made it possible to stop the forward engine with the Renault ticking over very comfortably astern.

The early-morning drill followed a definite pattern. Approximately a hundred ground crew lifted the ship out on to the airfield and the crew of four took up their positions (average age about twenty to twenty-one, except the Coxswain, who was an 'elderly' gentleman of thirty).

On the usual call of 'Hands off, ease up the guides', the ship stood solid to the ground. If the ground crew could just move the ship, that was good enough. The engines were started and the ship was held by forward guide-ropes only, the Bugler signalled the 'G', the forward guides were slipped, and wallowing like a grampus the ship took off for its patrol. If the flight was a long one the ship came down at the end of its patrol having lost a certain amount of buoyancy by expansion and contraction of the envelope in changing temperatures, and there was a risk of damage on landing, particularly in high winds. But in spite of the limitations of these airships they did help to check the submarine menace.

Rear-Admiral Sir Murray Sueter, whom many consider to be the father of the R.N.A.S., a short time before his death sent me some photographs which are reproduced in this book. I feel they illustrate the life and appearance of the ratings that served overseas. As one of the men who was stationed at Otranto in Southern Italy, Hancock has some further experiences to narrate.

After leaving Mullion Airship Station he was posted to No. 6 Wing R.N.A.S. Otranto. At one time Captain Murray Sueter was in command, but the O.C. he best remembers was one who was known as 'Snakey' Oliver. He was a regular R.N. officer who had transferred to the R.N.A.S.

At this station the original task was to spot enemy submarines breaking out of the Adriatic into the Mediterranean to attack our shipping. For this purpose Short seaplanes were used, but had very little, if any, success. It was then decided that the best policy was to attack the U-boats in their bases at Durazzo and Cattaro. To this end a considerable force of landplanes—D.H.4s and D.H.9s—was built up and over a period of months carried out a series of raids, which at least disturbed the slumbers of the resting U-boat crews.

Another of the base activities was the development of the Short seaplanes as torpedo-carriers. There were some Austrian warships in Adriatic harbours, but as they seldom put to sea our aircraft never got a target in the open. It was then planned to put in an attack on Durazzo Harbour. A 1000-pound torpedo was fitted between the floats of the Shorts. In front of the torpedo and holding the floats together was a strut that had to be removed before the torpedo could be launched. The aircraft were towed out into the middle of the Adriatic by naval launches and 'volunteers' (you, you and you!) from the launches swam out to the seaplanes and unbolted the struts. Sadly enough, the weather became so bad that the attack had to be abandoned. A pity after all that effort!

The 'Silent Service' has lived up to its reputation. Though there were R.N.A.S. detachments operating in very many places, particularly in Gallipoli, in Egypt and on the east coast of Africa, few of the ratings have written of their experiences. On shipboard or ashore their work was arduous, their living conditions singularly uncomfortable and few of them ever received any reward for their labours or their endurance. At this late date, in an endeavour to make some amends for the shortage of stories and other material from which this book has suffered, let me quote the words of Rear-Admiral Sueter, who was certainly in a position to speak with authority:

'The very fine work of our pilots . . . could not have been carried out without the skill of the ratings in keeping the aircraft in a highly efficient condition. Their maintenance work could not have been bettered, and Britain should always remember their fine record.'

If the officers appreciated the airmen it is true that the airmen appreciated their officers. In the *Bat* of 1917–18 (the story of Great Yarmouth Air Station) appears this letter to the Editor:

'Sir,

I trust you will be able to find space in your next issue to publish these few words of welcome from the A/Cs of the Huts to our new Captain [Samson].

We have all heard of the great prowess and abilities already proved of Commander Samson and we feel more than honoured that we are to serve under such a capable officer; we look forward with pride to future events on the Air Station, and our Commander can rest assured that every A/C will do his duty with zest and renewed energy. . . .

I humbly sign my own name to express the wishes of my brother A/Cs.

Terence H. Baizley.'

That Samson was a hero to his men is beyond doubt. But even he could not weld together completely the crews of the seaplane-carriers, such as the *Ben my Chree* that he commanded. Captain Wedgwood Benn (now Lord Stansgate), who was an observer in the *Ben*, comments in his book *In the Side Shows* on the relationship between the ratings employed solely on ship's duties and those looking after the aircraft: 'The ship's company was split up between the airmen and the seamen. It is surprising, although we were a naval unit, how distinct, even divisive, was the class-consciousness of these two groups. . . .' Even the wearing of the same uniform and following the same way of life could not wholly overcome this demarcation between two trades. Do not we see the same thing every day in the internal wars of our trade unions? I am forced to wonder therefore if today, when the ship-borne aircraft have gone back to the Navy with their attendant airmen in naval blue, there is this same trade-consciousness that Wedgwood Benn noticed in 1916. It probably does not matter, any more than it did then, but it points to the speciousness of some of the arguments that have been put forward by the Admiralty in past years to support their case for splitting up the R.A.F.

Seaplane-carriers such as the *Ben my Chree*, the *Raven* and *Anne* must have been a sore trial to their crews. Temperatures in the Red Sea in which the ships were operating rise as high as 120 degrees in midsummer. Remember too that these were coal-burning ships, the coal dust penetrating everywhere and clinging to clothing and skins that were wet with perspiration. At night all scuttles were closed and the fug in the lower decks must have been awful! Food was of the most unsuitable type for a hot climate—full of protein—and fresh vegetables were an unobtainable luxury. Refrigeration was in its infancy and air-conditioning unheard of. It must have been a great relief, after a period of desultory bombing of the Turkish forces on the Red Sea coast, when the ships moved north towards Palestine and Syria, where there were some useful targets and a lower temperature.

The active existence of the *Ben my Chree* was brought to an end in Castelorizo Harbour. Though the French were in occupation of the island they were apparently unaware that the Turks had established a heavy battery on the mainland within range of the harbour. Shortly after coming to anchor in assumed security the *Ben* was shelled and set on fire. Wedgwood Benn recounts that 'when the order to "Abandon Ship" was given the motor-boats were lowered and, filled with members of the crew, tripped backwards and forwards to the island. Scores of the crew, however, dived overboard, each man acting according to his temperament. I recollect a very quiet and shy man, who was our head photographer, coming up to me just before the last boat left and asking if I had any objection to his taking a few photographs.'

Though most of the personnel got safely ashore the shelling continued, to be followed later by torrents of rain. Lacking clothes and shelter, the survivors from the *Ben* passed a night of misery. Seamen and airmen were as one in their common misfortune.

Wedgwood Benn paints a lively picture of his appointment by the French Governor to a post in which he was expected to defeat a Turkish landing that seemed imminent. He had made contact with the meagre forces placed under his command by the Governor and had established his coast defence detachment in a whitewashed church. He writes:

'Soon the rain had stopped and the moon came out. The scene was worthy of the eternal beauty of the Mediterranean. I kept vigil all night in the little church and the picture it presented is with me now. The floor was covered with sleeping men in groaning, muttering, heaps; in the stalls were piled rifles, bayonets, and bandoliers; on the pews loaves of bread, tins of bully beef and jam; overhead in the whitewashed vault a little lamp. . . .'

A little lamp! Something to keep their faith alive after the loss of their ship, their military equipment and most of their creature comforts. Rescued by the French the airmen and seamen of *Ben my Chree* survived to fight again, with a heavy score against them to avenge.

Benn tells an amusing story of his batman, Stickell by name. Stickell was not a 'regular'. In fact his views on discipline would have made a regular officer expire in flames. Benn says that Stickell's greatest *bon mot*, when asked by his C.O. to say something in his defence against a disciplinary charge, was, 'Well, what I says is this, there's only a few of us 'ere, let's live in 'armony!'

The evacuation of the last remnants of *Ben my Chree*'s crew from Castelorizo had a dramatic quality. Benn's account is well worth repeating:

'Behind us in the harbour lies the shrivelled corpse, brown and blistered, of our ship. It is with sadness that we turn to march over the hills to our escape. We are loaded ... with certain material evidence that what remained of our ship was incapable of service to the enemy. For example, we had the breech-blocks of the guns. We scramble along in the darkness to a spot where we overlook a small cove. All round us rise steeply the rocks, wainscoted with foam. To reach the landing place we rely upon a hand rope fixed among boulders. A dump is formed but the swell grows and washes over our stores. It seems impossible that fifty men can embark from such a spot. Presently a trawler—*Paris II*—noses her way into the cove. One of our biggest men, a 6 ft. 4 in. Scots farmer, stands on a rock, sometimes waist-deep in water, holding steady the coracle that, two and three at a time, ferries us over to the *Paris*. It took three hours to effect the embarkation.'

Back to France and an amusing comment by Maurice Baring, Trenchard's faithful shadow on tours of inspection.

'We visited a naval squadron. Carpentier [the famous French boxer] was attached to them, and all defaulters were made, as punishment, to box five minutes with him. This punishment combined being a great honour and privilege and hurting very much indeed.' Could this have been Naval 10, O.C. Commander Redpath, a Canadian? It sounds very like him.

One of the flying instructors who did much to help the R.N.A.S. both as a civilian and as a commissioned officer was F. Warren-Merriam. Merriam's interest in flying had started very early in life. In spite of poor eyesight that was to cause him trouble time and again when he appeared before medical boards he became a very fine pilot. Indeed, in his book *First Through the Clouds*, he claims to have initiated blind flying in the naval air service. For some part of the Kaiser War he was training pilots at Chingford, one of the better-known schools, and he gave an outstanding example to the naval airmen of the manner in which periods of bad visibility could be faced and overcome by a courageous pilot.

Merriam started his flying career with the Bristol School at Brooklands, near Weybridge. I was one of the lucky pupils who fell into his hands, and under his skilful tuition I obtained my Aero Club certificate in a hour and fifty minutes' total flying time!

Merriam comments on the mechanics who, at Brooklands and elsewhere, kept the aircraft in the air. He seems to have had some regard for them, but, like all sensible aviators at this time, he was accustomed to check over their work before leaving the ground. To me it is strange that in a book of 160 pages I have been unable to find a reference to any one of these men by name. They must have rubbed shoulders with him from day to day, and yet their devoted service has remained anonymous. In my endeavours to break down this anonymity I have invited many of my old colleagues formerly in the R.N.A.S. to put me in touch with their ground crews. The answer is frequently, 'I cannot remember much about them—they were good chaps but I have lost touch with them.' There have, however, been rare and shining examples where names and credits have been forthcoming, and these have been incorporated in this one chapter. I should have preferred to have written two or three on the subject!

'Colonel' Cody

Cody's funeral

Larkhill Flying Ground, Salisbury Plain

Salisbury Plain 1906

4

'The Beginners'

L EAVING the R.N.A.S. and moving on now from the early days of the R.F.C. at Farnborough and on Salisbury Plain, Flight Lieutenant Oliver Day tells the story of his experiences as an airman in No. 2 Squadron. In 1913 this squadron was at Montrose, in Aberdeenshire, and quartered in some aged military barracks not far from a particularly smelly fish-manure factory. Day mentions in passing that these barracks were primitive even by 1913 standards. I can confirm his view from my own experience at this station.

Flying was conducted at Upper Dysart—a long narrow field fronting on cliffs that fell 200 feet into the sea. Day says that Upper Dysart was only a few minutes' march from Montrose, but my recollection is that it was several miles, mainly uphill. From this airfield a number of flights were carried out that won notice in the technical Press. The longest was that of Captain Charles Longcroft, who, in a specially equipped B.E.2a, flew from Montrose to Portsmouth and back to Farnborough non-stop. He was in the air for over seven hours and his engine never faltered. This was a tribute to the Royal Aircraft Factory that made the engine and to the airmen who serviced it.

Day had done his seven years' apprenticeship as a marine engineer before joining the R.F.C. and was therefore a skilled man. He was put in charge of 'B' Flight workshop lorry. These lorries had been built by Leylands and were equipped with a three-inch treadle lathe, brazing tools, bench and vice and a small auxiliary power plant, designed to provide lighting for repairs done at night. All the small tools were built to British Standards, in spite of the fact that 50 per cent of the aircraft were of French origin and therefore used metric nuts and bolts. It took some of the less well-trained mechanics several days to discover the nature of this particular problem!

No. 2 Squadron flew south to Salisbury Plain for the Review of the R.F.C. that took place in June 1914. Day comments: 'The taxi past was rather like that of a stage army! The leaders disappeared into a fold of the plain, and a few minutes later exactly similar aircraft reappeared at the end of the ground.' I was at this review myself and I cannot confirm Day's statement. But then I was busy taxi-ing my Blériot and did not see the whole picture as did the ground crews. Whether the M.P.s and foreign air attachés attending the Review were suitably impressed is another matter. At the outbreak of war No. 2 Squadron was confined to barracks. Then followed medical examination and kit inspections. At this time airmen were in possession of two sets of uniform, one for work and one for walking out. The latter set was packed in the kitbags and was to follow the squadron. Not unexpectedly the bags got left behind and the kit was used to clothe the new recruits. A slightly ridiculous note was struck when the mobilization maps of Northern France and Belgium arrived in a horse-drawn cart and quite unguarded.

The squadron transport drove across Scotland to Glasgow where it waited four days. One of the lorry-drivers, bending down too quickly, tore the back buttons off his trousers. Having no spare pair he had to enlist the services of a friendly Glasgow girl who took him home, made him bend down and hoist his jacket up, and sewed the buttons back on the spot.

A. V. Collett of the walking-out-uniform story also served in No. 2 Squadron. He told me that when the squadron moved to Montrose in the early spring of 1913 the airmen got a tremendous welcome from everyone. A rather unusual feature of the general celebrations was that the school children were given a holiday so that they could meet the squadron. But what was really needed was an interpreter. The Scots accent and speech was quite beyond most of the Southrons!

The hospitality of the Scots was amazing. They pulled the legs of the airmen about Panmure Barracks in which they were accommodated as it had been used as a lunatic asylum, 'but we all had a wonderful time from the C.O. downwards, ask any of the lads who were at Montrose about Ma Fraser's fish-and-chip shop, the times we turned out to help launch the lifeboat, the night a drunk cut the tow-rope with an open razor because the lifeboat was not launched quick enough, the gloom that descended on us the day when Lieutenant Arthur was killed in a B.E.2a'.

Weather conditions were very bad in the winter at Upper Dysart so the powers that be built an aerodrome just outside Montrose. Airmen still had to mount guard at Dysart for some time, and Collett says he will never forget the night when he was on guard, pitch dark, snowing, swish of canvas, clanking of chains, banging of tie rods. Suddenly a huge figure in an Inverness cape, long white beard covered in snow, with six enormous shaggy dogs, loomed up out of the darkness. 'Blimey,' he thought, 'this is it!' 'I quietly and quickly drew my Webley Uk4 pistol,' he told me, 'I thought I would shoot the dogs first and use the pistol as a club on "Old Nick", as I was certain that's who it was. I challenged him and much to my surprise he answered, "Friend", in a very strong Scots accent.

'After talking for a few minutes he told me he was the Laird of Lunan taking his dogs for a walk. He shook hands with me on leaving and I felt something in my hand, after a few seconds I saw it was 3s. 6d., then he called out, "That is for a bottle of Johnnie Walker to keep yourself warm." '

From Montrose to Netheravon. There Nos. 3 and 4 Squadrons were preparing for war. Their aircraft were a very mixed bag, three sorts of Blériots, the 50 h.p., the 70 h.p. and the 80 h.p., Maurice and Henry Farmans and the 'Bloaters', as the Gnome-engined product of the Royal Aircraft Factory were called. There were also some few of the B.E.2s, good aircraft, that came and went. On the whole the mechanics of the two squadrons had to compete with relatively simple problems. Basically, there were only two types of engine, the Gnome rotary and the Renault air-cooled stationary. The R.A.F. engine was merely a development of the Renault and was no better and no worse. So, with two reasonable and good-tempered commanding officers and a fairly comfortable camp, Netheravon was a happy station. There was overcrowding from time to time as when the famous Concentration Camp was organized. But apart from incursions of this sort the airmen were not over-worked—just hard enough to stop them worrying about the lack of amenities in Netheravon Village— pop. 250! Besides, the threat of war was enough to keep everyone on their toes.

One airman in my flight was called Webb. He was classified as a photographer, so that when I was carrying out some experiments in photo-survey he generally accompanied me. I think he must have been the first man to develop a photographic plate in the air. Kodaks had produced a developing box about as big as *The Oxford Dictionary of Quotations*—9 in. × 7 in. × 2 in.—in which a picture could be developed as in a dark-room. One of these was fitted to the back seat of my machine and Webb was detailed to take a photograph of Salisbury Cathedral and develop and fix the negative before we landed back at Netheravon—about a ten-minutes flight. Webb performed faithfully, but something I had not thought of rather spoiled the result. After a few minutes' flying at 2000 feet in winter the liquid in the developing box became too cold. The ensuing picture was just charcoal and whitewash.

Between the airmen and the villagers of Netheravon there was a certain mild tension. At night, when the two public houses, quite small as befitting the number of civilian inhabitants, were invaded by a large force of thirsty airmen the only villagers to be content were the pub-owners. And even they became a little peeved when the sign of the 'Dog and Gun' was removed and another sign announcing the presence of 'Ye Puppe and Pistole' was found in its place. Childish perhaps—but in keeping! Amesbury, a larger place, was within bicycle reach. But it was also the haunt of artillerymen from Bulford Camp, and the greater numbers told. The lucky airman who possessed a motor-bicycle would adventure as far as Salisbury or Devizes where there was *lebensraum*.

It was at Netheravon that a certain Mr. Grey pulled off a most successful hoax on the Government. The first we knew about Mr. Grey's activities was a warning from R.F.C. H.Q. that all pilots should practise 'dead-stick' landings (i.e. with engine stopped) and that the best mechanics should stand by, firstly to watch over their pilots' engines and secondly to be prepared to observe a scientific phenomenon—to wit the stoppage of an aeroplane engine in the air by destroying its means of ignition from the ground. Mr. Grey was very reticent about his procedure but very forthcoming in demanding £500 before he would carry out a demonstration. The War Office 'bought it', paid up and commissioned Grey to proceed. In due course large packing cases closely sealed, coils of wire and various electrical instruments arrived and were stowed safely in a locked building. Meanwhile the pilots practised madly and soon could be relied upon to do 'deadstick' landings without damaging their undercarriages. Days went by, telegrams flew between Netheravon and R.F.C. H.Q., but there were no signs of Mr. Grey, nor could he be traced. Finally airmen were detailed to open the packing cases in which they found bricks, scrap iron and a child's toy electric motor.

On the occasion of a Royal Review No. 3 Squadron moved up to Farnborough for the 'fly past'. Resting on Laffan's Plain, amongst others in the squadron, was a rigger who played the mandolin. One of the pilots, rather bored by the long wait, complained to the rigger that he should have brought his instrument to help pass the time away. 'Sir,' replied the airman, 'ain't there enough bloody wires on my aeroplane for me to look after without me bringing me mandolin as well?' The period aeroplanes were, indeed, very like bird-cages, and the care of their many wires was one of the riggers' great responsibilities. The rigging diagrams issued by the makers were not always able to answer the problems raised by continuous use and rough housing conditions. The riggers had to employ their common sense and inventiveness and it was quite remarkable how effectively they dealt with these conundrums as they arose. In the two years I spent in the R.F.C. before the Kaiser War I do not remember an accident that was due to faulty rigging. Admitted that twice I bowled out my mechanic who had fitted my elevator wires wrong way round, never once had I to complain about the safety of my aeroplane when it was airborne. Later on, after the war had started, some careless or mischievous persons joined the R.F.C. and gave the pilots anxious moments. But the vast majority of the riggers were competent, conscientious and courageous enough to go flying in the 'crates' that they had erected and made ready for flying.

While No. 1 Squadron grew up at Farnborough, No. 2 at Montrose, No. 3 and 4 at Netheravon, Gosport was the nest in which No. 5 was feathered. Early in the nineteenth century the great naval base of Portsmouth had been embattled with forts at sea level and on the downs behind the harbour. The garrisons of these forts had fluctuated in numbers and efficiency, but at the time when No. 5 Squadron R.F.C. was due to form there was room in the forts that were supposed to protect the approach to Portsmouth from the east.

So the R.F.C. were allotted quarters in these ancient monuments, that reeked of damp, lacked every sanitary convenience and were gloomy beyond words. I suppose, however, that these quarters were not much worse than the Panmure Barracks at Montrose and it is a fact that the sick rate among the airmen was by no means frightening. But perhaps such trying living conditions left a heritage of rheumatism and arthritis that was to show itself in the later life of these men. *Post hoc* or *propter hoc*! Who is to tell? What to me had always been so remarkable is the patience and endurance that the average airman has always displayed in circumstances of the greatest discomfort and hardship. Will he go on doing so once the 'Never had it so good' slogan begins to sap his toughness and morale?

Cecil King, who was posted to No. 5 Squadron on its formation at Farnborough under Major J. Higgins, R.A. (generally known to the troops as 'old eyeglass and bottom'), did his early training on Maurice and Henry Farmans. When the squadron moved to Gosport Gnome Avros were added and my personal recollection is that they replaced the Maurice Farmans. King obviously took a much better view of the quarters than I did because he says: 'The barrack rooms at Fort Grange, burrowed into the earth mound of the fort, were very comfortable. It was a happy station. . . .' King speaks of a very well-known young mechanic whose story is told in the next chapter. This was Byford McCudden, who did hair-raising stunts on a motor-cycle. His elder brother, also in the service, was an equally good motor-cyclist, so it might well have been he. All this is nearly two generations ago, and memory is a tricky jade.

June 1914! The squadrons assembled at Netheravon for the Concentration Camp. There the Commanders, Burke, Brooke-Popham, Raleigh and Higgins, announced to their respective squadrons that war with Germany was imminent. Whereas up till then the tempo of life in the R.F.C. had been only slightly in excess of that of the Army generally, a reappraisal of our readiness for war revealed such startling deficiencies in essentials that soon we were, officers and men alike, plunged into a fury of preparation. Raiding parties descended upon civilian aircraft factories and gaily signed vouchers for spares worth hundreds of pounds, for which act they had no authorization. Personally, I was pursued for two years by a bill from Messrs. Blériot (England) for a pair of wings valued at £50 for which I had signed and quickly removed to Netheravon.

As August approached, so the little handful of officers and men of the Royal Flying Corps nerved themselves for the part they were to play in the First World War. The future was completely obscure. We reckoned on 100 per cent casualties in the first month, but an end to the war by Christmas. How wrong we were on both counts!

Some amusing things happened when the squadrons flew to

France. Lieutenant G. I. Carmichael crashed his Henry Farman on the ridge and furrow of Gosport airfield as he was taking off for the war. (The H.F. under-carriage was a delicate affair.) As a substitute he was given a B.E.8 generally known, by reason of its shape, as a 'Bloater'. Carmichael had never flown a B.E.8 and his mechanic, sitting in the front seat, was well aware of that fact. In flight, the two of them had a divided responsibility. Before Carmichael's eyes was the gauge denoting the level of petrol in the service tank. In the front cockpit was the hand pump that controlled the flow of petrol from the main tank to the service tank. Carmichael writes:

'On the way over to France I had to shout to my mechanic to pump when the level in the service tank fell too low. When we landed he said he was very sorry, he had never heard me shout, and pumped when he thought it was necessary. In the result he pumped too often and petrol over-flowed everywhere and we were very lucky not to catch fire!'

Our designers of aircraft were not always sufficiently practical in their arrangements!

A personal story of the flight to France concerns my rigger Robins. It was he who nearly gave me heart failure in the air. We had started from Netheravon on our way to Dover in a new 80 h.p. Blériot, heavily overloaded with kit, and were about twenty miles north of Portsmouth. Suddenly Robins grabbed my shoulder (he was in the back seat) and shouted, 'Zeppelins!' Now we had been instructed that if we met a Zepp we were to ram it in a suicide attack. At Robins' cry and shivering with fright I looked to the south and saw—one of the Spit forts just showing above the morning mist! I was really very cross with Robins! He survived my wrath and the risks of war, leaving the R.A.F. in 1919 to join de Havillands in Canada. Gardner, my fitter, disappeared after demobilization and I have never seen him since. Robins turned up a year or two ago in a Swindon hospital—a very sick man—and died not long after.

5

The Trinity and Others

ONE of the early developments in the flying service was the establishment of a very close personal link between the pilot of an aircraft and the two men, the fitter and the rigger, who serviced his machine. They were a trinity bound together by ties of close personal interest. The pilot knew that his life depended very largely on the conscientiousness of his servicing team. They knew that, after an overhaul of any kind, or indeed as a matter of routine, they would be called upon to fly as passengers in their own aircraft. But over and above the feeling of self-preservation was the spirit of teamwork, of satisfaction in a job well done, and in pride of service. All the very early pilots who still survive must remember the two other members of the trinity. Mine are a living memory to me. Gardner, the fitter, a bit of a cross-patch, and Robins, the rigger, a gay and cheerful type. Some of these associations developed into a close personal friendship between officer and man and in my opinion this feeling was of the utmost value to the service as a morale-builder. Work in the flying services was not 'just another job'. It was labour divided between friends, each aware of the others' worth. When death came a personal loss was suffered by the survivors.

The first other-rank flying casualty in the R.F.C. was Staff Sergeant R. M. V. Wilson. He was flying as passenger to Captain E. B. Loraine in a two-seater Nieuport monoplane. On this machine, a rather hotted-up version of the standard model, Lieutenant Barrington-Kennet had achieved some records. It is possible that Loraine was trying to clip seconds off 'B.K.'s' time, and while doing a sharp turn he is said to have stalled and so crashed. I am inclined to think, fully equipped as I am with hindsight, that this was an accident caused by reversed controls. Owing to the steep angle of turn, the rudder had become the elevator and the elevator a rudder. Misuse of the controls in such circumstances very often produced a crash, particularly at low altitude.

Air Mechanic Strugnell, aged twenty-one (now Group Captain and wearer of the Military Cross), was standing with Major Brooke-Popham when Loraine's aircraft disappeared into a valley. After waiting for some minutes for it to reappear 'Brookham' climbed into his machine and, with Strugnell as passenger, flew over to the crash. Strugnell comments: 'It was very early in the morning and nobody was about. I remember I was desperately sad. They were such splendid people. I had never seen a dead person before.' In this accident the R.F.C. lost a most valuable officer and an excellent mechanic. Sir Walter Raleigh, author of the first volume of *War in the Air*, says: 'An order was issued at once that flying should continue normally.' This indeed became a tradition of the flying services. The order was good for morale, but in addition it put matters into perspective. All of us had started flying with a fairly clear idea of the risk we were taking. If we were killed it was just too bad. The others would carry on the development of an art, a science, call it what you will, that really mattered to the country we were serving. Among the other ranks the same spirit prevailed. The one ambition of the clerks, transport drivers and the 'Odds and Sods' of the service was to have a flight, and the sooner the better. Some of them managed to achieve their whole ambition—to learn to fly. Sergeant Dunne was one of these. He was a most promising pupil of the Bristol School at Brooklands and his instructor, Warren F. Merriam, was full of confidence when he sent him up to take his 'ticket'. Before take-off Merriam had warned Dunne that conditions might be 'bumpy' and so he must be careful. Dunne performed all the necessary evolutions laid down by the Royal Aero Club and then started to glide down to his landing. A few hundred feet up the aircraft went into a steep dive and Dunne shot out of his seat and fell to the ground even before his 'box-kite' wallowed its way to earth. I saw the crash next day and have never forgotten the lesson I then learnt. In the primitive aircraft of the day there was no provision for a safety belt. A pilot flying in rough weather might easily be thrown forward on to the controls and so end up in a fatal nose-dive. Not long after Dunne's death safety belts were fitted to all service machines, but not before I had a similar experience that frightened the life out of me.

In the Military Wing the name of McCudden was to be out-

standing. I remember two brothers, both of whom were in the transport section of No. 3 Squadron. The elder, W. T. J. McCudden, was
a motor-cyclist. On his own machine he performed remarkable feats
of balance, invariably winning the Tortoise Race at Squadron Gym-
khanas. He fitted a very light sidecar to his motor-cycle and on one
occasion took a much frightened passenger from Netheravon to Salisbury with the sidecar wheel well up in the air for most of the way.
George was one of those who flew from Lark Hill to Farnborough
in June 1912. By then he had reached the rank of sergeant, but it is
not clear from the record whether he actually piloted an aircraft on
this occasion. He was killed in a flying accident at Gosport in 1914.
His younger brother took to the air somewhat later, and was to become
a fighter pilot of the first rank. Both were short but splendidly built,
with chubby red faces and keen twinkling eyes. The younger one had
a very ready smile, but the elder was more serious.

The two boys were the sons of an Irishman from County Carlow.
I believe there was a third brother, whom I never met. In the family
was a French grandmother who must have given just that extra bit of
zest and dash to the grandsons. Father McCudden served in the Royal
Engineers and it was natural, at that time, that the sons should follow
suit. . . . In his autobiography, published very shortly before his death
in action, the younger gives us a certain amount of information. The
books says that he was born on 28th March 1895. He must have followed the usual routine of a service family—constant changes of
station, married quarters when available, otherwise scruffy lodgings
in a series of garrison towns. Education was provided by the Army!
He joined the Sappers early, as a bugler in 1910. Three years later he
became a private—in the Royal Flying Corps. On 6th May he was
put in charge of the 70 h.p. Renault engine in the Maurice Farman
flown by that remarkable character Captain George W. P. Dawes,
Royal Berkshire Regiment—generally known as 'Early Doors' because he was so quick off the mark. This engine was the first that
James McCudden had ever touched and he was very much in awe of
it. Whether he was equally frightened of Dawes is a matter of doubt!
Being of a very enterprising spirit he decided one day to get some
propeller-swinging practice on a Caudron biplane that shared a shed
with his Maurice Farman. Unfortunately this Caudron's magneto was
controlled only by a thumb switch on the joy-stick and so was permanently in circuit. In a matter of seconds the engine began to turn

and the Caudron was eating its way into the structure of the Farman. McCudden was placed under close arrest and remained locked up in the guardroom for five days. At his trial he was awarded seven days' detention and forfeited fourteen days' pay.

Captain Dawes apparently disapproved of the boy and he reappeared later in 'C' Flight No. 3 Squadron—Flight Commander Captain A. G. Fox, Royal Engineers. Lieutenant E. L. Conran, County of London Yeomanry and a wild Australian, took McCudden on as his fitter, and a better combination could hardly have been found. Eric Conran was the son of a well-to-do family and had two sisters almost as devil-may-care as himself. In the society of these three there was never a dull moment, but in spite of his love of gaiety Eric's real passion was flying. So McCudden found himself with a master who fully understood and encouraged the boy's desire to fly. His brother, W. T. J. McCudden, was doing a certain amount of piloting at this time and gave his young brother some surreptitious dual instruction. But it was mainly in the back seat of Conran's Blériot that McCudden enjoyed himself. Judge then his disappointment when, a few weeks before war was declared, his master was issued with a single-seater— a Parasol Blériot. These high-wing monoplanes were great fun to fly, as they were fully powered for their weight and had the engaging characteristic of landing—like a parachute—at very low speed. So, when No. 3 Squadron went to war, McCudden had to go by sea to France with the rest of the ground crew.

Very early on during his stay in France he was in trouble again. He and another airman, Beaumont by name, were brought before me by Flight Sergeant Ridd and accused of looting—a most deadly sin, in the ultimate analysis punishable by death. On the evidence presented to me, the taking of half a dozen apples from a wayside orchard, it did not appear to me that very drastic measures were needed to prevent a recurrence of such indiscipline. The mere fact that so serious a view was taken of looting would, in my opinion, prevent a recurrence. I was wrong! Beaumont was in a rather more nefarious foray some days later. Lieutenant G. F. Pretyman and his observer, Major Moss, did not return at the expected time from patrol. Beaumont and Webb, his buddy, decided that their officer, either dead or a prisoner, would not want his kit any more. So they divided it between them. Some hours later, wearing Pretyman's socks, they were horrified to see 'Master' returning from his forced landing. The loss of kit was promptly discovered and Webb, with ready wit, explained that it had been taken down to their billet to keep the clothes dry. Pretyman inspected the socks when they were returned, found them damp and, quickly suspicious, but uncertain how far to take matters, made a present of them to the airmen. He was a fastidious type!

McCudden records in his autobiography that he flew with me during the retreat from Mons. Certainly at Le Cateau he worked until 3 a.m. on the engine of my aircraft. He admits to having pinched more apples at Meaux, the farthest south of the R.F.C. retreat, but he was not discovered.

When the British Army advanced after the Battle of the Aisne the R.F.C. established itself in some comfort at Coulommiers. McCudden speaks feelingly of the bath—indeed the two baths—the first for nine weeks that he had been able to achieve.

At this time, September 1914, only the senior officers were accommodated in billets. The junior officers and airmen slept in the lee of haystacks, under their vehicles or the wings of the aircraft. Not until the winter set in were the French invited to give us better shelter. The young officers were then 'stabled' in farm houses and cottages and the airmen in barns. McCudden seems to have found life good, even in these conditions. He was a very hard worker and seldom ailing. Soon promotion came his way. By April 1916 he was back in Gosport as a flight sergeant and here he qualified as a pilot. Nine months later he was commissioned as a flying officer and so must leave this story of 'ground crews' only.

Though McCudden had a magnificent career, gaining the Victoria Cross for bravery in the air, he was just one of the many young men who found life in the R.F.C. a fulfilment of their desires.

One of these, a man with a long and valuable career in the flying service, is N. V. Piper, who, in addition to his own story, sent me some notes on other airmen who were his contemporaries.

Piper joined the R.F.C. at the age of eighteen and his early days in the service were spent working as fitter/rigger with 'Colonel' S. F. Cody in an isolated hangar on Laffan's Plain, near Aldershot. Cody had previously been a salaried employee of the Royal Aircraft Factory at Farnborough but, together with Lieutenant Dunne, R.E., another experimenter, had been axed by the War Office in a fit of economy.

Cody obtained permission from the Factory to erect his shed on Laffan's Plain and here he continued to work on his own designs. One of these was a monoplane intended to compete in the Military Aviation Trials of 1912. It was powered by a 120 h.p. Austro-Daimler engine. Piper claims that this machine was far in advance of anything in service elsewhere. Unfortunately, on a test flight ten days before the Trials, Cody landed on a cow, killing the animal and destroying the monoplane. Undismayed, Cody entered his biplane, with which he won first place. This machine and a companion were bought by the R.F.C. and formed the first flight of No. 4 Squadron. One was very quickly written off by Major Raleigh, the O.C., and the second broke up in the air and killed its pilot, Lieutenant Harrison. So ended Cody's enterprise as a builder of military aircraft. But he had other schemes into which Piper entered. One was to build a monoplane capable of flying the Atlantic. Piper was to be the navigator and co-pilot. During his leave he attempted to modify a marine sextant belonging to his father, a master mariner, so that he could use it in an aircraft. In the meantime Cody was building a form of seaplane—he called it a water-plane—and this he proposed to enter for another competition. It is presumed that the Record Office of the R.F.C. caught up with Piper, because he was posted to Hendon not long before Cody was killed in a flying accident, and thus survived. This was in August 1913.

Later Piper came back to Farnborough to look after the new stable machine, the B.E.2c that had been built at the Royal Aircraft Factory. This was a design that came from Geoffrey de Havilland's fertile brain. Geoffrey was then Chief Test Pilot and Assistant Designer at the beginning of a career that was to make him famous throughout the world.

One of Piper's duties (he was now a corporal) was to demonstrate the qualities of his aircraft to visiting pilots.

Major Brancker, from the War Office, arrived to test the B.E. Piper warned him of its peculiarities, and particularly of the fact that it was impossible to stall it. Even if the stick were held hard back the nose would drop into a dive until flying speed had been regained. Not until then would the controls work.

Brancker (not a very good pilot) took off with Piper in the front seat. After a couple of circuits of the aerodrome the gallant Major came in to land and, as was only too often his custom, flattened out fifteen feet above the ground. As was also his custom, he continued to pull back on the stick so as to make a pancake landing. The B.E. wouldn't have it. She stuck her nose down and hit the ground with a resounding thump. . . . Bouncing back into the air, she proceeded to hop like an infuriated kangaroo for a hundred yards before coming to a stop. Nothing unusual, perhaps, but what followed was quite abnormal. Corporal Piper got out of his seat, walked round to the Major and said: 'Didn't I warn you not to land her like that? I told you all about it and still you do it the wrong way and knock hell out of the under-carriage!' 'Consider yourself under arrest!' roared the Major, his dignity greatly affronted. Piper, realizing that he had committed a military crime of the first order, walked away. 'Come back,' bellowed Brancker. 'What do you mean by speaking to me like that?' 'I meant every word of it,' said Piper, 'and more.' Brancker paused and then grinned. 'You were quite right. Shake hands.'

Leaving Piper for the time being and returning to Netheravon and No. 3 Squadron, an incident occurred there which should be re-garded as of considerable significance in the relationship between officers and men of the R.F.C. In the spring of 1914 there was a fatal crash in which two officers, Captain Allen and Lieutenant Burroughes, lost their lives. The accident was attributed to a defective rudder which broke just as the machine was taking off. There was a very strong feeling in the squadron that the Royal Aircraft Factory were responsible for this failure. A year before Lieutenant Desmond Arthur had been killed in much the same way in a machine that had recently been repaired in the Factory. This coincidence led to a great deal of talk and much criticism, but both courts of enquiry could find no one on whom to pin the blame. The only way then that the airmen could express their feelings was by paying tribute to the dead men. I quote from a letter written to Captain Allen's family by a first air mechanic named Pratt:

'Dear Sir,
         I respectfully beg to request that this letter, on behalf of the mechanics of No. 3 Squadron, be accepted as a reply to your extremely grateful feelings and satisfaction in the way slight services were rendered. . . . Captain Allen was a talented officer whom everybody esteemed. He would stop and talk to labourers and give them advice and on one occasion succeeded in obtaining for one a rise in his wages. . . . In dealing with men he was con-ciliatory, firm and just. I have been in hot water myself and re-ceived a severe lecture from him; of course I deserved it. It taught

me a lesson. A subordinate officer caught it for the same offence, but he [Allen] did not differentiate between officers and men in discipline. He possesed a keen sense of duty and that is why he will be a great loss to the service.'

The letter goes on to express the squadron's sense of loss and finishes by asking for photographs as a memento of a well-loved officer. When the pictures were received (Allen's sister sent three), Pratt replied thanking her and finished with these words: 'When our generation ceases to exist and all danger connected with aircraft eliminated and [they] form the chief arm of the services, men "war honoured" will point and say, "These pioneer heroes were always on active service." '

A year later Piper was interesting himself in fitting armament into Maurice Farman biplanes. He seems to have carried out some radical alterations to the general design, and it is perhaps fortunate for him that the Aeronautical Inspection Department was then in its infancy and that Monsieur Maurice Farman was busy elsewhere!

With this modified Farman, boasting a front gun operated by the passenger, Piper flew to France with Captain Chinnery ('China' to us junior pilots), and survived a crash at Poperinghe in November 1914. On leaving hospital he was posted 'in command' of Hawkinge aerodrome but when Hawkinge was reorganized on a permanent basis Piper joined No. 15 Squadron at Hounslow Heath and this is where we met for the first time.

No. 15 and Piper with it moved to the Swingate Downs airfield at Dover. I was later posted to No. 1 Squadron in France so I did not take No. 15 overseas. In August 1915 the squadron moved to the 2nd Army front in the Ypres sector. A year later Piper, flying as gunner/observer, was shot down by one of the famous Boelke's pilots near Roulers. He was unhurt and taken to have breakfast at Boelke's mess. During the meal everything connected with the war was studiously avoided. Indeed, when one young pilot did raise a point of that nature, Boelke shut him up at once. Afterwards, however, Piper was closely questioned but refused to answer. This attitude was accepted quite cheerfully with the comment that they would behave in exactly the same way if captured.

Piper spent the rest of the war as a prisoner. On his return to Britain, where he joined No. 50 Squadron, he was treated in the way which drove so many prisoners of war to the extremes of exasperation.

He was regarded as worth no more than he was in 1916. Thus he had
the mortification of being retained in a lower rank than many of those
previously his juniors, who had not the misfortune to be captured
and so had climbed up the promotion ladder. Hence he decided to
return to civil life in marine engineering, a tradition of his family.
In 1935, foreseeing the likelihood of another war breaking out, he took
a job as instructor at Halton Apprentice School, and here and at
Henlow he served the Royal Air Force for another twenty-three
years, being awarded the B.E.M. in 1957.

Some of his stories about old colleagues are worth recording.
He speaks of Sergeant 'Taffy' Landman, ex-Air Battalion and of No.
1 Airship Squadron, R.F.C. Taffy's idiosyncrasy was to wear a large
pocket watch on his wrist, and when asked the time always giving it
in terms of minutes to the lunch-hour or to knocking-off time.

No. 3 Squadron had its own 'character' in Bill Pratt, who came
to us from the Duke of Cornwall's Light Infantry. Bill was an extremely clever chap, well educated, but with a gift for running into
minor disciplinary troubles. For example, he returned from leave
wearing boots with toe-caps—against orders. For this 'crime' Major
Brooke-Popham gave him three days' confinement to camp. Bill got
his own back a short time later. He was a good vocalist and something
of a calypso singer, since he improvised his own lyrics. Performing at
a camp concert, his song being the 'Army Alphabet', he came to the
letter 'O'. Wagging his finger at Brooke-Popham, who was sitting in
the front row, he chanted:

> ' "O" stands for orders,
> Some of which are brutes.
> Never come off Easter leave
> Wearing toe-capped boots!'

'Brookham'—bless his heart—nearly fell out of his chair with
laughter, while the squadron, most of whom knew of Bill's punishment, nearly lifted the roof in their enjoyment of this apt retort to
authority.

A simple little episode, perhaps, but then No. 3 under 'Brookham's' command was a happy squadron.

There was not much entertainment for the airmen at Netheravon,
but when a travelling fair came to the village it was something of an

THE TRINITY AND OTHERS

occasion. After a lively Saturday evening Paddy and Mick met each other. 'Sure, Mick, an' I met ye at the Fair last night! Was ye there?' 'No, Paddy! I was not.' 'Sure, so wuz I naythur.' In actual fact Paddy had been in Salisbury and Mick in Devizes. What a 'beat-up' they both must have had!

There was an odd character in No. 15 Squadron called McDonald. Living in France when the war broke out, he promptly joined the Foreign Legion. One day in the trenches, when opening a tin of sardines, a shell-splinter wounded him in the head. He was knocked out, and owing to the difficulties of evacuation he spent the day on his back in the trench. Suddenly he sat up and shouted, 'Who's pinched my sardines?' He started to rave and could only be pacified by being offered an open tin. In early 1915 McDonald was released from the Legion and joined the R.F.C., being posted to No. 15. Every time something exciting happened to him, or he had too much to drink, there would be a repeat performance with the sardine tin. He became quite crazy and only came round when he saw the open tin of little fish. At long last the doctors decided to do a trepanning operation, after which McDonald became perfectly normal.

In the winter of 1914–15 Beaumont, the looter of apples, was posted back to England and in due course found his way into No. 15 Squadron that was forming at Farnborough, subsequently moving to Dover via Hounslow Heath. It was at Dover that Beaumont put up a magnificent 'black'. He was acting as rigger in the repair section, and was entrusted with the job of changing the elevator wires of a Blériot monoplane. The job finished, the aircraft was wheeled out of the shed to be flight-tested by the squadron commander. This officer, an experienced Blériot pilot, took one look inside the cockpit, puzzled for a moment, and then roared: 'Who rigged this machine? The elevator wires are crossed! Oh, you, Beaumont! How long have you been a corporal? Two weeks? Well, you won't be much longer!' After a reprimand but no loss of rank in view of his past good service Beaumont was sent off to the R.N.A.S. Station at Eastbourne to help the sailors rig their Blériots. The C.O. felt that he had received a salutary lesson and that a little more experience in this type of aircraft would do the man good. There was no question of ill-feeling against the Senior Service!

Here Beaumont had a wonderful time. He was allowed to live off the station and was provided with transport to get to and from his

E

work. The R.N.A.S. were very lush with cars at all times! In due course he returned to Dover and went with his squadron to France in August 1915. After the war he continued to serve, and in the Hitler War, as a warrant officer in the R.A.F., he was awarded the M.B.E. in 1944. When he retired in 1949 he was the senior warrant officer in the service.

Beaumont and his friends were, however, men who had joined the R.F.C. in peace-time. When the Kaiser War broke out a flow of skilled civilians joined the service and it seems relevant to this story to give illustrations of the manner in which these men were handled by the recruiting organization. It must be remembered that they were all volunteers—'Your King and Country needs you'—and in considerable numbers they arrived at the Farnborough recruits' depot, to be attested, kitted up and drilled into some semblance of soldiers.

I was at Farnborough in the winter of 1914–15 under orders to form a new squadron. The basis of the new unit was No. 1 Reserve Squadron, on to which had to be grafted the budding organization. I was in a position of considerable advantage. Knowing most of the staff of the Recruits Depot, only a mile away from my office, I would walk over and inspect the new arrivals. So, it was possible to hand-pick the most likely members of the depot and have them posted to my unit. In this slightly nefarious manner the new squadron was equipped with some first-class technicians. Soon, however, the flow of skilled men to the R.F.C. began to dry up. Many thousands went straight to the infantry and so were lost to the technical services. The War Office at last awoke to the fact that some form of technical training had to be established. Luckily, machinery existed which was apt for the purpose.

With its headquarters in London and branches all over the country, the Polytechnic was already training young men in a variety of skills. When appealed to the 'Poly' gallantly undertook to recruit and train the technicians required by the R.F.C.

The Director of Education at the London Polytechnic, Major Robert Mitchell, began this great task in 1915, and by the spring of 1916 had accepted a special responsibility in this sphere of activity. 'Poly's' representatives in the big industrial centres were in personal touch with men in the requisite trades. Major Mitchell, writing to the War Office in March 1917, said:

'. . . very careful selection is made and a number of these sent forward . . . have passed the London Matriculation and the B.sc. . . . During the last two months some 3000 recruits have been sent forward . . . we have to interview a great many more than we select.'

But already in 1916 this scheme was inadequate to meet requirements. Field Marshal Lord Haig had asked for fifty-six squadrons in France by the spring of 1917. Later a further twenty squadrons were demanded. The 13,500 men necessary to man these units were manifestly unobtainable by the methods used up till then.

Resort had to be made to the up-grading and retraining of semi-skilled men, to the combing of industry, to replacing men by women (the birth of the W.A.A.F.) and finally to a Dominion training and recruitment project, the precursor of the vast organization born during the Hitler War. But it was late in 1918 before this new development began to bear fruit and by that time the war was nearly over.

During 1916 those recruits who had been passed through the Polytechnic filter were trained at Farnborough in drill and discipline, in wireless and photography. At Coley Park, Reading, they underwent instruction in fitting and rigging. There was also a recruits training depot at Blandford in Dorset. But now to look at some individual experiences as these men left civil life and embarked on a service career.

Air Mechanic D. E. Giles, now living at Northolt, Middlesex, has made his contribution to this part of the story. Aged seventeen years and nine months he enlisted in the R.F.C. at a recruits depot in a mews off Park Lane—a very small place. A lot of waiting about—attestation-form filling, medical examination, signature on the dotted line—then a wait outside until a party was collected to march to Waterloo Station. It was dark by the time they started and pouring with rain. At Waterloo, already soaked to the skin, they boarded a train to Blandford. Of course they had to stand all the way—the best part of three hours. Finally they arrived and imprinted in his memory is a picture of pelting rain, tall covered lorries and a shouting figure waving a hurricane lamp. Then a long bumpy ride, still standing, and a jump down into endless mud. The recruits were then allotted to tents, blue-black in the driving rain, and taken to draw blankets and palliasses—also sodden with damp. Only then did they get something to eat—cold bully, stale bread and margarine—tea stewed until a spoon would stand up in it. Back to the tents through the mud—guy-rope drill; the youngest out into the wet when they got too tight from shrinkage in the rivers of rain. One hurricane lamp per tent, lights out and a few hours of troubled sleep. Next morning early astir; ablutions in the open with cold water—no means of shaving in comfort! Breakfast—tea, bread and marge and a banger and then issue of uniform, infantry pattern. Also knife, fork, spoon, plate, cut-throat razor, two hand-towels, button-cleaning stick, thick vests, long grey pants and brown cardigan. Why did he leave his comfortable home with Mum to look after him?

There followed six weeks of foot-drill, gas-mask drill—and fatigues. Afterwards draft leave of fourteen days—destination France. Giles' friends thought he had just come out of jail—the service haircut had put a stop to his endeavours to grow a good crop to meet the needs of the newest 'swept back' style. His face was sunburnt, the skin peeling off, and his nose was raw from so much gas-mask drill. The gas mask of the time had a spring nose-clip! But on the other hand he was extremely fit. The food was atrocious—the mess tent was well named. Everything was prepared in the open, and cooked in field ovens (iron contraptions covered with baked mud) and in the primitive Soyer stoves. History has it that these stoves were invented by a gentleman named Soyer during the Crimean War.

On return from draft leave the men were told that the destination was not France but Egypt, where they landed a few days before Giles' eighteenth birthday after a fairly uncomfortable journey. First a very rough Channel crossing to Cherbourg, then by train through France and Italy to Taranto, and then by sea to Alexandria. On the train journey the draft was transported in the usual box cars, 'Hommes 40, Chevaux en long 8'. The sliding doors were left open during the day, but at night, owing to the cold, were closed. Rations were cold bully beef and biscuits. Whenever the train stopped in a siding, which was fairly often, hot water could be drawn from the engine for making tea.

Third Air Mechanic W. A. Tilbury has a similar story to tell. In August 1914 he passed his Civil Service examination and became a learner in the Post Office at a wage of 5s. per week. In 1915 he qualified as sorter and telegraphist with the princely salary of 14s. per week. The war was being brought home to him by the incessant recruiting appeals and so he began to badger his chiefs for permission to join up. Early in 1916 he received an official letter instructing him to join the R.F.C. at Farnborough in the trade of wireless operator.

Arriving at Farnborough some time in April, he found there a few thousand others, all with the same idea and all volunteers. Each morning a queue was formed in front of the attestation office, and by nightfall a fraction of the number had gone through the mill. At night the men slept on the hut floors. The lucky ones were those who had palliasses as well as a couple of blankets. Unbelievably, it took Tilbury five days to reach the office. Here he handed in his call-up letter to be greeted by one of the R.F.C.'s loving sergeants who yelled, 'And where the hell do you think you have been?'

Next to the depot for kit (a civilian tailor takes measurements now). The recruit walked past different people who threw different articles at him. One item was breeches; these came right down the calves to the top of the boots, under puttees. 'These are too small,' said Tilbury. 'Pull them on.' He did and it took two chaps to pull them off, inside out, with Tilbury hanging on a door. Two pairs of long pants were issued and he used to kill his mates later as one pair he had to fold across his stomach twice, roll back up to his knees and then they came up to his arms.

Training was at Blenheim Barracks, the R.F.C. Wireless School. As the recruits were nearly all G.P.O. telegraphists they could do morse faster than the so-called instructors and were all fit for overseas within weeks but the majority were too young—not yet eighteen and a half. About Easter 1916 wireless operators were badly wanted for the Hindenburg push and, thinking that France could not possibly be worse, Tilbury stepped out and said he was eighteen and a half. They didn't question him—he was just under eighteen.

Why did he dislike Farnborough so much? Here are his reasons. Before breakfast on the Queen's Parade—doing P.T., and in 'the hands down position', one of the sergeant-majors, a lovely person, marched up and down with his swagger cane saying, and striking one's backside, 'Get that down.' He was a real terror and it is probable that if he were in now all the Labour M.P.s in the House would be on their feet.

One day, as Tilbury had two sore heels as big as half-crowns, he just couldn't go out on the parade ground and drill, so miked it. Sure enough along came the orderly sergeant and caught him and sent him out on the parade to report. To his horror this same sergeant-major was taking the drill. He crept up behind him and presently the S.M. condescended to turn round. Leaping into action he told two men to fall out and between them Tilbury was marched off right into clink. That night he slept on a bed which was a slab of wood about six inches thick and was up before the C.O. next day and got seven days' cells.

All the cleaning, scrubbing and dishwashing, etc., was done by punishment men and of course one received three week-end fatigues for the most trivial things. Tilbury got three once for sucking a cough sweet on parade. During the whole of his time at Farnborough the only time off he was given was the three days' draft leave.

There were about a thousand in the school and the men lined up in alphabetical order for their money, which was 3s. 6d. per week. As he was a 'T' it took about two hours standing on Queen's Parade before Tilbury reached the Paymaster. One day, when marching back, he said to a man in front, 'Three-and-six, hurrah!' Followed a shout of, 'Come back that man,' and then, 'Your name and number,' resulting in three week-end fatigues. All the dining-hall greasy dishes, the enamel mugs and plates, everything was washed up with cold water and sand in the open. It can well be imagined what misery it was! The men sat about twenty to a table and it was always, every day, a large bucket of so-called stew and boiled potatoes, not peeled. The bucket was put on the table and each in turn dived in, the bucket being pushed along so that by the time it reached the end there wasn't much left. These buckets were then washed, and the tea served in them. There was no supper. Tea was the sixth of a loaf, a spoonful of marge, with either a spoonful of jam or a lump of cheese. It was absolutely impossible to get another crumb. Of course, the biggest joy of all was to be on fatigues and get detailed to the sergeants' mess, where one had a glorious feed. Tilbury cannot remember if one put butter on a slice of toast or toast on a slice of butter. He can still taste it.

On posting to France, and as he was a pretty useful telegraphist, he was sent to G.H.Q. at Montreuil-sur-Mer, attached to the R.E. Signals, to work a line to G.H.Q. R.F.C. at Doulens. This was a lovely job and food was good and plentiful. He was now getting 14s. a week as a second air mechanic. Tiring of this, as he had come to France to see the war, he put in to be moved and found the war in real earnest. Taken by a motor-cycle and side-car right up to Arras, he was left in a broken-down house all alone and told he would be picked up next day. In 1916 Arras was noisy with gunfire and Tilbury got his fill. Next day he was taken out behind the Hindenburg Line to an eighteen-pounder battery to be their wireless operator. The equipment consisted of dry-battery sets with ear-phones, and he would sit from before breakfast until evening with these ear-phones on, food being brought to him. Later he moved up behind Messines Ridge when that blew up, being now attached as W.O. to an observation balloon.

He was in Ploegstreet Wood behind the Portuguese when the Germans came through. Smashing his set, he set out for safety. He got lost and rode on the front mudguard of an army lorry, ending up near Calais.

Later he went back up the line, now a fully fledged first air mechanic at 28s. per week, caught dysentery and came home to hospital at Bristol, and to discharge at Favant.

6

The Kaiser War

S O FAR in following the fate of individual airmen it has been
necessary to make allusion to their activities in the 1914–18 War.
In this chapter it is intended to describe in some detail the day-
to-day life of men who served in France and in other theatres overseas.

It must not be forgotten that though the bulk of the R.F.C. went
to France in August 1914, there were small detachments in other
parts of the Empire. As the pressure of operations grew, so these
detachments increased in importance. Although there is very little
material available about individuals who served in these distant parts,
some attempt will be made to tell about their experiences and the
circumstances in which they served.

In the first year of the war in France the living conditions of the
airmen were far from good. But at least they were less unpleasant than
the miseries suffered and endured with the greatest courage by the
rest of the Army in the trenches on the Belgian front and in Northern
France. As an example of this fortitude I quote the case of a chauffeur
who had lived in great comfort as a servant in a private house, and
who fainted if he cut his finger. He found himself driving a lorry in
the Ypres Salient! Oddly enough the blood and muck that must have
been his daily experience passed him by. He carried on as though he
had been the toughest of the tough. How did this happen? What
strange reaction took place so that, sensitive beyond the ordinary
before the war, he became inured to the horrors of the battle in
Flanders? It was this acceptance of the extremes of danger, cold and
discomfort that was an outstanding characteristic of the British soldier
of the time. The airmen suffered the cold and discomfort, but few
ran much chance of death or disablement. The wireless operators who
worked and lived with the artillery shared the danger that the gunners
incurred and many of them were killed or wounded. But apart from

an occasional rescue operation, when an aircraft forced-landed in the battle area and had to be retrieved, the men of the R.F.C., comparatively speaking, ran few risks. Only occasionally in 1914–15 were they asked to fly in an operational role. Piloting and observation was, in the main, an officer's job.

The stalemate of trench warfare allowed the airmen little opportunity for fighting the enemy on the ground. As they lived anything from ten miles upward behind the lines, only the grumble of gunfire and the glare of Very lights shot into the sky gave them any indication that 'there was a war on'! When a break-through took place, as in 1918, they did have a chance to see the battle at first hand. But before the ground crews settled down to a period of static warfare in 1914 they had some unusual experiences. Moving daily, first to the south during the retreat from Mons, and then to the north-west after the victory of the Marne, they saw quite a cross-section of the French population and began to look on the *vin rouge* with a more favourable eye. Beer was scarce, but wine was in abundance.

Webb (previously mentioned) and Borrit of No. 3 Squadron had a real 'beat-up' one night at a local *estaminet*. Returning to camp they climbed into bed, but Borrit at once fell out and down some stairs. Webb rendered first-aid and calm was restored. Next morning, Borrit, in not very good shape, was swinging his pilot's propeller. The engine backfired and the propeller caught the sleepy Borrit across the shoulders. Webb arrived just as his friend was being taken off to hospital. He roared with laughter and when rebuked for heartlessness said: 'Wait till they undress him. He has got two pairs of my puttees wrapped round his stomach!'

Maurice Baring in his book *R.F.C. H.Q.* notes:

'When I got back about 10.30 p.m. I found Brooke-Popham asleep on the stairs of the hotel in which we were billeted. I asked him why he had not got a room. He replied that he had been upstairs but had found his room occupied by two of the H.Q. drivers!'

Baring continues: 'I turned them out. They said philosophically they knew it was too good to last! Brookham got his bed and a good sleep!' Brooke-Popham was one of those few—the selfless few—who believed that horses should have first consideration, as they could not help themselves, that men came next and the officers last of all.

We officers were taught those principles when we were commissioned, but not all of us observed them.

One of the problems that faced the squadron officers from day to day was the volume of complaints coming from the French house-holders upon whom our men were billeted. On the whole the airmen behaved very well and sometimes the complaints were ill-founded. Maurice Baring, the trouble-shooter at R.F.C. H.Q., recounts that some mechanics belonging to one of the squadrons had been billeted in an outhouse of a villa inhabited by a local lady. When the men left the lady sent a furious message saying that the outhouse had been left in a filthy state. Investigation at the villa, and a talk with the gardener's wife, disproved the accusation. 'The whole thing was spite on the part of my mistress because her husband was taken off to the war between two gendarmes!' Some of these billets were quite horrible. Dirty, broken-down, with doors hanging on one hinge and every window smashed, they were really unfit to use. But used they were, and one very wet stable in which many airmen were quartered was labelled by them 'Villa Rue Matique'! Thank heavens for the saving grace of humour.

The reactions of the British airman, drilled and disciplined in the manner of the Brigade of Guards, to his early experiences in France and the rather sloppy appearance of the French troops are described by Air Mechanic C. R. King, of the R.F.C.:

'When we got to France we took rather a poor view of the French soldiers with their rusty aeroplanes, dirty ungroomed ar-tillery horses and unshaven faces, but the civilians welcomed us and were always kind and helpful. They often helped me picket down my aircraft, and would hump tins of petrol when I was filling up. A very pretty girl helped me one day so I allowed her to sit in the pilot's seat for a moment, as she had never seen an aeroplane on the ground before.'

On one occasion when he arrived at a field by air his pilot was told to take off at once with another officer. King was ordered to take up a defensive position in a nearby farm with the remainder of the squadron and transport. They were supposed to be surrounded by Uhlans and had to hold the farm till help came from some of our cavalry. How he longed for a rifle! But he had only a revolver, the same as the rest of his comrades. They had just settled down in their positions when one of the officers came along and examined the ammunition. It was mostly flat-nosed, the same as had been used for target shooting in England. Quickly the ammunition was buried deep in the farmyard manure. The men were told that if they were captured using that ammunition by the enemy they could have been shot right away, so, quite unarmed, they just waited to see what happened. There was a Lewis-gun (it might have been the only one in the R.F.C. at that time), and one of the officers fired a few bursts with it. The Uhlans drew off after a time and the party got out of it safely, but intensely disappointed at not being able to fire a single shot.

Flight Lieutenant Day of No. 2 Squadron also has something to say on the attitude of the French civilians:

'We sailed from Glasgow in the S.S. *Dogra* and as we steamed down the Clyde the shipyard workers gave us a tremendous send-off by beating on steel plates with their riveting hammers.

At Boulogne the local ladies gave us a warm reception, but it was noticeable that they were wearing badges of regiments which had passed through ahead of us. Already the owners of these badges were forgotten. For the ladies the interest was the man on the spot!'

From Boulogne No. 2 Squadron moved to Amiens and then to Maubeuge. Soon aircraft were needing repair from enemy action and Day and his lorry were busy. At night the glare from burning villages showed in the northern sky and the realities of war were coming home to the airmen, whose trip to France had hitherto been in the nature of a holiday.

On Sunday, 23rd August, it was clear that the R.F.C. would have to leave Maubeuge and move south-west. Through Aulnoye the column of vehicles trundled along, halting from time to time, their drivers hoping that darkness would see them comfortably encamped. This was not to be. Late that night orders came for a further move, and head to tail, each driving on his predecessor's red tail-light, the transport nosed its way towards safety. By next day exhaustion was setting in and Day has little recollection of what was happening. He remembers the crowds of refugees. Did he see perhaps the famous crippled old lady being pushed down the road on her bed which fortunately was provided with castors? How devoted must have been her family!

One night when the transport was parked in a field a heavy rain-storm broke. The officer in charge at once ordered all the vehicles on to the road in case they got bogged down and so might fall into German hands. The language of the troops as they were dug out from their hiding-holes must have been in a class by itself! Next night their sleep was broken again by the invasion of a herd of cattle. The owners had decided to drive them south to escape the Germans and had started the operation well before dawn.

Baths were an unknown quantity. Passing a big château surrounded by a deep moat the O.C. Transport decided that the moment had arrived for an all-over wash. Stripping on the bank the troops plunged in—into a foot or so of water and several feet of mud! They emerged black and stinking and any thought of using the one towel that they possessed was soon discarded. Lying in the sun, they dried out. The mud caked on them and had to be removed by scraping with grass and leaves. All told, it was not a successful bathe, but Day and others have recorded that it was six months before they had the chance of another cleansing.

The retreat ran its course, and after the battle for Paris the R.F.C. started its move to cover the Channel ports. Day seems to have kept his workshop lorry in serviceable condition because it reached St. Omer in one piece. Here, he says, 'The workshops were opened up, major repairs were done and discipline enforced.' Good old R.F.C.!

Day writes of Christmas Day 1914, when by consent of the troops on either side of the line there was an 'Armistice'—the last until 1918! The miseries of war and weather had already struck deep into the souls of the common men of all races and there were a number of instances of fraternization. Civilization still had a hold which soon was to be loosened!

'The weather was very wet that winter,' says Day, 'and what was very bad, all airmen including myself were lousy. We were sleeping on straw, in our clothes and under one blanket. Our laundry, such as it was, had been done by French women but soon they refused to accept it because of the lice.'

When a peasant from the Pas de Calais at this date became so finicky the louse situation must have been fantastically bad. Ovens for baking out the vermin had been sent out to France but their efficiency was doubtful. A story was current about two Jocks who were examining their clothes after these had passed through the ovens. 'Fergus—they're a' there yit!' 'Aye, mon! But they must ha' got an awfu' frecht!'

'In January 1915,' says Day, 'we were told we would go in batches to bathe and get clean underclothes at a laundry in Estaires, part of which had been turned into a bathing pool. Into the pool we went, stripped, and on coming out we were given clean underclothes. Part of the laundry was still being used for its original purpose, and sacking had been put round the pool to shield our modesty. But while we were washing we could see the sacking moving and hear the girls from the laundry commenting on our appearance!'

Soon, dozens of holes had been made in the sacking and salaciously inclined young Frenchwomen were peeping and squeaking at this vision of young British manhood in the nude!

Day was once asked to go up as observer. He was at first delighted, but after the aircraft had crossed the trench line he noticed the engine was failing. He signalled to the pilot who made back for home, reaching the edge of the airfield with a useless engine and confronted by a flock of sheep. The aircraft was written off completely in a whirl of oil, petrol and bits of sheep, but no one was much hurt and the squadron enjoyed fresh mutton as a change from the never-ending bully beef.

Day returned to England in early 1915 on promotion to Flight Sergeant and was posted to No. 40 Squadron. He seems to have spent a year in England before going back to France to be stationed with the squadron at Aire. That winter of 1916–17, though not so bitter as the 1917–18 abomination, was quite cold enough. No. 40 was equipped with engines using vegetable oil as a lubricant. On return from a flight this oil was immediately emptied into a drum which was then placed next to a stove as near as safety permitted. The oil would then remain sufficiently fluid to be poured back into the engines next day. This was back-breaking and finger-freezing work at a temperature of zero Fahrenheit. Day speaks with feeling about this task. What seems to have struck him as particularly unfortunate was that even the beer froze solid, and in those days beer had some alcohol in it!

As the war dragged on conditions improved. Hutments were built and baths were available rather more frequently. Parcels from home arrived with regularity and thick socks, warm pullovers and Balaclava helmets took the edge off the winter wind. Though the battle swayed backwards and forwards seldom did the Army advance or retreat so far as to disturb the ordered living of the R.F.C. until the Battle of the Somme and its sequel—the German retreat to the Hindenburg Line. Even then it was only the squadrons in the southern part of the British front that suffered an upheaval. In the north the *status quo* continued, though there were rumours that there might be an early advance even on this water-logged front.

In the late autumn all the plans made to break through on the Channel front came to nothing. It had been intended by this attack to clear the Channel coast and so put an end to the depredations of enemy submarines based on Ostend, Zeebrugge and other Belgian ports. The enemy intelligence got wind of these plans, and, by the simple process of opening a number of sluices, so flooded our jumping-off places that there was nothing for it but to abandon the attack. The Belgians were not amused. More of their land had gone under water and they were very scornful about our 'fameuse offensive'. So the German submarines continued to sink our ships on the short run from Belgian ports to our sea supply lines.

Then followed the Battle of Cambrai when, for the first time, tanks were used on a large scale. Fog and a quick German reaction robbed us of an early success.

Meanwhile, at Caporetto, the Italian Army had suffered a major defeat, mainly at the hands of four good German divisions that, during the months of mud and fog in Flanders, had been spared to help the not so warlike Austrians. The 14th Wing R.A.F., my command on the Belgian front, had been abolished when it was decided not to proceed with the attack. It was revived and, with some operational units, dispatched to provide part of the air contingent that had already arrived in Italy to stiffen the resistance of the Regia Aeronautica. The story of its journey to the Lombardy Plain and the subsequent experiences of the Wing as a whole are described in the next few pages.

The Army that, under General Plumer, was sent to plug the gap in the Allied Front caused by the Caporetto defeat consisted of five British and two French divisions. The air contingent boasted a Fighter Wing, an Army Co-operation Wing, a Balloon Wing and an Aircraft Park named 'Z'. This park was manned by a number of Coventry sheet-metal workers who had struck for higher wages and had promptly been put into uniform and shipped out to Italy!

The 14th Wing H.Q. assembled at Candas, the Aircraft Depot, and after due delay—inevitable in the circumstances—was embarked in a troop train—on Christmas Eve! In a leisurely manner and in freezing weather the train meandered across France—the officers in unheated second-class carriages and the men in cattle trucks. The N.C.O.s and our famous cook McCarthy benefited by the fact that there were not enough officers to fill the second-class coach and so travelled in commissioned luxury!

McCarthy established his kitchen in one of the compartments. His oven was on the floor and his larder in the luggage racks. By some miracle of improvisation he managed to produce three hot meals a day. The N.C.O.s messed with him, but the officers' food had to be carried to their compartment along the footboard of the coach, regardless of the speed at which the train was travelling. The orderly corporal, when acting as food conveyor, had a very narrow escape from death. As he opened the door of his compartment the train went through a tunnel and the door caught in the brickwork. By the grace of heaven it was only a glancing blow, but a fraction of a second later man and door would have been whirled to destruction.

As the train approached Italy the weather became even colder. Icicles hung from the engine and in an endeavour to avoid freezing to death the men in the cattle trucks scrounged coal from the tender and built fires on the floor of their trucks. On arrival at Genoa in milder weather, and with some chance of getting a wash, they emerged, coal-black and bleary-eyed. Why none of them died of carbon monoxide poisoning is still to me a mystery.

In due course we reached our rail destination—Padua—at 4 p.m. on Boxing Day. Lorries were waiting for us, but again there were delays. The Germans were bombing the road to our destination at Villaverla and we were not allowed to start. At last, at midnight and in five degrees of frost, we arrived at our billet—an ice-cold villa. Its tessellated floors and immense windows and doors chilled us to the bone. Our camp beds were erected in this morgue and then—there was McCarthy lying on his belly in the drive, coaxing some damp wood to burn by blowing on it. He was anxious that the officers should have something hot to drink before turning in! Kipling has sung the praises of Gunga Din, the water-carrier, who gave drinks to wounded men in the firing line. Was McCarthy's sacrifice much less than that of Kipling's hero? I for one am glad to pay tribute to a middle-aged Irishman who brought us so much comfort. He learned from the Italians and before long his *risotto portuguaise* was one of the more popular dishes in the Wing mess.

McCarthy stayed with us until March 1919, when he disappeared into the welter of demobilization. I have never heard from him since, but to me his memory is still green.

There was one other man in the Wing whom I have never forgotten. One day the O.C. of my balloons produced a defaulter whom he claimed to be an incorrigible drunk. Would I please deal with him? A nice quiet little man was brought before me and his conduct sheet indicated that on no less than twelve occasions he had been drunk according to service standards, and that meant very drunk indeed.

This didn't seem to make any sense to me so I turned the witnesses and escort out of the office and asked him some questions. I got nowhere. He would not explain—he would give no reason. Finally I said, 'Will you promise me not to get drunk again?' This he obviously considered an unfair approach. He was ready to take fourteen days' field punishment, but a promise of this sort! No! He gulped, he fidgeted, I pressed him. Finally he promised and for three months he remained sober. Then he got his home leave—and deserted. The story came out. He was married and very much in love. Every time kind neighbours wrote to tell him of his wife's infidelity he would get drunk on *vino*. When he got home he sorted things out but the conclusion he reached—desertion—merely got him into further trouble out of which I could not help him.

More comment on the airmen of the 14th Wing! An order came from London that all were to be given an anti-typhoid injection. A number of the fitters were fallen in for punishment because they refused the treatment. When pressed for a reason the answer was that their sore arms would handicap their work on the aero engines! They were given the alternative of the needle or a posting to Iraq! Although Northern Italy had its discomforts it was a Paradise compared with life in the desert, so the doctor had no more trouble. To maintain the health of all ranks in the rather trying conditions that prevailed in

Northern Italy was a considerable task to which I devoted a good deal of attention. The food the men ate was one of my main interests—so much so that I earned the nickname of 'The Cookhouse King'. I thought that a certain measure of success had been achieved. Judge then of my dismay and disappointment when a long letter containing the following remark landed on my desk.

R. S. Hudson, a fitter sergeant in No. 139 Squadron stationed at Villaverla in 1918, writes: '. . . the food was awful, stew and boiled rice in a temperature of 90°!'

However, I can say in my defence that the men looked extremely well on this diet, and the sickness rate was so low that a deputation of doctors came out from the Air Ministry to make an enquiry. The deputation seemed satisfied because, after some amiable exchanges, they departed to Southern Italy to harass my friend and colleague Geoffrey Bromet, who was then in command. Apart from his dislike of his rations and the difficult working conditions Hudson seems to have enjoyed himself. In his letter he says:

'You probably remember us at Villaverla and, considering that we were a mixed crew, we soon settled down under somewhat trying conditions. Imagine what the airman of today would say if he had to haul up the wet heavy front curtains of the canvas hangars of the time before daybreak, and then manhandle the aircraft through knee-deep grass to the airfield. Incidentally we slept in those hangars. [Does memory fail? I seem to remember that only the night guards slept in the hangars. There were certainly some very serviceable wooden huts available.] I enjoyed the free life,' he continues, 'but I never really became accustomed to the casual approach and the blind faith that the aircrew had in the ground staff. Considering the lack of proper facilities I think the maintenance was astoundingly good. . . . I managed to get in a few flying hours as passenger on trips to Venice, Florence and other towns. . . .'

These trips must have been taken after the Armistice. With no operations going on there was some difficulty in keeping the men occupied. To relieve their boredom flights of aircraft, with accompanying mechanics, were sent round the larger cities of Italy to give exhibitions of aerobatics. In this the airmen of the Aircraft Park—the

F

ex-Coventry tinsmiths—could not share and they became restless and threatening. Word reached them from the squadron airmen that if there was any suggestion of a mutiny the trouble would be dealt with very firmly. I heard of this only indirectly, but was delighted to get such support from the other ranks. Nothing further happened and demobilization proceeded smoothly.

One of the first to be released was my driver, Maisey. He was reported as saying that once he had driven with me in the service car for 300 miles during which I had never uttered a word. A gross libel, of course! It was Maisey who had accompanied me on leave to Porto Fino Rapallo, a famous seaside resort much used by Italian socialites. As we were walking up to the hotel we passed a gorgeous vision just emerged from the sea, Titian-red hair to her knees but otherwise clad in black net. One quick look and I turned to see how Maisey was taking it. His eyes were firmly on the ground, his shoulders bowed under the weight of my suitcases and every line of his figure stating unequivocally, 'This is no place for the Colonel!' News reached me later that, released from my service to the rest camp at Genoa, he had passed a very enjoyable week, while I, under the firm control of some respectable acquaintances who were also at Rapallo, had to watch my step very carefully.

In 1917 the plans were laid for the bombing of Germany's war industry in the Rhineland. These led to the formation of the Independent Air Force under General Trenchard. As one who served in the I.A.F. Air Mechanic Welland has this to say:

'I suppose that the best way to begin this story is to start with my initial training with the R.F.C. I joined as an instrument repairer at the age of eighteen at Charlton Park. From there I went to the recruits' camp at Farnborough where I did my square-bashing, and took my trade test at the Royal Aircraft Factory. I must have done well at my trade test as my ranking was 2nd A.M., and strange to relate this made me the senior rank in my tent although there were men of forty or more there. This led to a peculiar situation, as before I had a uniform I was on the peg for having a dirty tent. I was told that as senior rank I was in charge, and it was no good explaining to the S.M. that the others were old enough to be my father as that didn't seem to matter, and as we were about twenty to a tent my position could be well imagined. I also got into trouble with the S.M. for not shaving, as I had never shaved before. Anyone who has had experience with the lumps of hoop-iron the R.F.C. served out as razors in those days can well imagine what my face looked like after my first shave. The medical orderly had a good laugh anyway.'

He was glad to be posted to Farnborough for training on aircraft instruments. After some weeks he was moved to Yate, near Bristol. The airmen here were busy reconstructing crashed aircraft, mainly B.E.2es. Air Mechanic Welland had his first flight in a B.E.2e which to him was a bit of an adventure, as it was the first aircraft to be rebuilt.

From here came his posting to 215 Squadron, then being refitted at Andover aerodrome. It was a R.N.A.S. Handley Page bomber squadron, and he walked into a load of trouble! The amalgamation of the two flying services had just taken place, and there was a lot of *esprit de corps* about. In a minority of one his predicament was complete. He couldn't even understand what they were talking about at times.

When he reported he was told to see 'Johnny the One'. Who he was Welland had no idea, but it appeared he could be found on the quarter-deck. This was another mystery, when all that could be seen was an ordinary army or air force camp. To crown it all when he wanted to go to Andover Town he had to catch the 'liberty boat', which meant going through a gate into the lane which ran alongside the aerodrome and catch the leave lorry. He had in fact another spell of training to undergo, and that was in the vernacular of the R.N.A.S., which was entirely different from that of the R.F.C.

His job with the squadron, and it was a big one, was to keep all the instruments in good order, and to see that the compasses were true. If any new metal parts were added to the aircraft it meant that the plane had to be taken to the compass course to have the compasses swung again. As there were two compasses in this type of aircraft, this took best part of a day. They had to be right, as in those days, apart from flashing beacons, there was no other navigational aid.

The C.O. of 215 Squadron was Major Jones, and when training and refitting was complete the squadron went overseas to France.

No. 215 found itself at a place called Alquines, not far from St. Omer. It was a night-bomber squadron, and the first baptism of active service was not happy. The aircraft were lined up on the airfield ready for the first night's operations when a blizzard suddenly blew up, and none of the aircraft were pegged down. It was a case of all hands to the rescue. Not much damage was done although it was an anxious time, and nearly gave Major Jones a heart attack. The aerodrome at Alquines was on top of a hill, and the road to St. Omer had a very sharp turn at the bottom of the hill. This led to a really smelly experience for the dispatch-driver one day. At the bottom of the hill was one of those awful cess-pools which abound in France. The driver had a Phelon and Moore motor-cycle combination, and on this particular occasion took the corner too fast. He couldn't quite make the turn and finished up in the cess-pool. Anyone who has seen or smelt the stirred-up contents of a French cess-pool, let alone been in it, can imagine the state of the poor dispatch-driver. It took two or three days for the awful stench to disperse and about three weeks for the driver to recover.

No. 215 assisted in the preparations for the great counter-attack which followed the retreat of 1918. Its job was to bomb rail communications at Amiens, and in one period of four weeks its aircraft dropped ninety tons of bombs. This was no mean achievement for those days, as a Handley Page could only manage about fifteen hundredweight of bombs each load. This meant almost continuous work in one way or another for aircrews and ground staff, and at times the mechanics never took off their clothes for days. About this time the great flu epidemic struck, and Welland was the first to report sick. 'Needless to say I was given "medicine and duty". Two hours later I was on my way to the Casualty Clearing Station at St. Omer where I stayed for three weeks.' There were many casualties from the epidemic, and when at last the squadron was back to strength it was ordered to pack up and make its way to join the Independent Air Force under General Trenchard, near Nancy.

The journey from Alquines to Rambervilliers took over a week, and there were some amusing incidents. The train pulled up one evening quite close to a truck on which was a huge hog's-head of wine. The temptation was too strong. As soon as it became dusk the carpenters got out a brace and bit, made a bung, and tapped the barrel. There was a continuous stream of erks back and forwards to the scene of the 'crime', and before long everybody was very happy. Everyone who went to get their ration of wine was enjoined to replace the bung properly as the train was likely to move off at any moment. Sure enough it had to happen; whilst 'Dusty' Miller, the squadron character, was filling his 'Dixie', his tenth, the train started to move off, and the last to be seen of him for a while was his running madly down the track and, yes, he had forgotten to replace the bung, with the result that a lot of lovely wine was wasted. Dusty turned up about three days after the squadron reached Rambervilliers, and was immediately put on a charge. But the squadron got an even rougher greeting. As the 'troops' were unloading the train it was bombed and the petrol dump set on fire.

The work of 215 now started in earnest with the I.A.F. and General Trenchard paid a visit and gave a pep-talk. The job of the I.A.F. was to bomb the German Rhine towns and some job it proved to be. Losses started with the first raid. These were mainly due to landing accidents, as there seemed to be a permanent night mist over the aerodrome. The mechanics were working night and day to keep the planes flying and on many occasions meals were taken to the hangars. It sometimes happened that for a whole week the men did not sleep in their huts. The uniforms were black with grease, and of course every man was lousy. On one occasion some French cavalry sheltered in a wood close by, and a bomb from a German raider killed a number of horses. Our men had been on French rations for some time, but it was a bit of a shock to see the meat ration cut up and delivered to the cookhouse from the horses that had been killed the night before.

Some of the Handley Pages had been fitted with an extra tank to enable them to reach Cologne. This was a very long raid and took about eight hours. Welland does not think it was worth it, as it cost the squadron some very good pilots and aircrews. There were times when the squadron could not put a plane into the air, and many were the tricks employed by the mechanics to make a plane airworthy. They would take the mainplanes from one plane whose fuselage was damaged to fit to a plane whose mainplanes were unserviceable. This made it possible to get one plane fit for service. Spares were very short, and any wrecked plane was stripped of parts which would prove useful. Welland continues:

'About September a bomb was delivered to the squadron which weighed 1750 lb. and was about twenty feet long. When it was first seen the astonishment was great, and many doubts were expressed about a Handley ever getting off the ground with it. The armourers fitted a couple of chains under a plane and the idea was to sling it, as no proper bomb-rack had been supplied. The runway was lengthened to allow the plane to rise, and the time came to deliver the bomb to its target, which was Bonn. We heard later that the bomb missed its target, and blew a small village to pieces. The pilot reported that the plane jumped about 500 feet when the bomb was released. I may add it was the only one the squadron ever dropped.'

Here is one of Welland's stories that to my knowledge has never been told. Someone had a scheme to land a specially trained crew on an airfield that was being used as a base for raids on French towns. Here they were to set fire to the hangars and then run back to the plane and take off. A Handley Page was especially modified for this, and became known as the 'bathing machine' because on either side, just behind the mainplanes, steps were fitted to allow easy exit and access. The training of the crew went on for weeks until the proficiency was 100 per cent. They were all granted a week's leave, and then came the time for the operation. This was fixed for the first bright moon period, 10th December 1918. Owing to the Armistice on 11th November, the flight never took place. Welland remembers the pilot, all keyed-up, standing in front of the 'bathing machine' and cursing his luck. Reaction was responsible, for undoubtedly he was just as glad as anyone else that the war was over. A pilot's life was not very long in those days.

Welland says that the angled lights fitted to the Lancasters that bombed the Moehne Dams, so that they could tell their height above the water (the idea being that when the two beams met the height was right), were used by the I.A.F. in 1918 and proved very efficient!

The men had their lighter moments, of course. Once the officers of 215 organized a boar-hunt in the Charmes Forest. Wild-boar meat would have made a welcome change from the horse-flesh and McConachie's tinned dinners. The hunt was arranged, and the officers had the guns, and the other ranks, acting as beaters, formed a long line. As they walked through the undergrowth they were instructed to shout as loud as they could, tapping the trees with long sticks as well. After a while Welland's section came to a bit of a clearing, and then things happened. One of these ugly-looking beasts suddenly broke cover, charging straight at the hunters. Welland had never seen anything like it before so he dropped everything and shinned up the nearest tree, which proved to be a sapling. Needless to say, the thing started to bend over, and he found himself hanging on, with his behind nearly touching the ground. The boar by this time had gone, but Welland gave up the hunt right away. It didn't seem safe to come upon one of these beasts armed with only a stick and a loud shout. He'd sooner do a raid any day. Welland adds:

'On our squadron pilots and mechanics were great pals, and it was often possible to go on a short raid, although not officially. Aircrew were always in short supply. It was the custom for mechanics on such occasions to drop the twenty-pound Cooper bombs. It must be said here that bomb-sights were very crude and in some cases non-existent. The Cooper bombs were hung on racks in the rear cockpit, and one just took one off as required, prepared it, then leant over the side, and judged the proper moment to let it go. We usually aimed these at searchlights. Didn't seem to do much good. Just to show what the pilot thought about the bomb-sights in those days, the plane that I was most interested in had the pilot's mascot tied to the sight.'

In France and indeed elsewhere in 1918 the year was to be one of movement even for the R.F.C. On the Somme the new airfields that had been occupied after the German retreat to the Hindenburg Line had to be abandoned very rapidly when in March the enemy made a deep thrust into our lines.

On the 5th Army front our aircraft were mainly engaged in ground-attack duties, endeavouring to hold up the enemy advance. To help the pilots to establish where lay the front line, airmen were sent forward to report the position. On one occasion Second Air Mechanic Knight of No. 84 Squadron, armed with a rifle and bicycle, was far enough forward to see an Albatross two-seater shooting up our troops. By a piece of singular good fortune he brought the Albatross down with one shot and accepted the surrender of its crew. There were many other episodes of this sort where airmen had to take on the role of infantry and act in support of our hard-pressed troops. It was about this time that General John Salmond, commanding the R.F.C., found himself not only with a disorganized force in the south, but with his squadrons in the north blocking the gap in the line when a Portuguese division broke under the impact of a fierce German attack. This was in the 2nd Army area near Cassel. For some hours, until infantry reserves could be brought up, the front was held by low-flying aircraft that pinned the enemy to the ground he had captured.

It was a very difficult period for the Army and Air Force. If the Germans could have reached the Channel, only a short distance from Cassel, they might well have won the war. In very truth the British had their backs to the wall. The R.A.F. fought desperately and successfully to aid their comrades on land.

These two thrusts—on the Somme and in the Ypres sector—were Germany's last fling. By August the Allied armies were advancing on a wide front and by the winter were in occupation of the Rhineland.

To Egypt and to Mesopotamia came small detachments of the R.F.C. during the early days of the war. 'Mespot' did not expand very greatly as operations developed. Indeed the Government of India, carrying out its usual policy of cutting military estimates to the bone, kept both the ground and air forces that it dispatched to this front at the irreducible minimum of equipment. Egypt was luckier. The importance of the Suez Canal was not ignored by the Home authorittes, and, apart from substantial military reinforcements, a trickle of aircraft also went that way.

Air Mechanic C. R. King (already mentioned) was one of these reinforcements.

In the autumn of 1915 he was sent from France to Egypt with No. 14 Squadron. Major Stopford was in command and the squadron sailed in the S.S. *Anchises* from Devonport to Alexandria, where it camped. Some of the equipment came along on the S.S. *Hunspill*, a captured ship. She had a load of petrol aft and a load of bombs forward. King was helping unload the bombs when a net full of boxes of bombs broke high over the quay-side, and twenty-pound Cooper bombs smashed down on the cobbles. Some of the bombs were broken, so that the T.N.T. spilled out on the ground, but there was no explosion. This incident gave the men greater confidence when handling bombs. On another occasion some delayed-action 100-pound bombs had to be dropped on the Turks. A specialist was sent from the artillery to put the detonators in. The airmen noticed his hands trembled so much that they were glad when he went away and left them to do the job.

From Alexandria the squadron moved to Heliopolis, near Cairo, and established an airfield on the edge of the desert. Here R.A.F.-type hangars were erected and the aircraft assembled as they arrived from England in crates. When eighteen aircraft were ready, the squadron split up into flights. King went with 'B' Flight, under the command of Captain Jenkins, with six aircraft by sea to Sidi Barani. From here the flight advanced via Mersa Matruh to Sollum, travelling in ships long condemned as unseaworthy. They were rusty, rat-ridden, verminous and stank. One was said to be the first screw-driven ship to travel from London to India. On another there was a queer lavatory up near the bows which over-hung the water. There was a very heavy iron door with no fastening which clanged to with terrific force when the ship rolled, and the sea slapped up from behind. On a rough day the sight of an airman emerging from this cosy little spot provided a great deal of entertainment.

The task of the aircraft was to patrol the sea for submarines and the land for hostile Senussi tribesmen. Co-operation was carried out with the *Severn*, a gunboat, and the armed yachts *Lily* and *Veronica*.

It was a wonderful life at Sollum in the pure desert air and although on the barest rations the men were extremely fit. All water had to come by sea from Alexandria. It was put in tanks (called 'Fantasses'), loaded on camels and sent up the cliff road to the airfield. Extra water was wangled by claiming a quantity for the engines, which were actually air-cooled. Captain Jenkins rightly guessed that the authorities at Alexandria knew nothing about aircraft engines.

One day in the middle of a sandstorm one of the two camels that had brought the water suddenly went mad and chased its Egyptian driver round the hangar. The driver crept under the canvas and the camel started to rip the hangar curtain with his teeth in an endeavour to get at him. The Flight Commander, hearing the noise, came out and immediately ordered the airmen to get some long ropes and throw the camel by entangling its legs. As soon as they started to do this, the camel turned on them. They managed to secure his hind legs, but he could still run. He chased round after those who were trying to fix his forelegs, with frothing mouth and bloodshot eyes, but the party on the hind legs, holding the rope, could scarcely stand for laughing. One man rolled on the ground with laughter and the camel nearly

had him, but the others just managed to put it off by throwing the
rope round its head. Then its forefeet were lassoed and down it fell.
A swarm of airmen pounced on to it and trussed it up, so that it could
not move. Then the native emerged from the hangar and wanted to
thrash it, but he was not allowed to touch it. Later, one of the British
Camel Transport officers came up and told the airmen to leave it
trussed up for three hours. Then it was untied and it got to its feet
and walked away with the other camel as quietly as a lamb. All this
time the second camel had been quietly chewing the cud and taking
no interest in what was going on.

From Sollum the flight sailed on the S.S. *Minnetonka* with the
5th Welch Regiment and the 7th Cheshire Regiment and went back
to Alexandria. Later the whole squadron was transferred to Palestine.

In Palestine No. 14 followed behind the advancing troops. The
airmen were up against many difficulties. The rain, mud, mosquitoes
and sand flies made the going hard, and rations were meagre. Most
men became weak and slack, and so many went sick that it made the
work even harder. The aircraft got soggy and would not take off with
a bomb-load. On one camp the aircraft had to be pushed up a hill.
The bombs were then carried up and loaded on, and a downhill start
attempted. Taking off, the wheels would sink in the mud and throw
up stones into the propeller, shattering it, so that the pilot had to
throttle down quickly and hope for the best, as there were no brakes.
No aircraft was lost that way, but they got severely knocked about.
Many men were stung by scorpions that got into the engine covers.
Soon no cover was left on the ground, in case some biting or crawling
insect hid in it. They even got in the propeller covers, but King found
that if you left a scorpion alone, it wouldn't sting you.

The men were all very glad to get out of Palestine when the war
ended. The squadron went by road to Kantara and those men due for
demobilization were attached to the general demobilization camp there,
to await a ship for England. King was one of these, and came back
via Taranto on the S.S. *Kashgar*. He stayed at Faenza for a bit and then
by train through the Mont Cenis Tunnel to France. On the way, the
train was delayed and shunted about for many days before it got
through to France and Le Havre. When the train stopped the men
ran up to the engine, which was one of the continental types, fearfully
and wonderfully made! They would open any cocks or taps till hot
water came out, to make tea or to shave, and took not the slightest

notice of the Italian driver cursing them from the cab. Once again the train stopped alongside a truck loaded with wine. It was not long before someone had tapped it, and every cattle-truck-load of men was filling mugs and dixies. The Italians naturally complained, and a British provost officer came up and said that where any truck even smelt of wine he would put the occupants on a charge, and, what was worse, stop them on their way back to England. Unfortunately for him the officers' batmen on the train had brought their officers some wine which they were enjoying in their own trucks and which smelt as strongly as the next. So, as all the trains could not be stopped, King and his friends were allowed to proceed, followed by a good deal of hate from the Italians. There was deep snow and frost and those who had been in Egypt for a year or two felt it very much.

Finally, when Folkestone was reached and the men had entrained for London, someone wrote along the carriages in large letters 'The Pankhurst Army'! Miss Pankhurst had said that all the men coming back from the East were 'tainted'. Little could she know of the stringent medical test undergone before they were passed for Home!

Victory in Palestine having brought about the collapse of Turkey, Bulgaria sued for peace. Austria followed suit in October and Germany in November.

For a while the airmen were content to feel that the shooting war was over and that soon they would be home again. There was the novelty of parading as victors in enemy country, of accepting a position of superiority—and enjoying it. But soon these minor fruits of victory began to pall. 'When are we going to be released?' was the question that officers were constantly called upon to answer—and their instructions were not really very clear. Broadly speaking the principle of 'First in—first out' underlay the demobilization procedure, but in the Royal Air Force the problem of the technical trades was to vex the authorities very much as it did nearly thirty years later. It was essential to retain a minimum of skilled men to keep aircraft serviceable, and many of these were the early entrants, or time-expired regulars. Besides the sense of grievance caused in this way there were many men who had been conscripted into the service and hence felt no other desire than to get back into civil life as soon as possible. They had heard tales of the high wages that were being earned by operatives in the reserved occupations. Their pay and allowances had been on the meagre side and so they felt that a considerable injustice had been done to them. Even the fact that women of the W.R.A.F. were being sent out, so far as was possible, as reliefs did not content them. So in many camps there were mutinies which did little to enhance the credit of the Royal Air Force.

These mutineers must be excused. Some of them had suffered great hardship and rough treatment. Read what Air Mechanic Collett has to say on this subject:

'On the outbreak of war I volunteered for flying duties and was posted to Farnborough. On 13th of August we took off for France in a B.E.2a. Lieutenant Emmett, a South African, was the pilot.

My armament consisted of a short butt Lee-Enfield rifle, 150 rounds of .303 in a canvas bandolier, a Webley Mk. 4 pistol and fifty rounds of ammunition.

We landed at Shoreham to refuel, took off for Dover, on coming in to land the engine cut out and we crashed badly on landing; the pilot had his right thumb broken, but I received serious injuries and was taken to Dover Cliff Hospital.

On discharge later in the year I was posted to "C" Flight No. 7 Squadron, Longreach, Dartford, Kent. Later we rejoined "A" and "B" Flights at Netheravon, and proceeded to France where we were based at St. Omer. We lost all our aircraft through various causes and were re-equipped with the French Voisin, a wonderful aircraft, a pusher type with 4-wheel undercarriage, with hand-operated brakes on the rear wheels. You could not turn this machine on the ground as the undercarriage would fold up. Mechanics had to bear down on the rear booms, so lifting the front wheels off the ground, and then pushing it round into the required heading.'

Subsequently Collett served in two of the aircraft depots in France and finished the war in very unhappy circumstances. He had been invalided home owing to an attack of poisoning, and because he had gained wide experience of engines and aircraft during his previous years of service he was, on discharge from hospital, posted to No. 1 School of Military Aeronautics at Reading. He writes with feeling about this place, and I, having known the personnel there employed on administrative duties, am forced to agree with his strictures on the way the School was run. He writes:

'I tried my damnedest to avoid this posting but it was no use —I went.

Every technical N.C.O. was scared stiff of being posted to No. 1 S. of M.A. and very soon I knew why.

The officers and N.C.O.s from the C.O. downwards were exceedingly strict. 95 per cent of the administrative duties were thrown on to the technical W.O.s and N.C.O.s who also had their own duties to carry out.

One was placed on a charge for the least thing. I stopped four reps in a month for crimes I didn't know I had committed. We had every nationality under the sun as trainees, so you can guess we had our work cut out, without having to carry out stupid admin. duties all hours of the day and night.

Three officers were relieved of their command whilst I was there, and there were two cases of suicide, besides outbreaks of spinal meningitis, measles, etc.

Towards the end of 1917 we had quite a number of ex-soldiers from all regiments sent to us as trainees. These men had been wounded and maimed and transferred to the R.F.C. for lighter duties. They were treated so badly that 400 of them formed up and were determined to march to Windsor Castle and see the King. Heaven only knows how they were stopped!

I know the senior admin.'s sergeant-major met a crowd of "Aussies" on a bridge one night and was promptly thrown into the River Kennet.'

There was a D.H.4 housed in a portable hangar in a field close to the School. The River Kennet ran at the end of this field. Every night an armed guard was mounted on the hangar. Once the river overflowed and flooded the field to a depth of three feet. In spite of this the guard was still mounted, its members having to wade to their post. Collett once waded with water up to his armpits, carrying his equipment on his head until he reached the hangar. On another occasion the water was so deep that a punt had to be fetched to ferry the guard back to dry land. How silly can orders and routine become!

It was this kind of treatment that soured the best-natured of men and the R.A.F. paid in 1919 for the imbecilities of officers and N.C.O.s who had learned nothing and forgotten nothing during their period of service.

This condensed version of three years' war service leaves something to be desired from a historical point of view. But as a sketch of what the airmen thought and felt, of what they endured, it has a great deal of merit.

The work of the R.F.C. in Mesopotamia was hard, difficult and unrewarding. The ground crews had to keep some rather antique aircraft sufficiently serviceable to reconnoitre for the Army, to carry out artillery co-operation, to bombard the enemy and, during one disastrous period, to drop ammunition and food on to our troops beleagured in Kut-el-Amara. In addition they suffered from short rations, an almost complete lack of elementary comforts, and were subject to a whole battery of diseases of which dysentery and sand-fly fever were the most prevalent. And yet they bore all these trials with considerable fortitude.

A squadron's camp consisted of several rows of ordinary bell tents, sunk two feet or more into the sand to give some protection from the blistering sun. There were a few E.P. (European Pattern) tents of double thickness that served to keep out some of the heat. These were for the officers. The mess 'tent' might be anything from a few trestle tables out in the open to a roughly contrived palm-leaf shelter, open on all sides. The cookhouse would be of the same sort.

The moment the wind blew strongly sand would be everywhere: in the food, in the few clothes that were worn, in the bedding, in hair and eyes and between the teeth.

In similar conditions in the Sinai Desert I have watched from the top of a dune an airfield sited on a salt pan below. Within a few minutes the ground was obscured. Only the tops of the sheds showed above the sand fog but soon even these disappeared as the wind grew in strength and the sand thickened. I thought regretfully, first, of all the grit that was drifting into the engines and which would cause trouble when they started up, and, secondly, about the troops as they huddled in any shelter they could find. These storms lasted a day or more and were the cause of a great deal of profanity and unavoidable misery.

In Iraq the Field Force Canteens, usually run by Indian contractors, and which were supposed to provide small luxuries and amusements for the men, were often short of both these commodities.

The financial experts of the Government of India (responsible for the war in Mesopotamia) could speak with pride of the strict pruning they had given to the Army Estimates. But it was the service men who paid in suffering for this success!

The story has been told, officially and otherwise, of the river steamers plying between Baghdad and Basra and conveying casualties to the relative comfort of India. On the decks of these ships and without adequate protection from the sun lay the sick—suffering from dysentery in the main. The scuppers ran with their excreta as there were not enough medical orderlies to give them aid in their agony. The stench rose to the skies and flies swarmed all over these helpless creatures. It is impossible to say how many of them died from lack of care, but the figure must have been high. Of course, amongst the sick were many airmen. Only the very strongest survived.

Twice have I served under the British Government of India. To this day I cannot understand how such a hide-bound bureaucracy was allowed to come into being to the detriment of the individual soldier and airman serving under a fantastic form of control.

Let me give two instances. In 1938 there was a surplus of 60,000 rupees (about £4600) in the Air Force budget. New wash-places and lavatories for the men were badly needed on the R.A.F. stations, and it seemed obvious that, one at a time, and year by year, these improvements could be built. The estimate was put forward—and turned down. Only if all the stations could have the same improvements in one year could this expenditure be allowed! A predecessor of mine as A.O.C. India, Sir Geoffrey Salmond, arranged for the R.A.F. workshop lorries to provide electric light for the airmen's barrack rooms. This dastardly act was discovered by the Army Department and he was told to 'stop it immediately'. Because the tens of thousands of soldiers up and down the country had only paraffin lamps with which to light their barrack rooms, the airmen had to conform.

It is almost impossible to speak calmly of the time, just after the Kaiser War, when the R.A.F. in India had to go into the bazaars to buy wire, steel rod, sparking-plugs and other material with which to keep their aircraft serviceable. The Finance Department was either unwilling or unable to make the necessary provision from England.

Peace on the ashes of the Government of India that died in 1947, lamented by few!

7

Technical Training at Home and Abroad

IN THE background of this story were the efforts being made in Britain and elsewhere to supply the mechanics and pilots essential to the conduct of the war in the air. In addition the rate of expansion of the R.F.C. must be taken into account.

There have been some references previously to the primitive training organization that had to suffice the R.F.C. in the early days of the Kaiser War. Studying the activities of the Directorate of Military Aeronautics at the War Office it seems fairly clear that at first the policy of the Directorate was to rely for its supply of skilled men on the Corps of Royal Engineers and on civilian industry. But it had not counted on the tremendous influence of Lord Kitchener's appeal for volunteers. Men who would have been invaluable in the technical corps flocked to the infantry so as to 'have a bash at the Huns'. In the mud of the Ypres Salient, on Messines Ridge, at Arras, Cambrai and on the Somme they died in their thousands. Thus was left a gap in our national resources that was hard to fill. The training organization of the Polytechnic went some way towards providing the men required, but it was most fortunate that at the start the R.F.C. expanded very slowly. It was some time before the military authorities realized that success in the war might well turn on a prior victory in the air.

Paradoxically, though the supply of officers for the land forces was always inadequate, by the end of 1916 there was no shortage of officer pilots. The flying-training schools, built largely on the civilian schools existing in 1914, had done their job.

The R.N.A.S. does not seem to have had any real trouble to find the personnel it needed. Civilians came forward in sufficient numbers from the engineering and electrical industries, and were knocked into shape by the regular officers and the technicians that the Grand Fleet

The engine shops, Farnborough. Rotary engines under repair

Fabric workers under training, Farnborough

Camp cookhouse

Woodworking shop, Farnborough. Wings under repair

felt itself able to spare. So, the Admiralty were able to build up a force of some 50,000 officers and men without going through the agonies that afflicted the War Office in its greater task of finally producing 330,000 all ranks in the budding Royal Air Force.

In January 1917 the pressure was on. Lord Haig's demands grew with the passage of weeks and the needs of Home Defence against Zeppelins and Gothas became more and more urgent. The training programme was a kaleidoscope, shifting in pattern and colour with every change of policy. Trainee engine fitters, after eight weeks at Coley Park, Reading, moved to the Scottish School of Fitters in Edinburgh, or to the Central Flying School at Upavon, now a very large organization. Here the men passed another eight weeks, after which they went to a training squadron as 'improvers'. In February there was a change. The men went first to the Polytechnic schools for eight weeks, after which they went to Edinburgh, Upavon or Coley Park. No part of this organization was adequate and overcrowding was endemic, with consequent loss of efficiency. In July, when accommodation had been built, fitter training moved to Halton, where it was named No. 1 School of Technical Training.

The association of the R.F.C. with Halton had begun during the army manœuvres of 1913. Lord Rothschild, who then owned a very large property on the Chiltern Hills above Wendover, invited the Brigade of Guards, a brigade of Royal Artillery and the Royal Flying Corps to stay with him for the week-end. A landing ground was established and occupied and officers and men of these organizations, some thousands of them, were accommodated in tents on Lord Rothschild's land. For three days all lived like fighting cocks! The host must have been impressed by the discipline and good behaviour of all ranks, in particular the R.F.C., because on his death he vested the Air Ministry in the title to his property, including the 'big house' which is now the main officers' mess.

To this day Halton's chief activity has been the training of technicians who do three years of general and technical education before passing on to service units.

In Egypt in 1916–17 the Commander of the R.F.C. was a highly intelligent and very progressive lieutenant-colonel called Geoffrey Salmond. He very soon made up his mind that the climate of Egypt was ideal for flying training and that, in addition, there was space and man-power with which to create a big technical training organization.

G

At this time there were two British squadrons, Nos. 14 and 17, and No. 1 Australian Squadron operating on the two fronts guarding the Suez Canal. To supply them was 'X' Aircraft Park in Cairo. When No. 17 Squadron moved to Salonica, and a reserve flying/training squadron was created at Abu-Sueir on the Sweet Water Canal, the need for a more exensive base organization became apparent. 'X' Aircraft Depot then formed at Aboukir, not far from Alexandria and on the Mediterranean coast. A large number of Egyptians were enrolled and trained as air mechanics and drivers. Some time later another training depot station was formed nearby.

What the conditions were under which the airmen lived at the T.D.S. are best described by Air Mechanic Giles, an eighteen-year-old:

'No. 16 T.D.S. camp was in course of construction and was situated on the edge of the Libyan Desert, just outside Alexandria. Sun-baked sand, tents and some stone buildings being built. In the officers' lines a few huts, H.Q. and Mess were built. Otherwise, personnel and cadets were in E.P. tents. As far as I can remember, discipline was slack. We went about camp dressed for comfort rather than looks. Treatment by our superiors was good. The food on the whole was rough. Practically every day for sweet we had boiled rice and dates, and bully-beef and biscuits! Bread (sometimes not available) was, I imagine, native-baked, a dry bluey-brown concoction. The biscuits could not be eaten unless soaked in one's tea. There was always plenty of marmalade (Needlers) and cheese was surplus to the general need. Never saw any jam. Eggs were plentiful, but we had to buy them from the native labour corps.

Accommodated in tents for a couple of weeks, then moved into a stone hut. Plenty of bed space per man. Had to construct own bedstead from airplane wreckage, odd wood and doped fabric. No palliasses, lay on folded blanket. Hut window spaces filled in with doped fabric also. Had plenty of company in the way of bed-bugs, fleas. During sand-storm, locusts, spiders, scorpions, etc. in addition blown in under the eaves. One could only lie under blanket till storm was over. Fresh water was transported daily from Amria village by donkey-drawn tank. Washing water was pumped up from well, but supply was poor. Lighting for camp was supplied from generators, operated on workshop lorries, one each end of camp, which closed down each night at 10.30.'

The operational squadrons on the Canal—a flight at Port Said, a squadron at Kantara, flights at Ismailia and Suez—were somewhat better served. In spite of the heat, the curse of sand-storms and the monotony of their existence the airmen maintained a very high standard of morale. Amongst them were some unusual characters and Hudson was one of these. In 1915 he was gardener to a wealthy man in the Midlands. Forty years of age, married, with children, in a well-paid job with a cottage, he could have spent the war in relative comfort and security. He was one of those moved to their innermost being by Kitchener's appeal. In spite of every pressure that his master could apply to him Hudson volunteered and, because of his age, was posted to the R.F.C. as an aircraft hand. He did his training, waiting for the day when he would be sent to France to fight the enemy. Instead he was allotted to No. 5 Wing H.Q. at Ismailia as batman! This was disaster, but he played the game. Being a Midlander he understood good food and good living. He hadn't a word of Arabic and yet he coped with the Arab cook most successfully. Wing H.Q. became a gastronomic centre of great repute, and later when he was transferred to Brigade H.Q. in Cairo (the Brigadier also liked his food) he continued to 'father' his officers until the end of the war.

Hudson was a very solid type, about 5 feet 11 inches tall and almost as thick, ruddy-complexioned and well moustached. He had the brightest and kindliest eyes. 'Hudson! There are some guests tonight. What can we give them?' 'Well, sir, as you know the chickens are tough and stringy, and besides there's only bully beef. Leave it to Cookie and me. We'll fix something!' At dinner there would be a most savoury stew of chicken, onions and small potatoes, tiny stuffed vegetable marrows (here the bully beef played its part) and whatever fruit was in season. This was in Ismailia! In Cairo he had greater scope!

The experiment of treating Egyptians as technicians proved successful, particularly as carpenters and riggers. The Arab is no fool and has good hands. But it was rarely possible to allow Egyptians to work without supervision, and it says much for the patience and adaptability of the British airmen that they worked well and willingly alongside the native Egyptian.

As the Middle East Brigade grew in size in preparation for the assault on Palestine, so the relief afforded by these measures began to disappear. Something on a vaster scale had to be undertaken and now was to appear the embryo of the Empire Air Training Scheme. Appeal was made to the Dominions, particularly to Canada, and within the Empire flying and technical training schools were set up. From England partly trained airmen were sent to Canada to assist in starting these establishments. One of these men, Air Mechanic H. M. Hudson, relates his experiences:

'As regards my trip to Canada, I left my station, Cramlington, and arrived at Catterick rather late on Easter Saturday 1917. The Station Orderly Sergeant dumped me into an empty hut and being tired I lay down on my bed. Later, in the dark, somebody else was dumped in and started asking questions. I found he had the same name and initial as myself—H. Hudson. This was confusing and when he told me he was also from Cramlington—No. 36 Squadron—the coincidence became startling. Next morning we met the rest of the Canadian party and were formed up. We were told that we formed No. 88 Canadian Training Squadron. From Catterick we went to Liverpool and boarded a White Star liner, lay for a week in the Mersey, presumably waiting for an escort. We heard that we had bullion on board—destined for the United States—so our voyage was important.'

Leaving Liverpool the ship set course south of Ireland—well to the south, for the weather became quite warm. In the end it arrived safely at Halifax, Nova Scotia, on May Day! From there the party went by rail to Toronto. The Eastern Provinces were still under snow, after a most severe winter, but Toronto itself was tasting the beginning of spring, and looked a pleasant city. But nobody seemed to know anything about Hudson and his friends and there was nowhere to go! After some delay they were bundled into spare buildings at the McGill University and later moved to the Toronto Exhibition. Once their presence was discovered the Press photographers were round like flies. But the Canadian troops at Camp Mohawk were far from welcoming!

This sort of general post went on for two months and at last Hudson came to anchor at Armour Heights. Barracks were being built and after a spell under canvas the party moved into permanent accommodation. Here they were joined by many Canadians and the unit blossomed forth as the School of Aerobatics. Amongst the pilots was Vernon Castle, the famous dancer and an American citizen, who had volunteered very early on to fly against the Germans. He was sent down to a school in Texas where he met his death in a flying accident.

Each week-end was 'open house' with flying displays, the main object of which was to encourage recruiting. The summer was hot and the British airmen had been 'kitted out' at Catterick with tropical clothing, pith helmet, shorts and open-necked shirts for which they were very grateful. In addition, and much to their surprise, they had been issued with heavy clothing, leather jerkins and fur-lined caps, soon called 'tea cosies'. This type of kit baffled the British for a bit, but the winter was to show how necessary it was. Though the U.S.A. and Canadian cadets went south to Texas in the autumn the 88th Canadian stayed in Toronto. That winter was bitterly cold. After three days of blizzard there were four feet of powdered snow on the airfield, while the drifts were twenty feet deep. During these three days the station was cut off from Toronto, only a few miles away. Going the rounds with the orderly officer one bitter night, Hudson went into a hangar to check the temperature. The corporal in charge, whether by accident or design, had put the thermometer above the hot-air stove. It showed 60°F.!

At this time alcohol was used in radiators as 'anti-freeze'. Unfortunately it evaporated fairly quickly. Was somebody drinking it? In the end it became necessary to drain every radiator and oil sump as soon as night fell. Next morning there was the laborious job of refilling with hot water and warm oil.

In the spring of 1918 the 88th Canadian moved to Camp Borden —now one of the permanent stations of the R.C.A.F.—some sixty miles north of Toronto and at that time in undeveloped country. Hudson was left behind at Armour Heights, forgotten by Headquarters and quite content. With him was Air Mechanic Witham, a married man, who was also 'by the world forgot' but as a married man driven completely wild because—in consequence of his abandonment by authority—his wife was not getting her allotment. This was the type of minor tragedy that, once it was known about, could be dealt with by the Soldiers and Sailors Family Association. S.S.F.A., which had come into being many years before the Kaiser War broke out, had been asked by the War Office to handle the huge problem of married soldiers' family allotments. It is amazing that nobody in that august body of generals and civil servants had ever seriously considered what would happen to the families of the men who were recalled to the colours or volunteered for active service. When the emergency arose S.S.F.A. was there to take over, and brilliantly it carried out this difficult and complicated task.

Air Mechanic Hudson was only one of many who made this trip to Canada. Before long the Dominions Training Scheme had begun to fulfil its purpose. From its establishments began to flow first a trickle and then a stream of pilots and airmen.

8

The Period of Expansion

WITH the help of technicians from the United Kingdom the Empire Air Training Scheme began to produce results. Though in its first stages there was, as Air Mechanic Hudson was to find, a great deal of bad administration and amateurish effort, the training wings and training depot stations began to take shape, and, with many a groan and hiccup from their primitive machinery, to produce the pilots and air mechanics that were urgently needed in France and elsewhere. Those from Canada were incorporated in the R.N.A.S. and R.F.C., but the Australian Government, advised by some far-seeing and ambitious officers, decided to create its own flying service. Squadron and flight commanders with war experience were recalled to build the new units and great use was made of Egypt as a base. Soon a high proportion of the Middle East air forces were manned by Australians.

In Egypt I had my first introduction to non-stop tea-drinking. In 1916 I had been posted in command of a wing on the Canal and one of my squadrons was Australian. The Digger seems to lap up inky-black tea, so sweet that a spoon stands upright in it, as the desert sands absorb water. Tea full of tannin is of course a good stimulant, and as beer and whisky were only available in small quantities there was some logic in this system.

Apart from their excellent fighting qualities the Australians were particularly interested in photography. Some of the best pictures taken from the air of the Palestine campaign were the work of the Digger. They were already catching the camera infection from the U.S.A., but they had other less peaceful attributes.

Everyone who served in Egypt during the Kaiser War will have heard of the 'Wazar'. This was the red-light quarter of Cairo, and much frequented by troops on leave from the Canal Zone. Some of them got the worst of the exchanges with the local citizens, and a considerable amount of ill-feeling began to accumulate. Who started the idea of inflicting retribution is unknown. It might have been one of the several units of Australian origin, but I would not be in the least surprised if the Australian Light Horse were at the bottom of it. This magnificent body of men reacted very badly to being fleeced, drugged and robbed and they were determined to get their own back. How many of our airmen were involved in the 'Battle of the Wazar' is uncertain, but I remember some types who would joyously have entered the fray. On a given date the war party assembled in Cairo and proceeded to do an immense amount of damage to the brothels, drink shops and other sinks of iniquity in the Wazar. Before long fires began to burn, and it took the full force of the military and civil police to bring the trouble to an end. But it must have been a most enjoyable evening for the boys.

Ever afterwards the sight of an A.L.H. trooper, bush hat, open-necked khaki shirt, and shorts so short that they barely covered his buttocks, would send Egyptians screaming for cover.

Apart from tea-drinking with my Australians, Christmas 1916 started badly for 'V' Wing H.Q., which had moved from Ismailia to the desert. The messing officer, primed with subscriptions from his colleagues, had ordered food and drink from Cairo. But transport broke down and on Christmas Eve all that was available was bully beef and biscuits to eat and chlorinated water to drink! The messing officer spent his time hiding from the Colonel and, when caught, swearing it wasn't his fault. The news spread to the Australian squadron. At once transport was organized, the members of Wing H.Q. were translated to the main officers' mess where officers and men were beating hell out of chickens, geese, sausages and ham, with lashings of beer and whisky to wash the food down. The situation was saved, and alcoholic tears of gratitude flowed down the Limeys' cheeks as they toasted their friends in borrowed ale.

A few days later the Wing moved on. The Turks were in full retreat and the German Air Force was taking less and less part in the struggle. The Wing had been promised a railway siding that was to provide its increasing strength with petrol, oil and spares, not to mention food and drink. 'D' Day arrived and no siding! The telephone sizzled and the Railway Construction Corps, mostly recruited from the London South Western Railway, counselled calm! At dusk the siding was laid, the trucks arrived and were promptly derailed owing to faulty points. Railwaymen these days are not very well regarded by the general public, but on this night I began to appreciate and to understand their problems. There was no hurry, no fuss, but the effort was applied at exactly the right spot, and after the minimum delay everything was working again. Nevertheless, I was maddened by this setback. Young and over-impetuous, I decided that I would help with unloading the trucks. Secure in the feeling that in the dark I would not be recognized, I joined the airmen's fatigue party and began carrying cans of petrol to the dump. After about ten minutes I heard an Aussie sergeant say: 'Christ! It's the Colonel!' Time to go!

I had hoped that I would be allowed to go with my 'outfit' that had fought in the Western Desert against the Senussi, towards the south against the Sultan of Darfur, prideful on his white charger, and to the east against the Turks and Germans until we had helped to rid the Middle East of the enemy. It was not to be! A great friend of mine who suffered from chilblains, and was known to be highly efficient, relieved me in the spring of 1917. Back to England then, once more in the Training Division.

Again I was able to make a comparison between the airmen overseas and those in more prosaic jobs at home. There was not a deal of difference. They came from the same sound British stock. The same sense of humour, of loyalty, and of a desire to get the job finished and so back to the life they desired and understood—Civvy Street! This year was, however, to see a considerable change in the pattern of life in England. For the first time, owing to the shortage of man-power, women were to be called in to do a number of jobs which previously had been done by men. The War Office, committed by the demands from overseas to a large programme of substitution, calculated that to meet the required expansion of the Royal Flying Corps alone 30,000 women would have to be recruited.

Up to this time the only women directly assisting the Army and Navy were shorthand typists—and nurses! But already in 1915 the lack of men cooks had turned attention to the large number of domestics who were ministering to the comforts of the upper and middle classes in Britain. Here was a fruitful field of recruitment. The difficulties experienced by householders in maintaining the supply of capable cooks and housemaids were to be aggravated, and indeed to become a permanent feature of British social life, as the demands of the services impinged on the ordered routine of the neo-Victorian households.

The leader of the attack on the Englishman's 'fortress'—his home —was the Marchioness of Londonderry, a strange paradox! This great lady created the Women's Legion—a para-military formation—in 1916. At first there were only drivers of motor-cars. In February 1917 the War Office formalized the use of women in this role for the Army Service Corps and the Royal Flying Corps. A month later it was accepted that women could serve overseas—but not many achieved this object. One woman worked her passage with some ingenuity. Having started the war as one of the Voluntary Aid Detachment— that is to say as an almost untrained nurse—she stuck a year of empty-ing bedpans and carrying operation screens about the ward. She then resigned and—as was possible at that time—went to stay with a relative in the South of France, ostensibly on a holiday. Here she joined the French Red Cross and within a year was theatre sister at a big military hospital. It had been borne in upon me very early in the Kaiser War that the general standard of nursing in the French Army was abysmally low. The Sisters of Mercy, in their flowing and germ-laden robes that swept the dust off the floor of the hospital wards, were the only substantial contribution that the French populace made towards the care of the men who fought for them. So there was nothing really astonishing in that a British V.A.D., who had at least been taught the elements of nursing, was allowed to hold so responsible a position. After a year in that post our 'heroine' wangled her way into a French Casualty Clearing Station on the Aisne. Here she was within sound of the guns, but she told me that this worried her much less than the chilblains from which she suffered during the bitter winter of 1917–18. By the next summer she had worked her way up to a C.C.S. in Calais and so was in a very strong position to get home after the Armistice in November!

In July 1917 the women were formed into the Women's Army Auxiliary Corps. But recruits were lacking and the problem of ac-commodation was serious. At this time Grundyism was still a strong force, and in any case the organizers of the women's corps felt a great responsibility towards the girls who, leaving behind all the sanctions on which they had been brought up, were faced in their new environment with many temptations. But the 'head girls' could do little to minimize the discomforts from which the other ranks suffered. Accommodation was crude; food was, to say the least, rough and ready, and the uniform, when at last it was issued, most unsightly.

In spite of these troubles morale was high. Gertrude George, the author of *Eight Months in the W.R.A.F.*, writes:

'It was a curious thing, though, that by the time one had been in the W.R.A.F. for a few weeks discomforts ceased to have much effect upon one. Bad accommodation, unserviceable transport that often kept the girls waiting for long periods in the cold and rain, jobs in icy hangars or stuffy offices, all were accepted as part of their duty. When these trials came one put up with them stolidly until they passed. Comfort was not looked upon as a natural thing, but if it came it was thoroughly appreciated.'

Did our present generation of women behave as well in the Hitler War? I hope to show that they did!

The W.R.A.F. did not last long, as the title of Gertrude George's book suggests. Officially constituted on 1st April 1918 it began its period of war service with sixty-seven officers and 6700 other ranks. By the Armistice it had grown to a total of 25,000, all employed in the United Kingdom. As demobilization reduced the ranks of the men, so W.R.A.F. were drafted abroad to take their place. The first draft went to France in March 1919, and a month later another batch was sent for duty to Cologne in the Army of the Rhine. Both at home and abroad the girls did an excellent job, and it was a sad day when, at the end of 1920, the W.R.A.F. was disbanded.

Though the Women's Services disappeared, a small element remained in the military nursing cadres. But the W.R.A.F. had left behind it a reputation as 'the best-disciplined and the best-turned-out women's organization in the country'. There may well be two opinions about that statement but there is an element of truth in it. Bless them all—they did their best under very difficult conditions, and they were supposed to be the weaker sex.

After the war there were enquiries and the less responsible newspapers, under banner headlines, publicized all the difficulties that had beset the newly born force. Scandals there were, without a doubt, but it was the men more than the women who were responsible for their birth. I have a very strong recollection of a dinner party in Northern France where I was the guest of the local R.A.F. brigadier. One other guest was a man who had been very much involved in the creation of the W.R.A.F. The Brigadier was determined to bring home to this man what the fighting troops thought of his activities in Whitehall. I have never listened to a more concentrated attack on policy and behaviour, nor felt more embarrassed on behalf of the unfortunate recipient of this verbal blast. The Brigadier believed firmly in the rumours that had reached the front line and he was basing upon them his accusations. But let us see what was probably the truth of the affair.

The report of the Douglas-Pennant enquiry, held soon after the war, makes very interesting reading. Miss Douglas-Pennant, who had spent some six years with distinction in the public service, was, on the formation of the W.R.A.F. in April 1918, invited to be its first commandant. After some hesitation she agreed to accept the appointment. Her task was to be one of exceptional difficulty. The women she was to command had been drafted piece-meal from the Women's Royal Army Corps and the Women's Royal Naval Service. There was a grave shortage of trained officers, sixty-seven in a force of 6700! As has already been said, accommodation was poor, feeding arrangements primitive and administration indifferent.

One of the first failings of the Air Ministry brought to light by the Douglas-Pennant Committee of Inquiry was the lack of any firm order bringing the W.R.A.F. into existence. In the rush and hurry of 1918, and under pressure of the disasters of early spring, the over-stretched machine had slipped a cog. So as far as can be seen from the Committee's report, Miss Douglas-Pennant's appointment was, in some respects, irregular. Add to this the Committee's view that she was a woman impatient of control and apt to make statements that were founded on rumour and not upon fact, it becomes hardly surprising that the W.R.A.F. got off to a bad start.

There were, of course, two kinds of W.R.A.F., the mobile and immobile. The mobile, a fully uniformed body, could be posted anywhere in the United Kingdom. The immobile, largely working in plain clothes, could not be moved from the vicinity of their homes. Here is the story of one of the latter sort.

Mrs. Guest, who has just completed twenty years as a civil servant working for the Air Ministry, recalls her days at West Ascot Packing Department. Here she was involved in the stripping, packing and dispatching of aircraft and aircraft parts destined for overseas.

'When the Kaiser War broke out I was still at school. At about the time when I was due to leave I saw an advertisement for the W.R.A.F. I thought here was a chance of service overseas, but this was not to be. I had to be content with service as an immobile W.R.A.F., living with my parents in Reading and going each day to Ascot by train. I must say we were all treated very well. We were not rationed, but brought our food with us or bought it from a little Italian who set up his shop in a tent near by the Depot. We ate our meals sitting on boxes of stores. If we wanted to wash there was a tap about 300 yards from where we worked. As our jobs were pretty messy, painting wires with anti-corrosion paint, packing and unpacking straw-filled boxes and climbing on to the rafters to sling aircraft wings up to dry, this was a bit of a hardship. Officers in those days were more human than they are now. Coming back after a bout of flu I met Captain Horlick. He said, "Glad to see you back!" Well, that gave me a bucking-up, like walking on air!

The morality of the girls was very high indeed. London perhaps was different but at Ascot there was never any trouble of that sort. The only time I was "absent" was when I missed my train back to Reading and had to sleep "hard" and eat very uncomfortably at the Depot.'

Clearly Mrs. Guest never was given one of the late-night passes to London of which the Douglas-Pennant enquiry speaks at length!

The Mobile W.R.A.F., dumped down on isolated airfields all over the Kingdom, were undoubtedly subjected to greater temptations. With few officers to guide them, a small proportion, probably no more than 2 or 3 per cent, succumbed. It should also be remembered that 1918 was a period of great strain. The spring had been full of disasters and in the south-eastern part of the country, including London, there was a definite food shortage. These ills produced in the minds of some women the thought that if they were going to be raped later on by a conquering German, they might as well begin by enjoying themselves with an Englishman. As more and better officers were posted to stations the situation began to improve. Some of these officers had a mixed reception from the men. Mrs. E. B. Hine tells of such an experience:

'I arrived to find that although they had had immobile W.R.A.F. on the station for two or three months, they had no W.R.A.F. officer to date, and I was received with mixed feelings by the R.A.F. officers. The C.O. was frankly terrified of me, but the Adjutant met me with open arms, as he had a pregnant waitress on his hands and did not know what to do with her!

There were no W.R.A.F. quarters ready, so I was billeted out at Eastham Ferry, and it was not until the 21st November that I was able to move into quarters at the Aerodrome.'

Mrs. Winifred Bailey, at first a W.A.A.C. and then a W.R.A.F., writes:

'When we were invited to sergeants' mess concerts, dances or dinners (in Aldershot at Malplaquet or Blenheim Barracks) we had to show the invitation to the W.R.A.F. officer, then, after being given permission in writing, were all called together, and roll call taken . . . then we had to march two by two to the function with a hurricane lamp front and rear. I often wonder what the girls in the Forces today would have to say about this. . . . I am afraid they would take a very poor view, especially the marching back after a dance. We did too, but could not do anything about it. It is not very romantic to say goodbye and march off home . . . no civvies and no escorts allowed.'

Mrs. Hine moved on from the London area and in August 1918 settled in at No. 4 T.D.C., near Chester. She reports:

'Until this date all airwomen were immobile and came in every day from Chester and the outlying districts. The new officers soon began to pull the W.R.A.F. section into order and discipline, and things moved smoothly. Early-morning drill was introduced and entertainments were arranged, as well as sport. As soon as quarters were ready, mobile W.R.A.F.s were posted in and two more officers were sent to help.'

The quarters, though adequate, were not exactly luxurious. All floors were concrete, the roofs of corrugated iron, extremely cold in winter, hot in summer. There was a water radiator central-heating system in the dormitories, common room and officers' quarters.

During the hard winter there was a good deal of intense cold, burst radiators and flooding; also on occasions the most exciting rat-hunts—really outsize rats!

Once the W.R.A.F. section was got into order the airwomen soon began to make their mark, and the R.A.F. ceased to resent their presence and began to welcome them as good co-workers. After the first week or two there was never any trouble as regards non-co-operation from the R.A.F., and everything ran very smoothly.

When the Army of Occupation went into Germany, volunteers for overseas postings were required. The majority of the airwomen at Chester volunteered, but only the pick of them were selected. These airwomen were eventually posted to France and Germany and had excellent reports. It is interesting to note that the W.R.A.F. was the only women's corps to serve overseas.

Let me attempt to sum up the situation that existed in 1918. To the officers and men of the R.F.C. in the early days women had presented no problem. They were, so to speak, extra-mural. But now they were to be within the walls, in the cookhouses, in the cipher offices; they were to be typists, batwomen, clerks—transport drivers even. And with their arrival would come a social problem of a major order.

When the war started men were torn away from their home background. Instead of the accustomed pattern of their life where church and chapel gave them guidance in their relationships with women, they had been condemned to a monastic existence for months, even years. Now the monastery had become a co-ed establishment. La Fontaine, author of the famous *Fables*, in his *Contes*—a book which is not universally available—has given a picture of the intrusion of one young man into a nunnery and the consequences that flowed therefrom. Something of the same sort might have happened in the early years of women's military service if a reasonable control had not been established.

Those of us who were overseas during this period of transition suffered a considerable shock when we returned to England on leave. We appreciated that a measure of substitution—women for men in certain jobs—was inevitable. But the influence exerted at the 'top' by a number of very ambitious females was to us in every way repugnant. No doubt some of them were imbued with a strong sense of patriotism and were reputable and useful. But there were others! As regards the rank and file of the Women's Royal Air Force they were no better and no worse than their sisters in Civvy Street, and they did an extremely good job of work. Poor dears! Their uniforms were designed by someone who had not a clue! Indescribably clumsy, ill-fitting and uncomfortable, it was quite amazing that when clad in this monstrous outfit the girls could still be attractive to men. To me the answer is clear! Their legs and faces were still visible! In Victorian days the legs were hidden in voluminous petticoats and the faces concealed under coal-scuttle hats. Picture to yourself a woman, clad in this manner, cleaning the wings of a training aeroplane! But she would still be a woman and a gust of wind might reveal those tormentors of the male mind, a pair of shapely thighs!

Naval airmen, Taranto

Recruits outside
R.F.C. Headquarters,
Farnborough

By Courtesy of the Imperial War Museum

W.R.A.F., 1918 model

By Courtesy of the Imperial War Museum

By Courtesy of the Imperial War Museum

Winter of 1917

The first military air-drop. Packing supplies to be dropped on the besieged garrison at Kut-el-Amara

By Courtesy of the Imperial War Museum

9

After the Armistice

THE shooting war stopped on 11th November 1918 and soon the
R.A.F. was on the move again. A small force joined the Army of
Occupation, and of the remainder some squadrons returned to
the United Kingdom where they were disbanded, and others were
prepared for their new role in the post-war Air Force.

This was a troublesome time. There were mutinies in units and
in the holding camps in France. In the training stations in England
there were thousands of Empire cadets whose one ambition was to
get back to their own country as quickly as possible. Discipline grew
slack and attempts to enforce it were resented—sometimes physically.
Unpopular warrant officers, walking unguardedly at night, would find
themselves plunged into smelly little streams such as the River Pinn
that flows through Uxbridge R.A.F. Depot.

It is therefore refreshing to read of men who were content to
remain in the R.A.F. and so make a life career for themselves. Amongst
these were many ex-naval warrant officers who had transferred to the
R.A.F. under the Air Ministry Order No. 138, and, of course, were
christened 'One-three-eighters'! These men were of the utmost value
to the budding R.A.F. There were others, too, like Welland of the
I.A.F., who also carried on.

One of the first tasks to which General Trenchard addressed himself when he was installed as Chief of Staff of the new R.A.F. was,
consciously or unconsciously, to do exactly what the Duke of Wellington did after the Napoleonic Wars. This was to hide as large a part
of his forces overseas where Parliament had little or no control over
them. Welland accompanied a squadron on a mission of this sort to
Egypt.

His squadron, No. 215, had moved back to Northern France
where it was gradually disbanded. Welland, with some others, was

posted to No. 216, then engaged on postal service to Cologne. Later, No. 216 was told to prepare for a flight to Kantara, in Egypt. The aircraft, Handley Pages, were to fly (shipping and railing aircraft was still common practice) and the ground crews were to go by train and ship. Although the men worked hard at getting the aircraft serviceable, many of these had seen long service and had been damaged on operations. There was something ironic about an article in the *Sunday Pictorial* headed 'Blazing the trail to Egypt' since of the ten machines that started on the flight only three arrived. Of the unlucky seven, several crashed and caught fire.

At the start of the flight the aircraft left Marquise airfield in Northern France, in groups of three, at one-and-a-half-hour intervals. Le Bourget, outside Paris, was the first stop, but there had already been a crash—in a cornfield. It didn't worry Welland. Though this sort of thing happened to others, it seldom crossed his mind that it could happen to him.

When Paris was reached by Welland's aircraft the early starters had completed the first leg, and gone on to Dijon. The rest were to take off for Dijon next day, so the evening was spent in Paris. Here the airmen saw a great peace parade, which turned out to be as big a battle as any of them had seen. It was over who should lead the parade, the Americans or the Australians, and eventually it was fought out, a wonderful demonstration of allied unity!

The next morning the engine fitter and Welland ran the rule over the plane, gave the all clear, and it took off for Dijon, which was reached without any trouble. Again they checked the plane, and the next morning flew to Lyons. On this leg there was trouble—a series of storms along the Rhône valley. The Handley Page was forced down to about 200 to 500 feet and during one violent storm if a suitable landing could have been found the pilot would have used it. As it was he had to keep going and eventually ran into better weather and reached his destination.

The first job was to thoroughly check the engines and rigging. It was surprising to find how the landing and flying wires had stretched during the buffeting received in the storms. It took some time to adjust so two days were spent at Lyons, where the crew were fortunate to see the 'Battle of Flowers'. Taking off again Marseilles was reached without incident. But evidently others had not been so lucky, as on top of a big stone hangar was a plane lifted there by the mistral. As it was evidently the season for this high wind there was no delay in leaving for Pisa. This was a most interesting flight along the coast, over Monte Carlo, and skirting the Italian Alps, a wonderful sight. It was on the coast that another of the casualties was visible on the sand near Monte Carlo. Pisa was reached safely and here there was a two-day stop, to give the plane a good overhaul before going on to Rome. In the evening the crew went to see the famous Leaning Tower. By this time the mechanics were 'broke', so sightseeing was all they could do. The wine might have been very good, but there were no lire with which to buy it. How often was this story to be repeated in later years!

Now came the journey to Rome, and on this leg the aircraft nearly came to grief. On the way it ran into heavy cloud, and as the country was very mountainous, and the ceiling only 7000 feet, the conditions were most uncomfortable. All of a sudden the plane started dropping away and the engines began racing. For over 1000 feet the fall continued and when it stopped there were several empty stomachs. In the end Rome was reached in safety and the sight of two other Handley Pages on the airfield cheered everyone up. There were now 'Three Little Nigger Boys'—the only three to reach Rome and indeed the only ones to reach Kantara.

At Rome a week was spent carrying out a major overhaul, and there was also time to see the sights. Work all day, and evenings in Rome.

When all was ready, the C.O. decided to make for Suda Bay, Crete, in one hop from Taranto, which was the next port of call. This cost him dear in time as on the way one plane had trouble through an engine over-heating. The ensuing forced-landing was lucky in that the aircraft reached the only flat piece of land in a remote part of Greece. It was a cornfield covered with stubble which burst two of the tyres. Welland says that the other two planes came back to look for the presumed wreck and also landed there. On inspection the engine fitter found a cracked cylinder, and here was a predicament. From where and how was a replacement to be got? The natives, looking very fierce and bristling with guns, eventually came near enough to talk, but there was no common language. The pilot showed a Union Jack, and one of them understood, and brought a man who turned out to be a Greco-American planter. The C.O. had a pow-wow with him and a day or two later a Greek policeman turned up. The situation was again explained, and it was learned it would take about a week for a man to reach the nearest town by donkey. It was therefore decided that Lieutenant Sawyer should go back to Athens. To do this all the petrol from the other two aircraft was transferred to Lieutenant Sawyer's plane. At Athens, after on-loading the new cylinder block, he had to fill his machine with as much petrol as he could carry in his own tanks and in cans to refuel the other two. To lift this overload he had to fly alone. He accomplished this mission in about three days, and for this he was recommended for the D.F.C. During these three days the marooned aircrew were fêted. A sheep was roasted whole at the dinner held in their honour. Everyone was seated cross-legged around a square stone slab on which was the roast mutton, some bowls of fruit, a jug containing wine and a single beaker. The presiding host was a priest, and the guests of honour, the aircrews, were seated opposite. After speeches, which took some time, the priest cut off chunks of meat and passed them to the various people around the slab, who took the meat in their hands (no plates or knives or forks were provided) and proceeded to gnaw the meat from the bone. The beaker was filled from the jug, and each in turn took a drink, passed the beaker on, which in its turn was refilled from the jug and passed round again and again. Needless to say by the time the feast was over most of the guests were hardly in a fit state to walk home.

Eventually Suda Bay, Crete, was reached after one false start and the flight got away for Mersa Matruh. It was escorted across the Mediterranean by a seaplane from Malta. There was trouble on the way. A corporal had to lie along the fuselage of a Handley, holding the gravity feed petrol-pipe together so that the plane he was in could return to Suda Bay for repairs. Before leaving Crete as much water as possible was on-loaded, as the post in Mersa Matruh was very short of it. A good load of grapes was also taken and this was very gladly received by the personnel stationed there. The next day the aircraft took off for Heliopolis, Cairo, and the following day Kantara was reached.

This marked the beginning of the squadron's sojourn in the Middle East which has lasted up to quite recent times.

At Kantara it was found that the hangars were not high enough to accommodate the Handleys so it was decided to dig the sand away to a depth of three feet. A band of 'Gippos' were engaged for this work, among them a number of women. Women were not allowed to work on the aerodrome, and as both sexes dressed alike it was difficult to sort them out. This problem was solved by the orderly officer in a very simple way, much to the amusement of all who watched, and to the great embarrassment of the officer. He lined up the 'Gippos', obtained a stick, lifted up the clothes of each worker, and had a look. It was taken for granted that all those he poked in the belly with his stick were women. He should have known!

It was hard work for the mechanics during the period after the squadron's arrival in Egypt. Gradually men and machines were brought up to strength, for it must be remembered that many of the old hands were 'duration of war' only, and were anxious to go home. Towards the end of 1919 D.H.10s began to replace the Handleys, and when Welland eventually left the squadron in December 1919 the change was nearly complete.

He did not sever his connection with the R.A.F. on demobilization, but got a job with No. 1 M.U. at Kidbrooke, and is now with Signals Command there, an unbroken period of forty-three years with the R.A.F.

By the greatest good fortune for the R.A.F. the Government had decided that General Trenchard should resume the post of Chief of the Air Staff he had vacated in the winter of 1917. Trenchard was a man who had his feet very firmly on the ground. One of the things he had realized during the welter of demobilization was the need to lay firm foundations on which to build the new Royal Air Force. The hybrid organization, half Army and half Navy, that had come into being in April 1918 was disintegrating. Only a skeleton remained on which to construct the organization that was to fulfil the national need for air power.

In the face of an ill-advised, almost hysterical, Press campaign that clamoured for new squadrons and new aircraft with which to maintain the prestige of 'Britain in the Air' Trenchard went quietly to work to provide the mechanics needed to maintain the aircraft of the future.

First, the technical schools had be to set up. He had something to build upon. The training organization that had been created so laboriously during the war was there to his hand. But how were the pupils to be enrolled? Trenchard decided that there were to be two breeds of mechanic. The first, the long-service men, who should form the hard core on which the aircrews could rely; the second, the short-service men, who would carry out the less skilled duties. To train the former to the requisite standard of efficiency a period of apprentice-ship was obviously necessary. So the aircraft apprentice scheme came into being. Boys of fifteen and a half to sixteen years of age, from every reliable source of education in Britain, were invited to enter for an examination which many people thought rather too testing. The lads came forward, many of them from families, now fallen on hard times, that had previously given officers to the armed forces.

Of the 500 who started the 1st Entry only 131 graduated at the first attempt, the remainder failing at various stages of training. Some deserted, and one at least committed suicide. This boy hanged himself in the Marylebone Station toilet on returning from leave.

Flight Lieutenant Akhurst was the No. 1 Halton cadet. He writes of his experiences as an apprentice:

'Fatigues and extra duties were far more numerous than today. Memories of Mess Cook particularly remain with me. This job included washing dishes, cleaning dixies, scrubbing mess-decks (in 1922 we still had many Navy and Army terms), scrubbing tops, bottoms and sides of forms and tables and then scraping with glass. The whole was then inspected by a corporal and if, in his opinion, it was not good enough a bucket of dirty water was thrown over the lot and the procedure repeated! This I did on one occasion five times after lunch on a Sunday and just managed to get cleaned up in time to prepare tea.'

Writing of dixies reminds Akhurst of the time at North Camp when one of the cookhouse staff, aiming for maximum cleanliness, used caustic soda in the washing-up water. The result became apparent about midnight with the whole Entry queueing up. The dixies weren't alone in having scoured insides!

Another well-remembered but embarrassing incident was in connection with the Duke of York's visit. The apprentices had re-hearsed for weeks and then, just at the moment of arrival, with the fanfare playing, two little dogs gave a display of tug-of-war in front of the dais but were quickly dispersed by an 'erk' with great presence of mind, but inappropriately dressed in overalls, using the necessary bucket of water.

Akhurst continues:

'Of personalities Warrant Officer Marshall stands out above all others—what a disciplinarian and how we feared him and his cane—not, I hasten to add, that he ever used it on the body! Corporal Clarke, the R.A.F. and Highgate Harriers long-distance champion (later to be killed as a sergeant-pilot on the North-West Frontier), who gave me so much encouragement in my own, comparatively limited, running career. The civilian schoolmasters —Ivor B. Hart and Captain Fanshawe, to mention only two— what a grand job they did, not only during working hours but helping us in our other activities, but above all being a very valuable link with civilian life and so different in their disciplinary approach from our superiors in uniform. They were real friends and, in my opinion, the apprentice of today is missing much by their absence. Padre Clarke, later to become Chaplain-in-Chief, and Father Beauchamp, the R.C. padre, both wonderful men, always understanding and ready to help in any way. Marshal of the R.A.F. the Lord Trenchard as our Reviewing Officer on graduation ("Passing out" in those days) and the fact that the great man had a word or two for me personally. The civvy instructor with the cocky hat and his smutty stories (which description is quite sufficient for the armament types of the day to recognize him!). The pilot of a 504K who gave me my first flight and said, "If you are sick do it over the port side and I shall then know where it is coming from!" Jock Clarke, the first Halton apprentice to gain a cadetship, later to win the Sword of Honour at Cranwell, but whose brilliant career was so tragically ended almost before it began.

Incidents? Having to kneel down to pray each night at the sound of a bugle-call. The queues and inspections before one could leave camp. The yellow bands of the janker-wallas. The complaining at the preparations for—and inspections on—church parades but that "something" one felt afterwards and how it all seemed worth while in the end. The feeling of being guinea-pigs as there were so many policy, training and syllabus changes— many completely unjustified yet have been continuously repeated ever since!'

So the schools were filled, and after three years airmen of high quality began to enter the service.

Not only did Trenchard provide the skilled men in this way, but he saw to their comforts. A well-planned building scheme was started, and barrack rooms were provided where the men of the new age could feel they had a home and in which they could take a pride. There was hot water, central heating, lock-up cupboards for private possessions and a standard of messing that would have made their fathers very envious.

The Press reacted unfavourably. 'The Royal Ground Force' screamed the headlines. 'Where are the new aircraft?' 'The Air Staff seem to think that bricks and mortar alone matter!'

Trenchard and his advisers had learned one supreme lesson during the war. It takes a long time to design new aircraft, and while waiting for the post-war novelties to show their utility and become worth the money to buy them there was the task of laying down what is now known as the 'infra-structure' of the R.A.F. How well was this work carried out!

Gradually the service began to grow in size and strength. In 1919 or thereabouts there was one serviceable squadron in existence in the United Kingdom. When the Government discovered that the French were still maintaining 1500 front-line aircraft in their Metropolitan Air Force, our leaders 'went to panic stations'! The Royal Air Force was to be raised to a strength equal to that of any European air force within range of Britain. The Air Staff laid their plans and ordered new aircraft. But then the League of Nations took a hand in the game. World disarmament seemed within sight and with a sigh of relief the British Treasury laid down the 'ten-year rule'. Although the Government had agreed to an air force of thirty-five bomber and seventeen fighter squadrons the Treasury ordered that the service estimates each year should be based on the assumption there would be no war for ten years. 'War' was therefore always ten years ahead and progress was negligible.

In fact this did not matter very much except for the stagnation in promotion that hit every rank. The 'infra-structure' was taking shape and the build-up of really good technicians increasing yearly. The aircraft industry, much reduced by the run-down after the war, had little to show in the way of new and existing machines. So the service was content to use the types that were coming into use at the end of the Kaiser War.

The life of the airmen in the early 1920s was, on the whole, agreeable. Even if there was plenty of work it was of an interesting kind. Though discipline was strict it was intelligently applied. In Britain week-end passes and annual leave kept the men in touch with their families while the married quarters were being built. The bachelors could enjoy the good facilities for sport that were everywhere available.

Overseas conditions varied. At first in the Mediterranean, the float-planes and flying-boats of the R.A.F. kept the flag flying, at Malta and Alexandria. But soon a few Handley Pages found their way out to Egypt. The training organization that had done such sterling work in the Kaiser War was still in being, though in a small way. The war-time stations of Aboukir, Alexandria, Heliopolis, Heluan, Abu-Sueir, Port Said, Kantara, Ismailia and Suez carried on at a greatly reduced tempo.

For the airmen it is farly certain that Abu-Sueir was the most unpopular station, Kantara and Suez following it closely. The other places were near towns which offered certain amenities, and, apart from the summer heat and the sand-storms, the Egyptian climate is quite tolerable. In time the tented camps were replaced by permanent buildings and soon wives and families were allowed to join the airmen. The Middle East settled down to an orderly, peaceful routine, with occasional flashes of excitement when trouble boiled up in Iraq, or when a long-distance flight to India or South Africa awoke some interest. The men were far from unhappy, and they were maturing in skill, in service loyalty and in the flexible discipline which has always been an asset of the R.A.F. Year by year the apprentices from Halton and Cranwell were being moulded into the structure of the R.A.F., and as they grew older and more experienced in practical matters they began to form the steel frame that was to support an immense expansion in the Hitler War. Without these long-service men as a basis it is doubtful if the flood of conscripts that was poured into the squadrons could have supported the strains of a total war.

Not that the apprentices were popular! Far from it! When a particularly bright boy of nineteen or twenty arrived in a unit wearing corporal's stripes (this I think was one of Trenchard's minor errors of administration) the old hands proceeded to 'take the mickey' out of him to no small tune. They had served their apprenticeship the hard way and Trenchard's favourite sons had to be taught their proper place in the scheme of things. It did the boys a great deal of good and many a flight sergeant of 1939–45 must have been grateful for the grilling he received at the hands of the 'old sweats' when first he joined a service unit. They knew their job and were conceding nothing to theory learned from textbooks and from instructors who may well have become old-fashioned. I met some of these ex-apprentices and old-timers at Habbaniyah in 1937. All through one hell-hot Sunday they worked on a troublesome engine that had caused me some anxiety over the Black Sea and the Turkish desert—the plain of Anatolia. They could well have left the job until the Monday, but because I was due back at my Headquarters at Simla in three days' time they gave up their leisure to help me!

In Mesopotamia/Iraq a formidable building scheme was undertaken, and though for some years the airmen lived 'rough', in the end the vast camp of Habbaniyah and the smaller ones at Mosul, Hinaidi and Basra offered very reasonable amenities.

Habbaniyah, planted in the middle of a howling wilderness, but by a big lake where boating could be enjoyed, accommodated some 7000 officers and men. The station was divided into a number of units, each self-sufficient. Thus a measure of *esprit de corps* could be maintained.

But one dreadful error in psychology was made. Every camp was built to exactly the same pattern. In consequence, when officers and airmen visited neighbouring units they found the same lay-out as their own camp. Within the barbed wire that surrounded the buildings there was an awful sameness. This sameness had a definitely bad effect on morale, particularly as there were few chances of getting into Baghdad by road or to Cairo by air. One escape was to go to the Imperial Airways landing jetty on the lake and quiz the passengers as they disembarked to stretch their legs or have a meal in the restaurant.

It was possible to leave the perimeter for a ride or some shooting, but there was always a risk of meeting unfriendly Arabs or getting lost in the featureless desert.

In the smaller stations near the big towns, Mosul, Baghdad and Basra, there was no trouble of this sort. Firstly, the units occupying them had every chance of taking part in the active operations that were denied to the men at Habbaniyah. Then the towns were within reach by station transport and though the delights they offered were either dangerous or dirty they might be exciting. Money that could buy nothing at Habbaniyah but the products of the N.A.A.F.I. was spent on possibly worthless but nevertheless exotic presents for wife and family.

In India the position was different. The airfields (except for the emergency landing grounds) were all near fair-sized towns that had a considerable European content. There were also the army cantonments and so there was plenty of sport—cricket, soccer and tennis. These pastimes sufficed for the majority of the airmen, but some were more enterprising. Buying, begging or borrowing shot-guns and small-bore rifles, half a dozen men would organize themselves on a shooting/camping basis. Karachi Aircraft Depot produced a number of these teams whose members, saving up their leave, would adventure into the desert where they could find mixed sport—sand grouse, small deer, jackals and of course the inevitable snakes and scorpions.

These expeditions were encouraged by the officers as it was felt they taught initiative and improvisation which might be most useful in war.

Scattered up and down the main lines of communication—Delhi–Bombay: Delhi–Calcutta: Delhi–Peshawar—were small detachments of airmen maintaining the emergency landing grounds that the doubtful behaviour of the contemporary aircraft engines imposed upon an over-loaded organization. These men were relieved from time to time, but it is questionable whether the more active-minded of them found this duty disagreeable. They were on their own—no disciplinary sergeant-major was there to harry them about unshaven faces and untidy tents. They were in contact with the local Indians who were, as a rule, friendly and prepared to offer whatever amenities it was in their power to produce. As the aircraft, the passage of which over their landing ground had been announced, passed safely overhead they could relax and carry on with whatever sport that interested them.

Some of these landing grounds were maintained by local labour —the nearest army regiment as a rule—and of such a one was Drosh in the Himalayas. To reach Drosh the Lowari Pass, 11,000 feet high, had to be cleared. In tribal territory on the North-West Frontier there were others permanently occupied by the R.A.F. and guarded by local forces such as the Tochi Scouts. At Miranshah the aircraft had to be wheeled inside the fort every night. Eighteen-foot mud walls were alone sufficient protection against raiding tribesmen who would creep through the boundary wire to damage anything they found in the open.

These small camps were often very uncomfortable. Close to the border in the North-West Frontier Province is the town of Dera-Ismail-Khan. This is one of the hottest places in India and just above it on a ridge jutting out from the tribal territory was one of these landing grounds. Having stored up its own heat during the blazing day this torture would be added to by the waves of hot air rising from the plain round Dera-Ismail-Khan and flowing into the R.A.F. camp.

Among the men cases of heat exhaustion were common and this was one of the most-loathed 'stations' of the R.A.F. India.

When the Air Ministry, with the agreement of the Government of India, decided to create the Indian Air Force certain problems presented themselves. It was necessary to recruit from a number of normally hostile elements, hostile on grounds of religion alone. The best mechanics were to be found amongst the Sikhs. The Sikh is a special kind of Hindu and very faithful in his religious observances. Parsis, a form of sun-worshippers, were the next-best mechanics. After them came the orthodox Hindus and then the Mussulmans. The Air Ministry decided that each of these religions should have its own barracks and its own cookhouses where the food could be prepared according to religious custom. It was very astonishing that a few months after it was formed the men of No. 1 I.A.F. Squadron demanded that all should mess together. While they were in the flying business there should be no more of these differences and please could they all live, eat and work as one?

At first white N.C.O.s and senior airmen were brigaded with the Indians, but as these learnt skill of hand the R.A.F. men were gradually withdrawn. It was noticeable that No. 1's aircraft were a great deal cleaner than those in a comparable R.A.F. squadron. This was due partly to beginners' enthusiasm, but also to the fact that few Indians have off-parade occupations, and a bit of extra cleaning-down helped to pass the time.

Hardly had the Kaiser War been officially terminated by the Treaty of Versailles than the Far East loomed as a trouble centre. The Japanese had passed an inexpensive and fruitful war as allies of the West. They had suffered few casualties and their navy had gained some experience in anti-submarine operations, mainly in the Mediterranean.

The British Admiralty, very conscious of the great contribution made by Australia and New Zealand to the defeat of Germany, were most anxious to develop Singapore as a great naval base. Only in this way, went the argument, could the flow of Dominion reinforcements reach Europe in safety in the event of another great war.

Given that this base was built, it had to be defended. The Chiefs of Staff argued interminably over the problem of Army and Air as the major factor in defending Singapore. Finally the money went into the fifteen-inch guns, only one of which ever fired a shot at the Japanese when the island was invaded. So the number of airmen who were based on Singapore was not large. India and Iraq were regarded as reinforcement centres from which aircraft could be drawn in the event of a war with Japan. Each year there were reinforcement flights east and west, and the ground crews on the receiving airfields had a busy time looking after their visitors' aircraft. One sergeant driving a crane lorry round the Singapore airfield neatly cut the starboard wing of my aircraft in half with the jib of his crane. The subsequent correspondence between Singapore Air Base to which the sergeant belonged, and R.A.F. H.Q. New Delhi, the home of my machine, threatened to swamp the archives of the Government of India.

There was much to keep the airmen interested. Though the climate was unpleasant—80 degrees humidity and 80–84 degrees of heat—there was a great deal of entertainment. The R.A.F. Yacht Club flourished—golf, cricket and football were available, and in the evening 'The New World', 'The Happy World', and some other 'World', the name of which I have forgotten, offered dancing with 'taxi' girls in an air-conditioned atmosphere. I tried this dancing once. For a dollar I got several tickets, each of which entitled me to take a girl—Chinese, Javanese, Malay—out of the pen in which they all sat. The band played and we circled around, the girl showing all the sultry passion of a kitchen chair! It was not surprising that the airmen went elsewhere for their fun!

In Hong Kong there was an air force detachment, and from time to time flying-boats from Singapore paid it a visit. There had been a coming and going of maritime aircraft in these eastern waters ever since H.M.S. *Pegasus*, a seaplane-carrier, had brought some Fairey IIID float-planes to Singapore. These aircraft were instructed to carry out a survey of Malaya and later of Hong Kong. Understandably, the jungles of the Malayan peninsula had presented an almost insoluble problem to the normal method of map-making. With the threat from Japan a grey shadow in the background it was thought wise to find out what the country would look like to the troops who might be called upon to defend it. The air survey was completed in about four months, while Hong Kong was mapped in less than four weeks.

Flight Lieutenant S. R. Pegg, now in active retirement in Dorset, educating and training the young in air affairs, was on this trip. He had enlisted in the R.F.C. in October 1913, and was a flight sergeant (fitter) when he sailed in *Pegasus* for the Far East in March 1924. I have tried to persuade the Flight Lieutenant to write his experiences of this trip, without success. I am sure he would call an effort of this kind 'shooting a line'. But, knowing something of the Malayan climate and of the sort of accommodation provided for the other ranks in ships such as *Pegasus*, it is not difficult to imagine the hell-hot nights between decks, the wet steamy days, the unpalatable food presented at mess and the constant struggle to control prickly heat, dhobie's itch and other joys of life in a tropical climate. The commissioned ranks could have recourse to a respectful medical officer. For the men it was 'medicine and duty', and the medicines of the day were not particularly effective in dealing with tropical ailments.

But whatever the airmen may have felt about this trip, the Air Ministry regarded it as a success and pressed on with its ideas on maritime air operations. At first the float-plane held sway in Coastal Area, but soon the influence of the Felixstowe flying-boat school brought about a marked change in operational development. Instead of float-planes carried in ships, flying-boats, capable within certain limits of maintaining themselves on long cruises, formed the basis of this part of the Royal Air Force. This change had some effect upon the activities of the airmen. The boats carried not only aircrew but ground crew as well—fitters and riggers. The skilled men in 'Coastal' became ambivalent—and enjoyed it. Of course the numbers carried could only provide a 'skeleton' service. Fixed bases where major repairs were to be carried out had to be established.

As a result, long cruises were performed in which these ground crews participated. The Irish Sea, the Baltic, the Mediterranean, the Indian Ocean, Australian waters and the China Sea were all logged up in 'Coastal's' list of achievements. To give an example of the kind of job these men carried out there is the story of the flying-boat refuelling at Malta. A clumsy Maltese dropped a full four-gallon tin of petrol which went straight through the side of the hull. The aircrew, mere dogs'-bodies on this occasion, had to sit on a wing-tip so as to raise the hole above the water-line. Their temper was not improved by the thought that the fitter who was putting a patch over the hole was working in relative comfort, while they were being drenched by the waves that broke periodically over their uncomfortable perch.

This was also the period of the long-distance flights—to Egypt, India, Malaya, Australia, South Africa and across the Atlantic. Of necessity the ground crews' participation in these flights was confined to preparation. But the excitement and interest of these preparations unquestionably raised their morale and the need to be 100 per cent right in their work was good for their skill of hand.

The Air Display at Hendon, where each year the R.A.F. performed before a very large audience, also improved the efficiency of the ground crews. In a restricted area, surrounded by railways and houses, some hundreds of aircraft carried out very complicated evolutions. In the dozen or so of displays staged by the Headquarters Air Defence of Great Britain and Fighting Area there were few failures attributable to technical defects. None of these failures caused civilian deaths or damage, and there was only one fatal casualty to a R.A.F. officer at the Display itself.

10

Quality and Quantity

THROUGHOUT the R.A.F. in the middle 1930s the influence of the Halton and Cranwell apprentices was being felt. The general standard of education in the service, already high, advanced at a quickened pace. It was something of a shock to me, when I wanted to check a poetic reference, that my L.A.C. clerk offered to lend me his *Anthology of British Poetry*. I thought ashamedly of my own very limited library consisting mainly of Kipling's stories and 'Whodunits'. The skill of hand, too, was very high indeed. The number of engine and aircraft failures that were due to bad maintenance was incredibly small. Usually accidents could be traced to defects in design, or to what is now known as 'pilot's error'.

This general level of excellence was a tribute to Trenchard's wisdom in establishing the apprentice schools, but even he could not have guessed that one of these apprentices would invent the jet engine.

It was shortly after he emerged from his training at Halton that Frank Whittle began to think about jet propulsion. It was not long before his thoughts crystallized into a design. Unfortunately, official discouragement hampered him and it was some years before drawings became moving parts and finally a completed jet engine. The full story of Whittle's remarkable invention is told in his own book *Jet* and gives a very fine description of the way in which a stout-hearted youngster triumphed over inaction, prejudice and jealousy, and so became the producer of the first jet engine to fly in Britain.

It was the high quality of this new entry, grafted on to the existing force of long-service airmen, whose experience stemmed from the Kaiser War, that gave the Air Staff the assurance that the newly formed post-war R.A.F. was a most worthy successor to the old Royal Flying Corps. It was no mushroom growth. Its numbers were small, some 30,000 by 1934, and the annual increase was slow.

Although in 1923 the fifty-two squadron Home Defence programme had been approved, in actual fact it took nine years, until
1932, to bring the strength up to forty-two squadrons. Of these
thirteen were week-end fliers, the auxiliaries that were to prove their
worth when war started, but inevitably were not as highly trained as
the regulars.

That the Air Staff were not displeased by this slow progress is
clearly shown in the discussions that followed the Government's discovery of the extent to which Germany had built up an operational
air force. The story of these discussions is very well described in the
first volume of the official history of 1939-45, *The Fight at Odds*.
What emerges most clearly is that the Government had suddenly
become anxious that a scarecrow Air Force should be built up as soon
as possible, while the Air Ministry, concerned in maintaining quality
in the face of a pressing demand for quantity, applied the brakes whenever opportunity served.

The argument raged round the expressions 'first-line strength'
and 'total strength'. The Air Staff clung to the first of these while
the Government wanted numbers, any numbers so long as there were
lots of them. In this way they thought to scare Hitler into abating his
pretensions. In fact the result was exactly opposite. The Luftwaffe
speeded up its aircraft production, its training and the formation of
new service units.

In the face of this development the Air Staff perforce gave way.
The Government demanded an increase to 123 squadrons by March
1937, though the Air Ministry had suggested 1939 as more suitable.
This figure would have produced a first-line strength of 1500—parity
with Germany.

So far as the airmen were concerned a very large training programme had to be undertaken. The apprentice intake was boosted,
and the recruiting of men for the less-skilled trades stepped up. But
we still were far from the German principle of 'guns before butter',
there was still plenty of butter on *our* bread!

The usual shifts and dodges had to be adopted. One of these, most
hurtful in the event of a long war, was to deprive the reserve of skilled
time-expired men by persuading them to re-engage for further service.
Another of considerable importance was the expansion of the Auxiliary
Air Force.

To provide the aircraft that would be required the new Secretary

I

of State for Air, Lord Swinton, developed the 'shadow factory' scheme, whereby the existing aircraft industry 'hived-off' new factories and the motor-car manufacturers were called upon to switch a part of their capacity for the same purpose.

There was still a lot of 'backing and filling', as sailors would say. By 1937 the Air Staff were beginning to catch up with the Government, so much so that the Treasury interfered on grounds of economy. It needed the seizure of Austria by the Nazis to get the 'all-clear' on the financial front.

Vital time had been lost, however, and in August 1939 the Royal Air Force was still ill-prepared in numbers for the war that lay before it. In five years, from the time when the Government began to think seriously about the Nazi menace, the R.A.F. had increased to some 1550 first-line aircraft at home and to 435 abroad. Personnel had risen from 30,000 regulars and 11,000 reservists in 1934 to 118,000 regulars and 68,000 reservists in 1939.

The German Air Force strength in 1939 was half a million, with another million men in A.A. defence!

It was intended that this enormous deficit should be balanced by the French Armée de l'Air. But the French Air Force was deficient in many of the things that really matter—amongst others suitable aircraft! It would not be unfair to say that, even before the fall of France, the R.A.F. was the sole effective contender for air superiority with Germany. The Russo-German Alliance was still in being and in any case the Russian Air Force was not a startlingly efficient organization at this time.

When war broke out in August 1939 the plans that had been laid for a British air and land expeditionary force to proceed to France were put into execution. Looking back on this period one is struck with the similarity to the same operation that took place in 1914. There was the same old trouble about reservists' uniforms and boots. The transport had the same makeshift look about it. Austin Sevens were used as reconnaissance cars. Our Battles and Lysanders were already years out of date, and there was the usual shortage of mechanics' tools. The official history comments that at one moment there was only one plug spanner available to several aircraft! Cockpit heating, de-icing equipment, R/T gear, all were either in primitive form or totally absent. The French *Système D* (Anglice beg, borrow or scrounge) was, as usual, in full blast. 'Firm' arrangements for accommodation,

stores and rations were found to be more than shaky. The staff work
for which, in the past, our ally had achieved a great reputation, seemed
notably deficient.

It was an act of Providence that Hitler, too, was unready. The
period of the phoney war was to follow, in which some of these deficiencies could be repaired. By Christmas time our airmen in France
were fairly well settled in, rations were available in due quantity, and
the minor pleasures of the French scene were available to those who
had the necessary francs. But though there was a token force of
Hurricanes, the Battles and Lysanders still formed the major part of
the R.A.F. in France.

Back in England the R.A.F. was really at war. Bomber Command at
first attempted in daylight to attack the German Navy in its harbours.
These sorties were carried out with the utmost gallantry in the face of
strong opposition. The results were negligible. The airmen on the
bomber airfields had their first experience of waiting and watching for
aircraft that would not return. The scale of loss was most depressing
and this feeling was enhanced by the lack of any success with which it
could be off-set. In consequence of these losses daylight attacks gradually faded out, and were replaced by pamphlet-dropping sorties over
Germany at night. In this work the casualties were at an acceptable
level and the airmen felt there was a strong probability that their own
aircraft would return unharmed. In any case, even if the aircrew were
not killing Germans they were gaining very valuable experience which
would help them when the shooting war started.

From the fall of the flag 'Coastal' was plunged into its own private
shooting war. Submarines and raiders were active around our coasts
and the 260 mixed aircraft that provided its main strength were employed day and night by the Command. The airmen were taxed to
the utmost of their strength and willingness, since, for every aircraft
available, there were six jobs crying out to be done. Serviceability had
to be as high as it was humanly possible to make it, and this involved
almost intolerably long hours of work. Fortunately a number of the
squadrons were operating from their peace-time bases, with good
workshops and comfortable barracks. Also involved in the war at
sea was Fighter Command. From the German coast came bombers
attacking our coastal shipping and—most dastardly—our light ships.
Flying at wave-top height, JU88s and Heinkel 110s played tip-and-
run with our convoys of unarmed ships. At first it was easy meat. But

when the low-level radar was established by our scientists, and fighter patrols followed our ships on their tedious voyage through the shoals and shallows of the east coast, things began to look up. Admiral Dryer's anti-aircraft crews, after a period of training in his ingenious 'simulators' that gave the pattern of an air attack on a ship by films shown in a mobile cinema, began to use their Lewis-guns and Bofors with greater effect against the enemy.

And then our fishing fleets were attacked when they were on their lawful occasions in the North Sea. This was a new form of blockade that for a while did us harm. The solution, admittedly only partial, was the 'Kipper Patrol' of our fighters round the trawlers as they dredged the sea floor for the fish that took the edge off the hunger caused by our meagre rations. For all these reasons it is fair to say that even in the period of the 'Phoney War' aircrew and airmen of the R.A.F. were busy fighting the Germans, each in his particular fashion. Often the airmen must have wondered why we had to be on the defensive: why the aircraft that they serviced with such care should not be hitting the enemy where it would hurt him most.

Dealing first with the Battle of Britain, let us take a look at the men and women who operated the radar screen that fed enemy information to Signals, and hence to the control rooms and finally to the pilots who did the fighting.

At first the radar screen was manned entirely by scientists. Soon, however, airmen were introduced to its mysteries. Finally W.A.A.F.s took over a large part of the duties connected with the chain of stations, long-range and high-level, short-range and low-level, and finally those immeasurably valuable organisms known as G.C.I. or 'Ground Controlled Interception Stations'.

Being in the front line—the coast-line of Britain—the radar stations were an obvious target for the Luftwaffe. In the summer of 1939, before war was declared, a German airship had patrolled the whole of the east coast, and wherever there was a radar station plotting its course it flew in to the coast and established the source of signals beyond a peradventure. Later it was discovered that our enemy was very scornful of our radar devices. He believed he had something better in the same line of business! But then his problem was entirely different from ours. We needed long-range early warning, even if it were not very accurate, since our coast-line is so near our vulnerable points. In the case of the Germans the North Sea coast is some con-

siderable distance from, say, Berlin. Long range was not their need—
it was accuracy in positioning the enemy aircraft so that guns could
shoot it down.

So, from the Humber to Poole, the masts of our radar stations
showed the bombers where their target lay, and for a while in 1940
a concentrated attack was made on the buildings which housed the
transmitters and receivers. The men and women manning these instruments behaved with great bravery. There is a tale of the Poling
W.A.A.F.s relieving watch in the middle of a raid. The new watch
was marching from the hutments and was within a few hundred yards
of the site when the bombs began to fall. It is recorded that they did
not break step but continued on their way!

Air Ministry Experimental (Radar) Station at Rye gives a further
example. A W.A.A.F. member of the staff tells the following story:

'Here we had the smallest possible establishment, about thirty-
three W.A.A.F. consisting of domestic staff and radar operators on
the W.A.A.F. side.

Shortly before the big show-down, the senior R.A.F. Flight
Sergeant and a Sergeant R.A.F. came to my office one morning,
and having completed their business, asked me when the W.A.A.F.
were going to be removed from the Station, as in their opinion it
was much too dangerous a spot for women, and anyway they
would have enough to cope with in the event of invasion or bad
bombing without hysterical women to look after.

I eyed them with an icy stare, and said that according to the
Air Ministry, where the R.A.F. remained the W.A.A.F. remained,
and that anyway they would not have any "hysterical women" to
deal with, and informed them they could now get out of my office.
A few days later, after a bad raid, the same two men came to me
and, hat in hand, apologized for what they had said on the previous
occasion, and said that they were proud to have the W.A.A.F.
on the Station with them. This gesture was greatly appreciated.

On 12th August the Station was bombed in the morning, and
in the afternoon when I was up in the Operations hut there was
another alarm.

The Ops. hut was a sandbagged wooden structure. Five of the
airwomen were there on watch, and they carried on serenely,
intent on their work, and deeply excited. Three were actually

working, and two were doing that extremely difficult thing in danger, standing immobile behind the workers.

The deep, snarling roar of the bombers and protecting fighters grew closer and closer till the whole hut vibrated with it. The Watch continued steadily giving height and speed and direction of attacking hostile aircraft to Fighter Command without a tremor in their voices. Suddenly the roar changed its note as the bombers dived. The R.A.F. Officer-in-Charge called: "They're diving! Get down!" and only then did those airwomen move, and they moved as if you'd pressed a button! We all fell flat on the floor as the first stick of bombs burst. Clouds of dust came up and a few things shifted, but not too badly. The officer's quiet voice cut through the ensuing silence with: "Keep down and keep quiet!" There wasn't a movement, and we waited for what seemed hours and was probably a minute. Then another bomber screamed down in its dive, and another "stick" exploded, this time nearer. Everything loose shot off the tables, shutters were blown in, and glass flew in every direction. The floor and hut shuddered, and chairs and tables overturned on to us. Through clouds of dust I saw legs and arms protruding from underneath the debris; to those in reach I gave a friendly pat and an assurance that they were all right and must remain still. I heard one voice exhorting the owner of a head to keep its face in her lap, at the same time pressing that head down, and an indignant but laughing protest stating that the lap was full of glass! Just then another full-blasted roar which seemed to be coming right on to the hut, followed by a terrible and shattering explosion; doors and the remaining windows were swept away, and then huge lumps of things began crashing through the walls, high up where the sandbags didn't reach, and through the windowless spaces. Every second one expected to feel a huge lump of concrete fall on one, and they kept coming! Just as one thought, "That's the last bit," something else would crash through somewhere.

At last, after what seemed like hours, we dared to raise our heads. Dishevelled and dirty, with my tin hat well on the back of my head, I asked, "Is anyone hurt?" On fervent assurances on all sides that all was well, bar a few small cuts, I announced that I would like a nice cup of tea, which sentiment, although heartily agreed to, caused some laughter. Just as everyone was preparing to extricate themselves, the roar of planes was heard again, and we flattened ourselves on the floor, prepared for another basting, but they passed over and nothing happened. Later we heard that they were our own Hurricanes.

After a time we again reared up, and looked round. What a scene of wreckage and devastation it was!

The Station buildings were all wrecked. All the private cars, including the O.C.'s, were in flames, and there were enormous craters all over the place. But we were not U/S. Oh no! We were back again on the air in twenty minutes. Forty bombs had been dropped in the space of about four minutes, which had seemed to us more like four hours.'

That same watch went on again at midnight at their own request!

At Biggin Hill, after a direct hit on a W.A.A.F. shelter, when there were many casualties, a W.A.A.F. sergeant was heard to remark: 'They have broken my back! My God, they've broken my false teeth too!' Both remarks were true! I am glad to say the airwoman recovered, but was invalided out of the service, to her very great distress.

Elsewhere, operators continued their functions though the buildings might be on fire or crumbling round them. The only complaint of which I was aware was made by the W.A.A.F. of Dunkirk (Kent) Radar Station. 'Please, could we have some lighter food, salads, fresh vegetables and fish? The meat and bread ration may be all right for the men, but in this hot weather it brings us out in spots! Most unsightly!'

The views of a civilian wireless operator attached to the R.A.F. and working in South-East England seem well worth recording. C. E. G. Claringbold has written at length of his experiences in Fighter Command. He had served in the Navy as a wireless operator, and, in accordance with Air Ministry policy at the time, he was engaged as a civilian (cheaper and possibly more efficient than an airman) to take charge of a Fighter Command wireless transmitter. After a year in the R.A.F. he was regraded as a wireless operator mechanic, with an increase of pay,

'and because of this I moved my home from town to the nearby village. When war came we were nicely settled in our country bungalow. I spent many hours cultivating the garden and the greenhouse was my special joy.

After the first shock of the declaration of war we soon settled down to the easy optimism that prevailed during that first winter. [The only trial that the state of war inflicted on his household was the arrival of three evacuees, and the long and inconvenient hours of his duty.]

It was not until Dunkirk that we began to take the war really seriously. The feeling of tension became widespread, partly as a result of the defensive measures—pill-boxes, trenches and barbed wire—that began to litter the countryside. People lost their indifference to the air-raid sirens and gazed skyward expecting something.'

At the airfield there was great activity. Aircraft, many of them the sub-standard Lysanders, flew across the Channel to take part in the coastal battle. In the signals section this activity was almost frenzied: touch had to be kept with the field stations in France. As these, one by one, went off the air and the plain-language messages from those that were still working spoke more frequently about an impending attack, the superintendent of the watch would make the gesture of loosening his collar, saying, 'Any minute now!' To relieve his feelings he would shout for a junior to sweep up the flood of signal forms that littered the floor 'and be quick about it'. The strain of this work mounted daily until the evacuation was complete and France had capitulated. And then—silence. There was no friend with whom to communicate across the water.

Claringbold confesses to a hollow feeling in the pit of his stomach as he stared across the Channel and faintly saw the outline of the French cliffs—now enemy country. His wife was furious, however, accusing the French of letting down the side.

Then began the battle of the Channel convoys. Every day the sirens went and there were dogfights overhead, but at first few bombs were dropped on land. The glorious summer weather held, and life was not too unpleasant. On the wireless there was the tonic of Churchill's speeches and confidence was great that 'we could go it alone'.

Claringbold was shocked when he was ordered to move to an airfield farther inland. To abandon his comfortable home and beloved garden was to bear a bitter blow. A new home had to be found, and by contrast all that offered was unsatisfactory.

On the day of the move there was heavy air fighting just over the house, probably a convoy air battle that had drifted inland. Claringbold cheered his wife with the remark: 'Anyway we are coming away from the continual siren and dogfights. Where we are going the alarm went a fortnight ago and they are still talking about it.'

Sunday, 18th August, was to shatter this illusion. The airfield was heavily attacked and he and 'Tubby' the wireless corporal spent a very uncomfortable half-hour crouched under a workbench. One of the younger telegraphists, caught in the open, bolted to the transmitter block and hid in a cupboard.

During this attack not only the airfield but the neighbouring village was hit. When Claringbold cycled back to his bungalow to see what had happened to his family he passed three cars ablaze, the village pub a shambles, with the owner lying on a stretcher outside, the post office in bad shape and several houses much damaged.

Casualties had been heavy but his family was safe. Twelve days later the airfield was again under attack:

'Quite a lot of W.A.A.F.s had been detailed to use our shelter. These girls deserved every praise. Some were nervous and uneasy, but most of them just sat and talked about things in general. Then it started! I felt my mouth go very dry and would have given anything for a drink. Some of the girls went to the shelter door to see what was happening. To a chorus of, "Shut that bloody door," reinforced by some physical violence on the part of "Tubby", they were shoved inside just as the blast of a nearby bomb slammed the door to!

The bombing stopped. A lot of chatter broke out, pent-up nerves seeking an outlet after strain. Then someone suggested that there might be a second run of bombing and there was immediate silence.'

In the subsequent clearing up it was found that there had been a number of casualties and a great deal of damage.

Claringbold's wife had been out shopping with her children when the attack started. As she was trying to take shelter a soldier stopped his car beside her and pulled the children down between the car and the roadside bank, using his body as an additional shelter. The children were frightened by this rough handling but what really worried them was the wet tar from the sunny road that had stuck to their hands and clothes!

By this time the ground crews were getting a little jittery. A series of concentrated attacks on a small area such as an airfield can have a punishing effect on the nervous system of the bravest. But the work of maintenance went on; the fighters took off, each aircraft serviceable and effective, manned by a stout-hearted pilot furious at the destruction of his comfortable quarters and longing for revenge.

The third attack did a great deal of damage, particularly to the airfield communications. The telephone exchange was hit but no one was killed. The Signals warrant officer lost his tunic and a considerable sum of money that was in a pocket. He was not amused! Two of the W.A.A.F. telephone operators earned decorations for the courage with which they kept the exchange 'alive' in the middle of the debris.

Other attacks followed, without grave consequences except to the nerves. During this period of waiting for something to happen the men's minds worked in this way: 'If only we could do something, mate, we should feel better. If we were manning a gun and ready to hit back it would ease this waiting to see if we are going to be the target.'

The bombing of our fighter airfields was becoming a real danger to our defensive effort when, happily, Hitler's fury at a successful attack by Bomber Command upon the Reich made him order a concentrated assault on London. So the well-calculated strategy of the Luftwaffe, almost within reach of success, was brought to nothing by the little Corporal's petulance. Hitler, in the ultimate analysis, can be considered as one of Britain's most valuable allies.

The feelings of the airmen working in the target area must have been very much akin to those described by Claringbold—dry mouth, a beating heart, and a strong desire to run rather than walk. But at least they had the satisfaction of dispatching their aircraft in pursuit of the enemy, and the pressure of work was such as to give little time for thought. Scratch meals snatched whenever there was a pause in the alerts; sleep broken by 'noises off' and very little of that in any case; and the sorrow felt when aircrew were 'missing, believed killed'. Group Captain 'Sailor' Malan has been kind enough to contribute two personal letters that he received from airmen who had served with him. These letters seem to epitomize the sentiment that existed amongst the airmen of Fighter Command during the fighting over Dunkirk while the evacuation of the Expeditionary Force was going on and afterwards during the Battle of Britain. There was trust, affection and the deepest respect that seldom found expression in words, but in service done with most willing hearts the men tried to repay what they felt they owed to the pilots who daily 'pulled the whiskers of death'!

The airmen who wrote the letters had been transferred from Fighter Command to South Africa under the Empire Air Training Scheme, and were indeed homesick and sad at being taken out of the fighting. They had seen an article written in a magazine by 'Sailor's' father and this was the reaction:

> 'A Flight,
> R.A.F. Kimberley,
> Cape Province.
> 24th September, 1940.

Dear Sir,

It was with proud feelings that I read your article in the *Outspan* in reference to your son, Flight Lieutenant Malan, D.F.C. It was only a few days previous that I was wondering if my Flight Commander of 74(F) Squadron was still batting, as it seemed a miracle to me that he was not bowled out. I always made it my job to see my Flight Commander off to Dunkirk and on his return which consequently caused me with pride to spend many hours patching his battered Spitfire up ready for the next trip over. Having done the repairs myself I could well realize the marvellous escapes he must have had. Although his Spitfire came back battered each time, Flight Lieutenant Malan would not part with it in exchange for a new and more modern one. His instructions were to his crew—"my machine has got to be serviceable". There was no excuse, his engine had to go first time, the Radio Telephone just had to function even if his junior pilots' Radio failed at times, and his guns weren't allowed to have stoppages. On one occasion it was my job to work out in the open all night with a hand torch to renew his battered tail-plane. I don't know how I managed it but I knew it just had to be done by 4 a.m. Flight Lieutenant Malan got in his cockpit and said, "Contact," without asking if I had finished, in fact I was struggling with the last stubborn splitpin. The day came when we were shown the films of his combats which was a tonic to us all, after eight terrible months of waiting but always ready.

The greatest thrill of all was the night of the first raids when Lieutenant Malan went up alone through the intense gunfire and shot down two German machines in what seemed less than ten minutes. In my heart I knew this was another award for our Flight Commander. A few weeks later I was detailed for overseas and eventually arrived at Kimberley. The first stranger I made friends with whilst shopping conversed about the R.A.F. in England. Of course I told him about my Flight Commander, who also was a South African. In the conversation he said the day previous it had been announced that a Flight Lieutenant Malan had been awarded the bar to his D.F.C. I then excitedly shouted, "He is the officer I was referring to." Again only last week I was telling the story of a lady living near Kimberley who then informed me of a relation of hers who had been awarded the D.F.C. and afterwards mentioned the name. I then jumped out of my chair shouting, "That is him, my Flight Commander." For the moment I cannot think of the lady's name who afterwards showed me your article in the *Outspan*. Although his name has followed me out here I have been very disheartened since the day I left my Squadron behind, who have been in the thick of it since I left, while I am here practically on a Cook's Tour and cannot assist in any way for the safety of my people in London. I am trying to obtain a copy of the *Illustrated News* June 29th which give pictures of the two enemy planes shot down by Lieutenant Malan. This I will forward on to you in case you have not already seen it.

I trust, sir, you will not consider my writing to you a liberty: but being so proud of Flight Lieutenant Malan, I just had to write. With all my faith in 74 Squadron and wishing them all Good Luck in their struggle for the freedom of the Empire. I am, sir,

Yours faithfully,
A. E. Still, Cpl. R.A.F.'

'744562 L.A.C. Wright, A.,
R.A.F. Detachment,
P.O. Box 989, Durban, Natal.

Dear Sir,

Picking up a copy of the *Outspan* in our hut yesterday, I came across your article about your son, and it was especially interesting to me as I was on "A" Flight 74 Squadron until September 4th of this year.

In my trade of flight rigger it was my privilege to work on your son's aircraft for some time and feel I ought to write and let you know of the high esteem and admiration in which he is regarded by all ranks on the Squadron. His fearless courage and leadership is certainly an inspiration to all who come in contact with him and not a man on the Squadron who would not follow him anywhere.

It was a proud moment for us of the "other ranks" to be paraded for the King's visit to pin the D.F.C. on your son's breast, and the night operation which earned him his bar will surely go down in history and will be talked about whenever the members of 74 Squadron forgather in the future.

With all best wishes for Mr. Malan's continued success.

I remain,

Yours sincerely,

A. Wright.'

For the next three years the work of the airmen in Fighter Command hardly varied, apart from those in the developing night-fighter force. Even here it was merely exchanging daylight for darkness, though with the advance of airborne radar the electricians and wireless mechanics had to increase the basis of their knowledge of electronics. But the general pattern remained the same—sudden rushes of frenzied activity when every available aircraft had to take to the air, to be followed by long periods of routine work at normal speed.

From Bomber Command's men a steady development of effort was required. At first the number of aircraft available for the attack on Germany was strictly limited, and, owing to the relative weakness of the enemy's defences, casualties were not high—between 2 and $3\frac{1}{2}$ per cent per attack. But as more of the heavy bombers became available, and the enemy's defences grew stronger with consequent casualties between 5 and 6 per cent per attack, so the airmen's burden grew heavier. In addition, as aids to bad-weather flying became available, so the number of attacks increased, and the periods of pressure came more closely together. What this pressure meant for the ground crews can best be illustrated in the following manner. An aircraft would return from operations with its starboard fuel tank holed by a splinter, port and starboard elevators and the fin shredded by blast from a near burst, all emergency exits blown in, 200 or more holes in the hull which required flush patching and the engine cowls distorted. All the electrical and hydraulic gear needed testing for faults. At a conservative estimate and provided spares were available this was a forty-eight-hour job. It would be completed with hours to spare!

In addition to this work it was part of the ground crew's duty to stand by at the dispersal point after their aircraft was airborne in case it returned early after developing some fault. Imagine the conditions in the war-time winters! Rain is incessant and the cold crippling. The men sit huddled up on the bomb-trollies or toolboxes, sheltering as best they may under the engine and cockpit covers. They are cold, wet and aching all over from fatigue. Occasionally a figure bent over his bicycle handlebars against the driving rain pedals his way to the canteen in search of a warm drink. Returning with one hand holding a can of hot tea he is the saviour of his comrades, but a very dangerous hazard to others moving about in the black-out. No lights of course and his navigation mainly by guesswork and long experience.

So these servicing parties sit and wait, so numbed with cold that they can scarcely move, listening for the drone of an engine and praying for the dawn.

In addition to this misery the normal working conditions of the ground crews were far from good.

As a protection against enemy attack, the hutments that were their dwellings on most of the airfields were widely scattered. The aircraft themselves were stabled in isolated revetments around the airfield perimeter. Finally, owing to restrictions placed on the use of mechanical transport, movements to and from the place of work and the quarters had to be carried out on foot or on bicycles. The average mileage covered daily in this way could not have been less than eight or ten.

Ground crews would often arrive at their huts, after a day's work in biting wind and rain, so exhausted that, in spite of wet clothing which would not be dry by next morning, they would tumble into bed to sleep the sleep of the dead.

Sometimes there was an amusing episode. An airman, inexperienced in the new four-engined bombers, arrived at No. 76 Squadron's station. He was soon one of a crew, and one day he was waiting for the return of an aircraft from operations. The machine landed and taxied to its dispersal point. The airman, Wadsworth by name, rushed forward, right into the blast of the four airscrews. He was catapulted into a duckpond by the force of the slipstream. Emerging and wiping mud and duckweed from his face, he was greeted with cat-calls and cries of 'Don't forget the diver!'

The strain of operations took its toll! In Bomber Command alone 8000 men and women died from illness, from bomb accidents, and from road crashes, the latter two causes probably flowing from inattention due to fatigue. Occasionally, too, there would be deaths from a night-intruder attack on an airfield busy with the dispatch of bombers to Germany. And there would be injuries suffered by brave men and women seeking to rescue aircrews trapped in crashed and burning aircraft.

An aircraftswoman, Margaret Hughes, gives her impressions of this period:

'My first few months in the service were overshadowed by very heavy aircraft losses and a vivid memory of a dignified Alsatian dog sitting outside Station H.Q. He took no notice of anyone and I learnt that he had belonged to one of our aircrew, recently missing. Someone took him away in the end. The Station Commander was a jolly, rotund man, greatly loved by us all. He was the first Group Captain I had ever seen in battledress. On his sturdy figure it looked just like a romper suit. One night I was on duty alone in the Met. office, on the top floor of Station H.Q., when he came into the room and told me to drop whatever I was doing. He wanted a younger pair of ears to help listen for an overdue aeroplane. It was a horrible night. North Sea stratus was drifting in, threatening to blot out the flare-path. For some time we stood straining our ears and just as I thought I could detect a faint rumble the telephone rang inside the office. The Station Commander went in from the roof where we were, answered the phone and then ran downstairs. By this time I was sure I could hear the plane and thought that the mist seemed a bit thinner. The throb grew louder and suddenly they were down safely. A few minutes later the mist had become fog and the station was blotted out. It was my first miracle and I shall never forget the blessed relief from the tension of waiting and listening.'

One of Margaret's room-mates was a girl from Southsea. She looked after batteries from the aircraft, and starter batteries—'trolley accs.' she called them. She was one of the most dedicated and devoted slaves of the aircrews in the whole of the service. Each morning she went off, smart, clean and sweet, to her dirty and tiring job. By lunchtime she was incredibly dirty but perfectly happy. Night after night when the Station was operating she would be down to watch 'take-off' and later for the return. When Margaret remonstrated with her and begged her to get a good night's sleep she would say: 'I can't sleep till I know they're back. I always feel so responsible for them. After all, those trolley accs. are all mine. Supposing something went wrong.'

A new squadron came to the station later in the year. They had what was regarded as a very dangerous scorn for the 'Cloudy Joes' in the Met. Office. They had been told at a morning briefing that a cold front bringing violent conditions with heavy rain and possible thunderstorms was due to cross the area later in the day. In view of their known attitude the Met. Officer paid particular attention to timing the frontal passage and, when the office was invaded by a crowd of cheerful leg-pulling pilots and navigators, he forecast rain at about 11.55 a.m. or noon. One of the visitors threatened to 'make a book' on the probabilities and work became a bit disorganized. By 11.39 the frontal clouds in a line-squall could be seen approaching from the north-west, by 11.55 they were overhead and just before noon down came the rain in torrents, closely followed by hail. Met.'s reputation was assured—until the next time.

Margaret has a funny memory of a sports afternoon when a very tall handsome Canadian officer came out to play hockey in extremely brief bright-red shorts! There was a gasp of surprise from the spectators and a stern command from the C.O. to 'send that man in to get properly dressed!'

Some time later that year Margaret Hughes was posted to a station in Huntingdonshire. Here the Met. Office was in the Flying Control building on the airfield. One night of maximum effort, after the 'tumult and shouting had died', she was working on the midnight chart when she heard a heavy aeroplane land and move off to one of the far-side dispersals. Very busy at the time, she was but mildly surprised, but about fifteen minutes later the door of the building opened and footsteps were heard along the passage. Then the office door was opened and in came seven weary Australians. They said they had run out of fuel and seeing lights had lobbed in with just enough to get off the runway. Margaret suggested that they should report their arrival but they said they were too tired to move. They really did seem 'all in' so she decided to make some tea first as the kettle was nearly boiling. She went into the kitchen to do so and when she returned they were all fast asleep, two in the only two office easy chairs, the other five in various attitudes on the floor. A couple of hours later, as dawn was breaking, she made some toast and some more tea, woke up her guests and in due course, after an effort to smarten up a bit, they made their way to the appropriate quarters. Margaret concludes her account: 'Demobilization came all too soon. The comradeship found in war will always be one of the most precious things I ever knew!'

Of the Coastal Command airmen it is sufficient to say that the troubles suffered by their fellows in Fighter and Bomber Commands were theirs as well. In addition, however, they worked in some of the most isolated and uncomfortable spots that any airmen was called upon to occupy. Their airfields ranged from West Africa to Iceland —even as far as North Russia. In the flying-boat squadrons the mechanics worked ten or fifteen feet above water-level, in the certainty that if their frozen fingers let go of a tool or spare part it was infallibly lost in twenty feet of water. The flying-boat anchorages, if dredged today, would give up a substantial assortment of scrap metal! One of my most lively memories is that of No. 10 R.A.A.F. Flying-Boat Squadron. Discipline on shore—Australian! On operations that of the Guards. No Christian names—only prompt and willing obedience to authority. They were regulars!

In the background of these events were the airmen and airwomen of Transport, Training and Maintenance Commands. As a flying command on an international scale Transport Command has a place in this chapter. At first modest, by the end of the war its activities covered a very wide field. In origin it stemmed from No. 24 (Communication) Squadron, of which the story follows.

In the years after the Kaiser War the Royal Air Force faced a problem of air transportation. To meet its requirements a squadron was formed out of the communication flights which had at first satisfied the day-to-day movements of the Air Staff. It was given the number 24.

This number had belonged to the first single-seater fighter squadron to take part in World War One. Formed in September 1915 the

K

original No. 24 went to France a few weeks later, equipped with a small pusher biplane, the D.H.2. At first it had some successes but soon it was outclassed by the faster German fighters. Amongst its losses was the tragic death of its Commanding Officer, Lance Hawker, v.c. He was shot down by the German ace, Baron von Richthofen —the famous Red Baron whose fighter circus caused the R.F.C. so much trouble in the early years of the war. In spite of this disaster the squadron battled on, and when it was re-equipped with the new fighter, the S.E.5a, it covered itself with glory during the fighting in March and April 1918. In 170 encounters with the enemy air force it gained sixty-two certain victories.

On one occasion towards the end of the war fourteen of its aircraft, in a running battle with at least fifty Fokkers, drove them out of the sky above our advancing troops and caused them heavy loss in some of the fiercest fighting of the war. When given the right tools No. 24 did the job magnificently.

The war over, No. 24 was disbanded, its records finding a home in the R.A.F. Depot, Uxbridge.

The squadron was reactivated in 1920, and in 1924 it was finally established as the Air Ministry's means of air transport.

In 1926, still flying the rather sordid left-overs of the Kaiser War, it carried Government mails, with some irregularity, due to engine failures, during the Coal and General Strikes. For these failures the airmen could not be blamed. The material was worn out and defective.

From then on the work of the squadron grew. The tale of Very Important Personages that made use of its services ranges from Princes to Prime Ministers, from Emirs to Envoys. Once a clutch of four field marshals was carried in one aircraft, a heavy responsibility for the pilot and for the crew that had serviced the machine.

Gradually, aircraft designed for the purpose took the place of the war-time makeshifts, and as this happened so the claims on the squadron's services grew apace. It is noticeable how the serviceability of the aircraft improved in the late 'twenties and early 'thirties. Crashes were few, and fatalities most rare. The pilots were carefully selected, but the ground staff were also hand-picked. No. 24 was building up a magnificent record of reliability, and officials and politicians showed a lively appreciation of this fact.

In the dark years before the Hitler War the squadron's aircraft ranged more widely, shuttling between the capitals of Western Europe with cargoes of anxious politicians. These flights wove a pattern that conformed to the changing international scene. They were full of interest and the lucky airmen who travelled on them saw Europe in a big way.

During the months of phoney war the squadron at first had little to do. But by early 1940 it was once again working at high pressure. Winston Churchill and his staff went backwards and forwards between Paris and London, and senior officers from the Departments harried the lives out of the commanders abroad by the frequency of their visits.

The peaceful trips to France came to an end with the German advance. By the middle of May transport aircraft were being destroyed on Allied airfields, and the airmen were withdrawn to Britain.

When France surrendered, 24 rested. The record book notes that 'owing to the evacuation of France the Customs officer was withdrawn'. The Customs and Excise are always with us. Many years ago the preventive officers looked for the 'Gentlemen' going by, their 'five and twenty ponies trotting through the dark' with 'brandy for the parson, baccy for the clerk'. Now the smuggling tendencies of air and ground crew had to be 'prevented', a simpler and less dangerous operation.

1941 wasn't an interesting year—mainly one of routine flights in the U.K.—but by April 1942 the new Hudson aircraft of the squadron were carrying out a shuttle service to Malta. 6000 passengers and 600 tons of freight were carried by night between Gibraltar and the beleagured island, giving some ease to a desperate situation. When the King awarded the George Cross to Malta it was a Hudson of 24 that carried the decoration to the Governor.

The tale of the flights in 1942 evokes many memories. One to Gibraltar reminds me of a meeting with the Governor. On the table between us was an envelope damp with sea-water. It contained a letter giving the dates and places of the 'Torch' landings in North Africa. It had been found on the body of a drowned pilot washed up on the south shore of Spain. The Spaniards had returned it and the rest of the kit without, to all appearances, passing on the information to the Germans. Was this bluff or double bluff, or just the result of a friendly feeling for Britain?

In 1943 and 1944 the squadron's flights continued to lengthen. For example, Lieutenant J. F. Rhykof flew from Hendon to India—Ceylon —Abyssinia—the Sudan—Kenya—Rhodesia—Durban—back to the Sudan and then across Africa to Accra and so home along the west coast of Africa and Europe. He was away four months and his laundry and that of the crew must have presented a serious problem. Did it ever catch up?

By the middle of 1944 the field was enlarged. Iceland, Persia and Burma were taken in the pilots' stride, with amazing regularity. Even the Azores, where, temporarily, the R.A.F. reigned, were frequently visited.

From this small band of air and ground crew Transport Command Royal Air Force was formed. Squadrons multiplied as the needs of the overseas theatres grew, and as the possibilities of parachute landings and glider attacks became more important.

After 1945, during which a thousand flights were made to liberated France and the Low Countries, carrying supplies and evacuating wounded at the pilots' discretion, Transport Command reached its peak, and its ground crews carried their burden with complete success.

In time, of course, the requirement of air transport declined, and with it the number of squadrons in the Command. For some years little remained but the tradition of good service established by No. 24 Squadron. But as the strength of the Army diminished its need for increased mobility increased. Thus once more there was a build-up in the number of transport squadrons required to move our land forces to the danger spots as they appeared. Today Transport Command is strong and efficient, and if present plans are put into effect it may find itself employed in offensive action against an enemy. Its ability to carry heavy loads at high speed, perhaps even armed with the stand-off bomb, will make it a most useful supplement to the V. Bomber Force.

11

The Women's Auxiliary Air Force

A N EX-MEMBER of the W.A.A.F., A.C.W. Horton, who served for ten years in the ranks and has written of her experiences in a most engaging style, begs me not to give the W.A.A.F. a chapter to itself. She insists, and rightly too, that the pattern of the women's service was so closely interwoven with that of the men of the R.A.F. it is impossible to make a distinction between the two.

But before one can write of the women's doings it seems to me essential to give special attention to the manner in which the W.A.A.F. was born and some of its major characteristics. To this end is this chapter devoted.

Although in 1919 the Air Ministry had been far-sighted enough to propose the creation of a permanent women's service and had again put forward the suggestion in May 1936, nothing was done by the Government.

It was not until 1938 when the threat of war became perfectly clear that reluctantly the War Office, and with enthusiasm the Air Ministry, began to act. At the start the new scheme envisaged enrolling the women on a Territorial basis and clothing them in khaki. They were to be called the Auxiliary Territorial Service—the A.T.S. This was in May, but only in September, when the War Office awoke to the fact that many women were taking on other commitments, was the scheme published.

From the very beginning the R.A.F. sections of the A.T.S. showed a strong desire to be more closely associated with their parent service. To be in khaki—a drab colour for a woman—did not appeal to them. They preferred the air-force blue. Besides, there was a great deal more glamour about the R.A.F. and there might be a chance of flying with some distinguished pilot!

Gradually the inevitable happened. By slow degrees the hybrid organization was broken down and a complete R.A.F. system took its place. On 28th June 1939, with the King's approval and Treasury consent, the Women's Auxiliary Air Force came into being. But the original muddled thinking had its expected effect. When war broke out few of the women in the service had undergone more than three months' training, and in the administrative branch in particular there was a most serious shortage of efficient officers.

So it was 'by guess and by the grace of God' that the W.A.A.F. came into being, and how gallantly the women met their difficulties!

Officially they rated as equivalent to two-thirds of a man and their legal status was that of a camp-follower, such as the locally recruited labour overseas. A very high percentage of the regular R.A.F. officers regarded them as an unmitigated nuisance and gave them no help. Their accommodation was abominable, their food most unsuitable and their uniform unattractive. But the volunteers that came forward to enrol had amongst them some outstanding characters, and all had a burning desire to be of use to their country in whatever capacity they were called upon to work.

In the main they were women of a middle- to upper-class status —well educated and accustomed to a high standard of living, but perfectly prepared to endure discomfort, and indeed hardships, provided they could help their country in war. There is the well-authenticated story of an A.C.W.2 who, after a fortnight on her station in Fighter Command, put in an application to be allowed to keep her two hunters in the near neighbourhood. War or no war, she was going to hunt if this was in any manner possible! It would not be as good as Leicestershire, but there was some open country in Kent and a few fences to be jumped.

There were two conflicting schools of thought that caused a great deal of trouble in the W.A.A.F. throughout the war. On the one hand there were senior women who considered the administration of the service should be carried out by a hierarchy of females, in the same manner that the senior men ran the men's service. Others were all in favour of integration with the men from top to bottom. They considered that apart from advice given by women officers the men's system should apply to the W.A.A.F. as well as the R.A.F. There is little doubt that there were insufficient skilled administrators to make the first system workable. So, with many a hiccup, the second method was applied. It was not easy to work. The Judge Advocate General had thrown a very large spanner into the works when he ruled that the Air Force Act could not be held to apply, from a disciplinary point of view, to the airwomen. This threw the whole system of punishment for bad behaviour into complete confusion. Up to the end of the war there were anomalies and weaknesses in the W.A.A.F. that arose from this narrow legalistic interpretation—probably right in law but wrong from the point of view of commonsense. At the outset it did not matter much because the W.A.A.F. were mostly of a type that had a sense of responsibility and an enthusiasm for their work. But later, when conscription was applied to women, the picture changed in a radical manner. I remember well, in 1943, when I was called upon to inspect the stations of the R.A.F. in Great Britain, that I found a very difficult situation. So concerned did I become with what I saw that soon, on arrival at a station headquarters, the first thing I enquired into was the disciplinary state of the W.A.A.F. It was astonishing to find Borstal girls, trollops and thieves amongst a mass of decent women. On the average there were 2 per cent of illegitimate pregnancies every few months, and desertion and other major crimes were common form. The women officers did their best, but not many of them had the training and none the authority that would have helped them to control their unruly flock. In spite of all this trouble I hope to show later on that the W.A.A.F. did a magnificent job, and if there were many black sheep there were ten times that number of gallant, hard-working and responsible girls.

A woman who served in both wars has written of her experiences after she joined up in 1939:

'The general structure of the W.A.A.F. organization in 1939 was similar to that of the W.R.A.F. in 1918. There were minor differences, but on the whole the organization and administration were easy to pick up if you had been in the service in the First World War.

As usual people said, "Of course the young people of today are not what they used to be!" Naturally they were not the same, but they proved themselves equally capable, and courageous.

The Training Depot Station of West Drayton during that first dreadful winter of snow and intense frost, when the water in our buckets froze solid overnight, as did our sponges and other washing gear, was a good proving ground. We were overcrowded, and at night in the blacked-out Nissen huts it was a case of asphyxiation from the smoking stove, or freezing. We generally froze!

Early morning ablutions after a tramp through the snow to reach the rows of basins was not an exhilarating event. Later we squelched through creamy mud everywhere. Then came the flu epidemic which swept the camp, filled the hospital to overflowing. Sleeping huts were hastily turned into wards, the convalescent nursing the sick. At one point for some days there were only one senior W.A.A.F. officer and one senior N.C.O. (myself) running the place, with the help of a few R.A.F. N.C.O.s.'

West Drayton was a tough place for women, young or old. Miss Horton writes with feeling about her stay there. Apparently no one was allowed to walk from one block of buildings to another without permission. This discipline was enforced by the women officers, but on the whole Miss Horton found the male N.C.O.s, instructors and disciplinarians, more reasonable and perhaps more biddable.

Whatever the miseries suffered at the Training Depot, there is little doubt that, when posted to stations, operational, training or maintenance, the women were happy and interested in their work.

In the rest of this narrative I shall attempt to weave the W.A.A.F. and R.A.F. into a composite pattern, gay in places, sober in others, and with one or two sombre patches—the result of the usury of war.

12

The Royal Observer Corps, and its 'Mates'

IN THE days when Zeppelins and after them the Gothas were a danger to our country an air defence system was created. One of the important parts of this system was the Observer Corps, later to become the Royal Observer Corps.

At first it was a mixture of police officers and soldiers who, in a rather ramshackle organization and with the minimum facilities for communicating their observations, endeavoured to plot the course of enemy aircraft.

I remember late on Christmas Eve 1914 being warned by the local police, who were in a hilarious mood, that Zeppelins were about in large numbers. Unable to do anything as I possessed no night-flying aircraft, and in any case more than doubtful as to the validity of the warning, I wished the police a Happy Christmas and went to bed.

Later, a big volunteer force was created, culled from every walk of life—the squire, the postman, the blacksmith, the farmer and the cowman—each giving of his spare time with no reward other than a sense of duty done.

On their isolated posts, scattered over the open country in the east and south-east of Britain, night and day these devoted men watched for the enemy. From the coast-line to the heart of the country they reported what they saw and heard to the control centres from which the day- and night-fighter aircraft were alerted.

During the latter part of the Kaiser War the Observer Corps did a wonderful job. After the Armistice the organization flagged, but under the impulse of Air Ministry policy its numbers later grew and prospered. The annual air defence exercises gave the observers something to look forward to and they felt they were an important part of the defence organization.

When radar came into being their authority was challenged. Here was something with a range of observation not of a few miles but of

120 or more. But the conservative commanders of the fighter force were not prepared to accept this new device as a complete substitute for the observations of men trained and wise in the ways of aircraft. So, even until the end of 1940, the observers played a great part in the day and night defence against air attack. This is understandable. All that radar could do at this time was to give early warning of attack. The plotting of the enemy, after he had crossed our coast-line, was in the hands of the observers, who visually by day, and by sound at night, could follow the course of the enemy. Sometimes they went wrong! 'You can't tell them by the sound' was a slogan in the winter of 1940–1. One observer post near Maidstone reported a twin-engined aircraft— possibly Blenheim, probably Beaufighter—to the centre at Maidstone. Some five minutes later a tired voice from 'Centre' called the post: 'You know that Beaufighter you just reported? Well, it's dropped a bomb on us!'

The observers in the posts, as this story illustrates, did not run any great risks. It was mainly the long hours in inclement weather from which they suffered. But the 'Centres', usually lodged in built-up areas where communications were good, often shared with the rest of the population in the results of enemy bombardment.

The position of the Corps during the Hitler War was twice challenged. Our scientists had been busy working on a system whereby radar could be used not only for long-range warning of enemy attack, but for short-range interception of their bombers after they had crossed our coasts. By 1941 the first Ground-Controlled Interception Stations —G.C.I. for short—had been established. As the G.C.I. stations increased in number and experience so our night fighters, with their assistance, shot down more and more of the Luftwaffe's raiders.

Throughout the Hitler War the Observer Corps gave splendid service. Today the question may be asked whether it can still help against the bomber flying at 70,000 feet and the missile travelling at ever-increasing velocity. It would seem that its usefulness is at an end. But the Air Ministry, not entirely devoid of sense, considers that the Observer Corps is well worth maintaining. Obviously there are still many tasks that it can perform. Enemy aircraft will not always fly at great height. Indeed, low-level attack may well be a great danger in any future war. Then there is the matter of atomic 'fall-out' that I believe it is one of the duties of the Observer Corps to watch. Thus the Corps will remain of great value in the foreseeable future.

The work of the G.C.I stations was most interesting to watch. I have a very vivid recollection of a night in one at Sopley in Hampshire. After supper in the mess I went into the Operations Room with the Station Commander just as the watch was changing. After a certain amount of orderly disturbance the new watch settled down to the nightly routine. There was a very gentle buzz of conversation and some of the girls were knitting, others reading, to pass the time away. Out in the Channel the coastal convoys were creeping along, their movements followed on the operations board by the plotters detailed for the purpose. South of the Isle of Wight a solitary Beaufighter was on patrol. Suddenly two plots came up on the board, just west of the Cherbourg Peninsula. One of them 'faded' very quickly, but the other came on steadily towards the island. Everyone in the Operations Room was on the alert. The Controller radioed the Beaufighter to proceed on a course that would bring him astern of the 'Bandit'. On the board the drama unfolded. The enemy flew straight and level towards Portsmouth, his probable target. Behind him the Beaufighter steadily closed in until, just over the coast, the plots of the two aircraft coincided. Within seconds the pilot of the Beaufighter radioed: 'Have shot into something! Give me a position, please!' He was flying above cloud and needed help. Two minutes later an Observer Corps post reported an aircraft crashing in flames within a few miles of the last plot on the board.

This was the perfect interception and kill, but it was relatively a rare occurrence.

Herbert Jones, an airman employed during the war at Trimley Heath and Martlesham Heath G.C.I. stations, has a more normal story to tell.

These G.C.I. stations were situated in open fields on the Suffolk coast. The Observations Block was of bungalow construction with no windows so as to be poison-gas-proof. It was also called the 'Final' because its design was the final one approved for building in view of the radar requirements of that particular part of the coast defence. The Ops. Room was manned throughout the twenty-four hours by crews worked like a ship, W.A.A.F. and R.A.F. personnel mixed, Controllers, radar operators and plotters, with ancillary army personnel for searchlight and A.A. control. Being in such an isolated position it was rather a 'family' affair and personalities were much discussed, and their doings reported even when they went to far-off G.C.I. stations in England, or, as sometimes happened, to Burma or North Africa.

The R.A.F. and W.A.A.F. people were distributed around the village in private billets, and this idea stemmed from the early days of the war when it was thought necessary to conceal the true nature of the Ops. from the public. Civilian clothes were worn off duty by most of the operators. However, as the need for secrecy passed away some men did live in Nissen huts in a field opposite to the camp entrance and they got along quite well, and even felt superior to their mates in civilian billets. They made their own amusements in the huts and always went out together for a drink, each man with his 'oppo' or pal. Probably this term sprang from afar off in the Royal Naval Air Service days of 1917, like 'Chiefy' for flight sergeant (cf. chief petty officer). A floor also was always the 'deck'.

Let the reader imagine a cold early January morning, grey and biting with first light only just starting to creep over the horizon. The day crew are coming on duty to relieve the night watch. Overhead the first Flying Fortress is circling, firing a red rocket to its friends who soon come up in dozens, circling to make up a formation to raid the German Forces in France or maybe near Arnhem. As the incoming crew enter the Final they meet one of the 'night bind-crew' (English— night watch) and ask, 'Had a good night, Corporal?' 'No—hell of a bind. We were up all night, went to bed at 0400 hours, and up again at 0700 for air/sea rescue. The "Shagbat" [i.e. Walrus] picked up two Yanks ditched in the drink near the Dutch Islands. So-long, I'm for breakfast now.'

The first duty of the new watch is to clean up the Ops. block, including the canteen, polish the floors, and set operators to sit on plotting lines, liaison lines and radar sets. A lot of chaff ensues amongst the 'busybodies' and a constant twittering from the W.A.A.F.s who usually have lots of news to impart to their pals, especially if they have just returned from a pass to Town, where some new show has been visited, or new dance place. The sergeant-in-charge watch is some-times a young W.A.A.F., and although it may seem strange, since many middle-aged men are under her orders, things generally go amicably enough. It is natural for a woman N.C.O. to be a bit regi-mental with her girls, but on the whole easy-going with men old enough to be her father.

On this point Jones tells of one incident which, although it did not concern an airman, may be of some interest from another angle. A very competent W.A.A.F officer was Controller one night when a Mosquito was airborne over the North Sea. When the pilot (a woman-hater) took off he was under the control of the male Flying Control Officer who, of course, handed over the aircraft to the G.C.I. Controller for Ops. against night intruders. After some half-hour the W.A.A.F. came on duty, took over control, and sat there waiting for something to turn up. Nothing did, no customers, as the pilots say, and the pilot called up the Controller, requesting permission for a 'homing' vector, or bearing. The W.A.A.F. officer replied that he must stay on patrol for another half-hour. Back came the pilot on the R/T saying he wanted to return, as he was very cold. The lady still told him to stay where he was. The irate pilot came in again on the radio and wanted to know who said so. The W.A.A.F. told him, 'I do.' 'And who the hell are you?' shot back the pilot. The Chief Controller then intervened from his cabin, where he had a loud-speaker relaying all this back-chat, and rapped the pilot over the knuckles well and truly. Afterwards peace was restored.

One of the less-publicized jobs which airmen had to carry out during the war and which carried a very high degree of risk to life was the manning of the decoy fires and the decoy airfields that were designed to attract enemy bombs away from more vital targets.

Some of the decoy fires 'pulled in' hundreds of tons of high explosive and incendiary bombs, and the airmen in charge of them went through the most hair-raising experiences. Usually, however, no more than an unfortunate cow was offered up as a sacrifice.

Operations Room personnel sometimes got these queer jobs wished on them. Aircraftsman Jones, normally on Ops. at the G.C.I. station, was sent for by the flight sergeant and told to report to Corporal-in-Charge 'Q' site in a nearby hamlet in remote Essex. Jones had no idea what this might mean in the way of duties, but it was summer time, and in the R.A.F. 'anything goes', so what the heck! Off he went on his bike for about three miles to a small country pub where the Corporal had his billet. Here he found two young men, very pleasant Sussex men from the downs of that county, who told him that they had been on the same job for some months, and that their basic duty was that of minding special Diesel stationary engines which supplied power for certain installations to which Jones would be introduced within half an hour. The airmen were billeted at the pub, where they had rooms and food. In practice they were always away on night watch and had all the days free, which was excellent work in summer! Also generous passes weekly.

The Corporal and Jones mounted their bikes, turned out on to the main road and proceeded about a mile to a small lane which led off the main road to a farm, where there was an iron Nissen hut earthed up and sandbagged, bearing on its top a small searchlight. Inside was another airman 'cleaning up' preparatory to his relief. The hut was fitted with a small desk and telephone, two beds and a coke stove. Beyond was a smaller hut housing a big Diesel engine that fed the electric lights.

The Corporal and Jones had brought their rations, and Jones volunteered to cook a stew over the stove with a view to a late supper. It was explained to him that his only purpose in life was the service of a flare-path, and to keep watch on the telephone line which led to the Ops. Room. This line served to keep the flare-party informed each hour as to the wind speed and direction, upon which depended the alignment of the flare-path. Jones was invited there and then to take a walk across the fields as it was now dusk and time to 'light up'. The Corporal switched the Diesel on and at once two lines of lights appeared, running through the fields. These two lines made a V or 'The Funnel' and then two parallel lines ran ahead for some three hundred yards or more. Each light was mounted on a short wooden post planted in the ground, often in ploughed furrows, and the bulb was in a tin box with one side open and rotatable. The idea was that when a hostile bomber flew over the pilot might think the careless English had left their aerodrome flare-path on, and forthwith proceed to drop a bomb or two on the English dimwits! In addition, to entice the Nazi to the spot the searchlight—about two feet in diameter—was shone recklessly about in the black-out to make sure some enemy pilot would definitely have a go! During the period of Jones' stay not one of the Luftwaffe saw fit to do so. Of course, the lights of the flare-path and searchlight only went on to the orders of the Controller at Ops.— mostly during air-raid alerts.

Jones' first night went well, with a good supper and reading in the warmth of the stove. He soon found out (at 0200 hours!) what happened when the wind veered round. Out into the cold cold night, to turn round every one of the lamps, stumbling over clods of earth, and expressing in vivid language his opinion of the fool who thought up the idea of using so many dozens of lamps. However, it was a fine night and dawn came very early. The relief arrived, and the night watch went back to breakfast at the inn. After about three days of this procedure the crew got a forty-eight-hour pass and were told to report to the Ops. office to collect passes at the hand of the Flight Sergeant. As this man was rather inclined to find new jobs at very short notice Jones walked into the spider's web with some misgiving. For all the interest shown it was very hard to believe that for a year or more Jones had worked under him in that very building. 'Flight' gave out the pass with a good grace and Jones quickly scurried down the passage, out into the yard and down the street to the railway station before some other idea could be dreamed up about his employment.

What with passes and summer night work the time passed pleasantly, but unfortunately, at the end of three weeks, Jones was recalled to the Ops. Room duty, and soon forgot the flare-path in the dreary round of day and night watches.

Other forms of deception intended to divert enemy bombers from their target included the beam-bending devices that interfered with their navigation. Though many of the early 'transmitters' (radio-therapy equipment in peace) were mounted on the roof of police stations and were operated by policemen when the warning went, there were the more refined devices such as the 'meacon' that upset the Germans' beacons and the complicated electronic equipment that obfuscated 'Benito', 'The Rivers' and other code-named beams that the enemy used.

The point I wish to make about these contraptions is that they were manned by small detachments of airmen, working in isolated spots. When called upon to do their duty these men were deliberately inviting death from the skies. Not a very attractive war-time occupation but a necessary one.

Mr. Jones recalls that he met me, when he was acting as door sentry at his station, and that we had a friendly chat together. At least, he did not treat me as the door sentry at Sopley G.C.I. station treated His Majesty some time in 1941. The King arrived with his entourage and was moving towards the Operations Room when the sentry, determined to make his mark with the monarch, pushed forward and, with his bayonet at the King's chest, shouted, 'Halt, who goes there?' Nobody was amused, least of all the King.

13

Transport, Mechanical and Foot

I N THE Kaiser War the R.F.C. transport ran serious risks only
during the Retreat from Mons and at the time of the Germans'
successful thrusts in 1918. Some unhappy people, like Corporal
Goodchild, took a wrong turning in the night and joined the enemy
'for the duration'.

The evacuation of France in June 1940 was all 'one-way' though
there must have been some dangerous moments when vehicles broke
down, were misdirected or forgotten in the rush of events. But it
required the war of movement in North Africa and, later, after D. Day
in France, to involve the M.T. drivers in the ordinary perils of the
infantryman or gunner. Many were unlucky and were killed or
finished the war in German prison camps. Others, like Corporal Hogg
of 208 Squadron, survived some active days of dodging and ducking
in an endeavour to carry out their duty.

On 23rd November 1941, while at an advanced landing ground,
Hogg was ordered to pack up and proceed with his ration lorry to
30 Corps H.Q. and remain there for the night. Next morning he
decided to move back to the landing ground as Corps H.Q. could find
no cause for alarm. The men of the squadron needed their food and
drink so he asked the army liaison officer for the position of the nearest
supply dump. Note the conditions of this desert warfare. They were
much like those at sea—over a featureless sand sea! Hogg was given
a bearing and a distance of fourteen miles. After sixteen miles the
dump was found. Hogg collected his water and rations for fifty-five
men for three days. On his way back to the landing ground he met a
large number of army mechanical transport. None of the drivers had
the slightest idea where he was going except that it was eastwards. As
he neared his destination he was challenged by an officer in a car who
fired on him with an automatic weapon. Hogg replied with two shots

By Courtesy of the Imperial War Museum

Open-air church service, 1918

The snowed-up technical huts and airfield at Reykjavik on 25th February 1945. Liberator aircraft of No. 53 Squadron, R.A.F., in background

By Courtesy of the Imperial War Museum

Men's dining-room, new style

A 'Trenchard' barracks

and his driver, putting his wheel hard over, sprayed the enemy with dust and small stones, just as the squid squirts ink when he is under attack.

Several unidentified tanks were seen, so, after shaking off the enemy car, Hogg proceeded due south for twenty miles. At this point he found seven British tanks proceeding east along the Divisional axis track—and with them he reached the British defences, and finally his squadron. Hogg, in his account, gives an impression of considerable panic in the 30 Corps area. The official account in No. 208 Squadron's record book is more restrained, as is to be expected. There is little doubt, however, that in this area morale was low. The enemy blow had been swift and unexpected and the consequences disheartening.

The account of the evacuation of the landing ground, Gaba Saleh, tends to confirm Hogg's view. The occupants of Gaba Saleh had pitched camp in fancied security, and one aircraft was dispatched on a bombing mission. Soon an air attack developed, and there were sounds of tank battles. The senior R.A.F. officer, Pilot Officer P. F. White, consulted the army liaison officer and the decision was taken to evacuate. Meanwhile disorganized mobs of British motor transport were streaming across the landing ground while aircraft were attempting to land. The measures taken by Pilot Officer White enabled a great deal of equipment and stores to be saved, but it seems that many of the airmen panicked. Though they had plenty of time to load their vehicles a great deal of their kit was lost. An explanation given by L.A.C. George of this failure is that these men were in charge of the ground-defence Lewis-guns. They received no orders to evacuate and a promised lorry did not turn up. Finally they were picked up by South African armoured cars. There was no room for their kit as well as their weapons which, to their great credit, they retained. I like to think that this story is the true one. George goes on to say that the armoured cars had a skirmish with the enemy during the night and captured an ammunition lorry. This vehicle, with two prisoners, George drove in triumph into our lines the next morning.

There must have been many episodes of this sort as the battle swayed backwards and forwards between Benghazi and El Alamein, but let this one example suffice.

At home M.T. work was routine—uncomfortable and dangerous particularly at night—but the enemy bomber was far less of a menace

L

than the black-out conditions and the perils of ice and snow on un-lighted roads. Nevertheless, there were some exceptional trips.

Corporal Williamson, a skilled driver of heavy vehicles, was based at Aintree in July 1942. At 2 p.m. on the 19th he was dispatched most urgently to Sealand in Cheshire to transport a Blenheim aircraft to Glasgow. He was to drive all night and get to Glasgow by noon on the 20th. The twenty miles from Aintree to Sealand were soon covered by his huge articulated vehicle, but the aircraft—far from being ready for loading—was still in the air. By the time it had landed, had been stripped down and put into its case there were only nineteen hours left to do 220 miles. The Blenheim in its box weighed seven tons and the box was 21 ft. 6 in. wide. Now the average county road in Britain is twenty-four feet wide, so clearly Williamson had to stick to the main roads if he was to get through. Official precautions were taken; the police were advised and two dispatch-riders were given the job of leading the convoy which by this time had grown to three vehicles. The vehicles were routed via Warrington, so as to avoid Liverpool. Someone blundered because the Liverpool police had held up the traffic for an hour so as to give the convoy a free run. It would have been better if it had gone via Liverpool! The dispatch-riders had been given a route unfamiliar to the drivers, who soon found themselves involved in narrow roads. 'Islands' and Belisha beacons came crashing down as the huge cases forced their way along. Shop-fronts, balconies, over-hanging signs, all in turn gave best to the Blenheims. Finally, owing to faulty map-reading, the D.R.s turned the convoy into a narrow country lane. There the cases became firmly lodged in the hedgerows. After an infinity of trouble the hedges were cut and trees felled to allow the lorries to reach a turning-point. With what pleasure the owners of the trees and hedges must have seen the convoy retrace its steps to safety! By then it was 7 a.m. on the 20th. Sixty miles had been covered. At this point reinforcements arrived! A detachment of the Pioneer Corps, the senior officer of the Western Command Military Police and mobile civil police.

Some sensible person then checked the height of the load as well as its breadth. As a result it was decided to reduce the height so as to give the necessary clearance under the bridges that lay ahead, and so the whole party went back to Preston.

The convoy started again at 1800 hours on the 20th. Williamson says:

'After that it was just one obstacle after another . . . more road signs (we were already blasé about them), shop signs, another balcony, bridges and walls. If we couldn't get round them we went through them. . . . I burned out my clutch on Shap Fell and had to get a new one from Carlisle and fit it on the spot. It was a nightmare drive . . . we hadn't slept for two nights and except when we were digging our vehicles out we had been at the wheel almost continuously. Past Shap Fell the road was easier and we arrived in Glasgow not in nineteen hours, but in fifty-eight. The Blenheim rather naturally missed the boat, the detours we had made amounted to 450 miles and *we had done over £2000 worth of damage.*'

One of the features of desert warfare was the probability that at some time or another air and ground crew might have to walk considerable distances in great heat and in sliding sand. Food might be non-existent and water—well, just not available.

A party from a Sunderland flying-boat wrecked on the Libyan coast had a very odd experience. There was a mixed air and ground crew on board, twenty in all, and they reached the shore in safety. One of their number was wounded in the air battle with German fighters which had caused the flying-boat's crash. It was midday and the party of twenty found themselves on a rocky beach which, they estimated, with reasonable accuracy, to be about a hundred miles east of Benghazi. A body of Italian soldiers suddenly appeared from behind a wall of rocks and the captain of the Sunderland, Flight Lieutenant Hughes, decided to go forward and surrender, as his exhausted party was without arms. To his astonishment the nearest Italian raised his rifle above his head, threw it away ostentatiously and advanced with outstretched hands. The British party had not quite recovered from seeing the soldiers behave as friends when another group of Italians arrived; these, about eighty strong, were more aggressive, and formally declared the British party to be their prisoners. Hughes, however, had one duty to fulfil and, with the pretext of searching for the wounded gunner's flying-boots, he returned to the wreck and, somewhat regretfully, jettisoned into the sea a bag of bullion, one hundred pounds' weight of gold sovereigns, which had been destined for the Malta Exchequer. Back on shore a stretcher made of oars from the dinghy was improvised for the wounded man, and in a long procession the mixed band started off along the coast. It was raining, and streaks of lightning lit up a leaden sky. Night came, and with it small comfort. There were no blankets, rations or water, and no fires were allowed since the Italians feared Arab sharp-shooters. The second pilot and the gunner were both suffering from shock, and the party huddled around them, massaging them constantly in an effort to keep them warm. With the dawn another start was made. Suddenly twenty Italian officers ran forward from a cluster of bushes. Highly agitated, they indicated to Flight Lieutenant Hughes that the Germans had taken their vehicles and told them to get to safety as best they could; they offered help to the party in exchange for favoured treatment should they be captured by the English. Now for the fourth time the party was increased in number, on this occasion by an Italian major with about one hundred men. The Major was a unique personage, middle-aged, with a heavily tanned face, deeply lined; he carried a cat-o'-nine-tails at his belt, presumably as a fly-whisk, but he used it for its original purpose later when one of the British party indignantly announced that an Italian soldier had stolen the wounded man's flying-boots. The thief was flogged in front of his comrades. Later that day the wounded air-gunner died and the Major conducted a form of military burial.

In due course the party arrived at the Senussi village of El Hania. Here they were given macaroni and coffee: three eggs were bartered for a wrist-watch and a two-shilling piece, and a bag of dates cost one Egyptian pound. The Major sent for Flight Lieutenant Hughes and stated that he proposed to leave for Benghazi. The question arose as to who actually held the town, and finally bets were made on it. The Italian decided that he would leave with his men, allowing the British to remain with the Arabs, and offered to leave rifles as protection. Once the Italians had gone the Senussi freely disclosed an abundance of food, and sent a messenger towards the advancing British lines. Hughes and his party decided to follow, hoping to reach an Indian Army unit which the Arabs reported to be some fifteen miles away.

The end of this incident was equally remarkable. After walking for an hour, the Royal Air Force party overtook some of the Italian major's men. One of these ran over to the group, drew his bayonet, propped it against a rock and jumped on it until it snapped. There were some two dozen Italians, and each one threw away his rifle or handed it over, to join cheerfully in the procession. Similar incidents happened on four occasions and after three hours the company was more than 150 strong. The British lines were soon reached, for the 8th Army was making a bid to take Benghazi by Christmas, and Flight Lieutenant Hughes, who had successfully led his men through the whole grim, yet whimsical, adventure added his prisoners to those of the Army.

Another desert walk carried out by a number of ground crew started in January 1942. No. 260 Squadron had to make a hurried exit from Benina airfield and Warrant Officer Cable's getaway was full of incident. With his party he reached Barka airfield on the outskirts of Benghazi, but their stay there was short.

An army dispatch-rider came up to say the enemy were trying to cut the road east of the town, so after dispatching the aircraft the airmen decided it was high time to get out. To their dismay they found the road cut approximately two miles east of the town. The padre who was with the party went forward to investigate and was fired on. His car was seen to plunge off the road and then an enemy armoured car approached. The airmen scattered and opened ineffective fire with rifles. Nevertheless, the armoured car retreated and the party resumed its march to the east. By this time it was almost dark so they plunged through the marshes towards the beach. The enemy must have sensed as much because he sent a few bursts of machine-gun bullets after them. No one was hit, and after walking along the beach for a while the party turned inland, crossed the coast road and got lost in the green belt around Benghazi. Finding the road again, the nineteen Army and R.A.F. plodded on for five days, setting their course as near as possible by the stars, as none of the party had either maps or compass. Of course they were very hungry and some of the men were already in pretty bad shape and were ready to give in. However, they met a Senussi boy about fifteen years of age who said he would take them to a track used by British transport. On approaching the track they could see the transport but could not recognize it. Warrant Officers Rixon and Cable left the party and crawled ahead, just to make sure. One vehicle stopped approximately a hundred yards away to refuel and although the truck was British the uniform of the occupants was doubtful, so they waited for another one to come along, but their luck was out, nothing came. The time was then about midday. Some of the men gave up the attempt to escape and started to walk along the track regardless of what happened. They kept this up for best part of the afternoon. Towards evening L.A.C. Dick Scully, who was in front, looked back and saw the little column spread out for approximately a quarter of a mile with Rixon and Cable bringing up the rear. Scully decided to rest and wait for the rest of the party. A few moments after they had caught up and sat down three trucks pulled up farther down the track. This caused the party to scatter. Rixon, Scully and Cable, although off the track, doubled back in the direction they had come and lay down on the rocks watching the trucks, which started off and in doing so sent out clouds of black smoke. This smoke spelt Diesels, and the British didn't have Diesels! The trucks stopped, rifle-fire broke out and through the gloom some of the men were seen walking towards the track. Cable and the others lay still hoping for the best. Then there was more rifle-fire, and more men walking with their hands up. Cable whispered to Rixon and Scully, 'Are you glad you joined?' Finally the trucks moved off and the party decided to put as much ground as possible between them and the track in case the enemy came back. Eventually they bedded down in the camel scrub and tried to sleep, but it was too cold. About three o'clock, while they were walking down an escarpment, somebody coughed. Turning left they heard German voices. As they dodged back two engines started. These were tanks coming towards them so they dropped flat in the sand. After the tanks passed they got up and 'got crackin' ', walking out of the enemy camp as easily as they had walked in. When daylight came they sat down to rest and found they were in a spot which had at one time been used for a camp. A quick search produced a German loaf which was almost as hard as the rock on which they were sitting and it was green with mildew. With it was an almost dried-up lemon. This was the first food eaten since 28th January when the trek started. It was now 3rd February. After the 'meal' they slept, and from then on decided to sleep by day and walk by night because the nights were too cold. Two days later they met an Arab shepherd and persuaded him to sell a small sheep. The Arab killed and skinned it for them and it cost forty piastres! Cooked in an old petrol tin it made good eating and when they had finished there weren't even any bones left. They burned the bones and ate those too. After this they did a little better for food, as the following day they came across a band of friendly Arabs who gave them a meal, some tobacco and a water bottle and put them on the right direction for 'home'. Approximately two days later, while resting under a small bush, a Fiesler Storch aircraft flew over them at about twenty feet off the ground. Cable dived back under the bush, but the pilot must have seen him for he circled the bush a few times and then made off. The party got going as well, just in case! While they were walking along a wadi about two miles wide, with Rixon and Scully some yards in front of Cable, the latter saw them duck and run. As Cable rounded a small escarpment he saw two Jerries leaning against a truck. He also ducked and ran and found the other two hiding among some rocks. While lying among the rocks another Fiesler Storch flew directly overhead, and on the far side of the wadi clouds of dust were rising where JU88s and ME109s were taking off. Creeping along the edge of the wadi, they came across a cave which seemed a good hiding-place, but away in the distance there were some camels attended by an Arab. Scully wanted to go to the Arab on the chance of a meal. Cable wasn't keen, nor was Rixon. After a while Scully and Rixon went to see what they could do, and Cable stopped in the cave. Some time later he heard someone whistle, and recognized Scully calling 'Harry' in a loud whisper. An Arab was with him who introduced himself as Suliman. Scully said that they had left Rixon in another cave, to which Suliman took them. There they found Rixon feeding like a lord, and wasted no time in joining him. Suliman left and said he would come back. Later he took them straight across the airfield they had previously been watching. This was Martuba.

On reaching Suliman's camp they enjoyed another meal of camel meat, milk and army biscuits. At sunset the Arab came back, with a camel loaded with food, and led them off eastwards. Cable thought it would be a slow journey, but was very much surprised at the speed of a camel's walk. At dawn they stopped; Suliman made strong sweet tea and again they ate. Afterwards he left with strict instructions not to look at any vehicles that might come near. The party slept well through the day, but when it started to get dark there was no sign of Suliman. Cable says:

'We thought he had deserted us, and had almost given up hope of seeing him again when out of the darkness a voice said, "Sarjn Major come." We started walking again and Suliman told us that while we had slept he had done a recco. during the day and said we must be extra quiet this night as we would go through the enemy front line. Although this was serious it cheered us up as we knew then we hadn't much farther to go providing all went well. At dawn we stopped again, ate another meal, more sweet tea and then down in a slit trench to sleep. Suliman went to do his daily recco. I was just dozing off when it seemed all Hell was let loose. We were bang in the middle of an artillery battle. How long it lasted I don't know for I eventually fell asleep. The next thing I knew was Freddie Rixon's excited voice saying, "Come, Harry, there's a British camp two miles away." '

The time then was 9.30 a.m., and at 1.30 p.m. they were still walking, the camp was still two miles away. Cable never wanted to walk any more Arab miles. Finally Freddie Rixon could go no farther, the trek had knocked him out. Suliman was impatient to keep going, and eventually Freddie gave him a note to take to a camp. After what seemed an age Scully spotted two trucks coming towards them over the desert. Suliman was conspicuous on account of his white Arab gown. On the trucks were an officer and about twelve men of the 7th Field Coy. R.E.s, who said they were some miles south of Gazala. Cable ends: 'The date was the 13th of February. Freddie said 13 was his lucky number and it proved to be ours too, and so ended the worst sixteen days of my life.'

There were thousands of W.A.A.F. motor-transport drivers employed on R.A.F. stations in Britain. I have been driven by some of them but none so shy as the heroine who graces the following yarn. She was driving an elderly air commodore from Plymouth to London, and halfway on this journey she decided that certain measures must be taken immediately whether the Air Commodore was shocked or not. Somewhere on Salisbury Plain she drew the car into the grass verge near a convenient spinney and disappeared into the bushes. The Air Commodore, a family man with no inhibitions, felt that the opportunity should not be missed and did likewise. Reappearing and averting her glance from the passenger's seat the W.A.A.F. leaped into the driver's seat and was halfway to Basingstoke before she realized she had lost her passenger!

Flight Sergeant Wordsworth, writing to me from Sharjah—that steam-heated spot in the Persian Gulf—sends me another W.A.A.F. driver's story:

'I was N.C.O. in charge of station transport at Melbourne, Yorkshire. No. 10 Bomber Squadron operated from here, and on the strength was a young W.A.A.F. driver. She was responsible for a 30 cwt. Ford truck and one day she was detailed for a run outside the camp boundary. Shortly after leaving she returned in a terrible state of excitement and claimed that she had been accused of damaging a steam roller.

Apparently, on turning from the camp entrance into the main road, she had passed in front of the roller and had felt a slight bump. I examined her truck and all I could find was a small black mark on the wall of the off-side front tyre. I went to the scene of the accident and sure enough there was the roller, stuck at an awkward angle in the middle of the road. The driver was doing his best to steer the traffic round his machine. He explained to me that the W.A.A.F.'s truck had hit a part on the roller called the "elephant's head". This had so damaged his steering that he could not move.

It took a long time and much argument to convince the subsequent court of enquiry that an undamaged Ford truck had been responsible for a £100 bill for repairs to a steam roller!'

There was something about Fords, the old Fords such as the T model, that enabled them to resist the brutality of even Arab drivers. They seemed to be almost indestructible even if they were unlovely. A friend of mine—ex-sergeant M.T. driver R.A.F.—once suffered a collision between his ancient Ford coupé and a brand-new French car of popular make. After the remains of the French car had been stowed on the breakdown lorry the Ford drove away accompanied by the felicitations of the local gendarmerie. *'C'est un cuirassé votre Ford'*!

Finally the story of a long walk in Greece. Again the men involved were aircrew, but as they did this trip on their feet—bare feet for some of the time—they surely qualify as ground crew.

A Wellington of No. 104 Squadron was shot down in the region of Salonika in September 1944. The aircraft appears to have received a direct hit from an A.A. gun, as an engine and a wing fell off. Somehow four out of five of the crew baled out successfully, two of them landing in Salonika Bay. They were fished out after three-quarters of an hour by friendly Greeks, given dry clothes, food and a drink of the local firewater. At first they were hidden on board, but after twenty-four hours of troubled sleep they were allowed ashore and given more food—black bread, grapes and twenty cigarettes. Later they joined up with a body of Partisans and were taken to a farmhouse.

The woman of the house had been beaten and bayoneted by the Germans, as scars on her face and neck showed. From here they were taken by a party of armed Greeks across country, past a railway station guarded by Germans (here the noise made by the local dogs nearly gave them away), reaching a village where the reception committee gave them a vast meal of bread, eggs and fruit and clothed them in British battledress. One member of the party, who had been given a very tight pair of dancing pumps to cover his bare feet, did not enjoy this three-hour cross-country journey. But a further five hours of walking was to follow before shelter in a priest's house was reached at 1 a.m. The place is described as filthy, with pigs and fowls as fellow lodgers. In the lavatory was a large stack of worthless Greek notes—being put to useful purpose. Bugs were active, but the party was so tired that they slept well.

Next day they were given a cart on which to ride to the next village, seven hours away. That night they danced with the villagers to the sound of an accordion. Their feet must have been better after the ride in the cart. On the morrow mules were provided and after a further night of discomfort in a little village they reached the H.Q. of the British Mission to the Partisans at Ano Melia.

Here they rested for a while, later taking part in the activities of the mission. They helped to lay the signal fires for the supply-dropping Dakotas (the wireless operator was nearly brained by a bundle of boots that had become detached from its parachute), manned the transmitter 'working' Cairo and generally made themselves useful. As soon as they were rested they pushed on with their mules. The passage over Mount Olympus was very hard going. In the pitch dark and pouring rain the party was very glad to find at four in the morning a house occupied by some Greeks. The Greeks were most friendly. They produced food and built such a huge wood fire that the chimney caught alight. A pistol-shot fired up it put out the blaze, but scared the occupants of the house out of their wits. 'After eats retired about five—very tired and sore through riding mule!'

The party was called with tea at 8 a.m. but this luxury was more than compensated for by the attentions of bed bugs and lice. That afternoon, about 4 p.m., the party resumed their journey on muleback and in darkness crossed the main road in enemy-occupied territory. When they reached the village which was their destination they found it completely destroyed. In the hills above the entire population was living in improvised shelters, tripods of poles interlaced with fern fronds. A family and two pigs cleared out of one of these shelters so that the English could have some cover. 'Once more bitten to death by bed bugs and clothing more alive with them. Have ridden and walked for eleven hours.'

The next day the muleteer and his mules left the party, who had still a very long walk before them. After six hours over hill and valley legs and bodies were beginning to fail. Recourse was had to the energy tablets in their packs: '. . . worked wonders—although still tired weakness relieved from legs and head cleared. Came over a hill and saw in the distance the camp we were making for. Passed the secret runway on which the supply Dakotas could land and met R.A.F. types and many Yanks. Ate a massive meal and got very merry on the local brandy. Went to bed early but awakened in the middle of the night by the Commanding Officer and his boys conducting a rodeo and firing guns—all as drunk as lords!'

Next day the party obtained flea powder from the Medical Officer and thoroughly deloused themselves and their clothing. 'It was fine to have nothing crawling up and down back and head!'

Quite a journey and what an excellent illustration of the failure of an occupying army effectively to control a country like Greece—rugged and undeveloped and peopled by fiercely independent individuals! The camps of the Allied Missions, large and well organized, survived in spite of every effort that the Germans could make to destroy them. Good intelligence and the support of the native population brought this about.

Eventually the party were taken off by Dakota and flown back to Italy. Here at Foggia they rejoined their squadron and once more became—'airborne'.

Finishing this chapter on an entirely different note, let the story of 'Chips' Circus' be recorded in the briefest form.

No. 309 Supply and Transport Column (the Circus) was formed in Southern England in 1943. Its duties were to be the following-up of R.A.F. flying units as they advanced from airfield to airfield, and their maintenance in food, fuel and stores.

Warrant Officer Blades seems to have had some influence in the operations of the Circus, and earned a special citation all on his own from the Burgomeister of Veldhoven. It took the form of a Christmas letter of appreciation addressed to 'The Commandant of Warrant

Officer Blades'. This was after the advance from Normandy to the Low Countries, when the column drove over 600,000 miles and carried 17,000 tons of supplies in 180 vehicles. By the end of the year the mileage was one million and a half and the tonnage 64,000. By V.E. Day two and a half million miles had been covered and 110,000 tons of supplies carried.

In the record there is one curious but significant remark. It foreshadows the present demarcation troubles that plague so many of our industries. The drivers in the column were surprised when they were asked to help in loading their vehicles! The deduction that I draw from this reaction to military necessity is that while the vast majority of airmen in the 1914–18 War were integrated into the service, by 1943 there were many men in the R.A.F. who were only civilians in uniform.

14

Flying Training

URING the early inter-war years and so far as the airmen were concerned the pattern of flying training did not vary. The Central Flying School produced its 'patter', a development of the verbal instruction carried out in the air by the School of Special Flying at Gosport during the Kaiser War. It also conducted some advanced instruction and periodically tested the instructors at the other flying-training stations. The Air Ministry issued manuals on the subject of flying training for war, but for the men life was relatively simple. Their business was to get as many of the rather limited number of training aeroplanes into the air for as long as possible. These trainers came, in the main, from Hawkers, Avros and de Havilland's, the Tiger Moth being the outstanding model. They were uncomplicated, their engines were reliable, and provided they were reasonably handled killed nobody and gave good service. By 1930, however, things were changing. An enterprising young flying officer, Johnson by name, had been investigating French progress in blind-flying. '*Le pilotage sans visibilité*', P.S.V. for short, had caught on in that country. Britain was lagging far behind. Of the eighteen pilots with whom I flew to the Brussels Exhibition in 1935 only three had done a blind-flying course. As a result of an attempt to fly through a severe thunderstorm, fifteen out of the eighteen had a very rough passage. From then on the instrumentation of the aircraft and the training of the pilots underwent a material change. This affected the airmen in no small measure. The primitive instruments of the early days could be looked after by the aircraft's rigger. The compass could be swung once a month by a technical officer. Now not only the radio mechanic, whose job it was to service the wireless gear, but an instrument repairer were breathing down the necks of the fitter and rigger as they serviced their aircraft. The days of the 'trinity' were over. Though the pilot still had his personal aeroplane, and for a while his own technicians, the writing was on the wall. Flying was no longer largely a matter of enjoyment. It was becoming a serious technical business, shared between a number of individuals of varying capacity. The lot of these technical airmen in the flying-training schools did not vary greatly from that of the men in the operational and maintenance units. They had more opportunity of 'getting a flip' with an amiable pilot and in the crowded airfields and congested air space over them they could see some tangible and visible results of their work.

In Britain in peace-time, however, all this was chicken feed. When the Empire Air Training Scheme based on Kaiser War experience really got under way then the airmen came into their own. Their wives and families may not have liked it but for the men themselves, as they travelled widely through the Dominions and Colonies, the scheme gave them a wonderful experience. How otherwise could a young fitter have seen what there is to be seen in Canada, South Africa and New Zealand—indeed in America when the States came into the war on our side? The food may not have been to their liking, the local customs difficult to understand and above all there would be homesickness. But on balance the advantage was great.

This expansion brought the women of the R.A.F. into jobs which, earlier on, everyone would have doubted they could perform. They became fitters, riggers, instrument repairers, starter-trolly 'minders', refuellers, armament experts in charge of explosives and pyrotechnicians, meteorological assistants, electricians, parachute packers and photographic experts. All this in addition to their more normal duties of radar and Operations Room staff, of cooking and butchering, of clerking and issuing stores, of driving every kind of mechanical transport. Miss M. I. Horton, in her book hitherto unpublished, but which I hope most sincerely will reach the bookstalls, writes about the individual W.A.A.F. as being only two-thirds of an airman. That may have been her official rating, but what of the airwoman who, singlehanded, pulled the rear-gunner out of the turret of a blazing crash? And what of the girls, previously mentioned, who withstood dive-bombing attacks with the greatest fortitude? Some of them may have been so small that they had to fetch stepladders with which to do their jobs. Some of them, not so muscular as their male colleagues, took a little longer to do a job—but in the end it was well done. I believe that the 'missing third' was more than made up for by the women's enthusiasm and their greater sense of responsibility. Is there a man who washes up properly, who dusts in the corners, who doesn't sweep the rubbish under the carpet, who will not put off until tomorrow the boring or difficult job? There are mighty few, but on the other side of the ledger the female sloven and slattern in the services is hard to find.

Miss Horton says the women 'served their turn'! I would put their claim to usefulness very much higher. In any case they were, on the whole, very good for the men's morale!

A.C.W. Horton first joined a bomber group H.Q. at Abingdon. Here, as she was a good short-hand typist, she was immediately put on to teleprinters, about which she knew nothing and of which the touch is somewhat different from that of a typewriter. But it must be said that the service displayed rare intelligence in this posting. A.C.W. Horton might have been sent to the cookhouse to peel potatoes.

Horton seems to have been worried by mixed parades of men and women. A lanky youth muttered, when a little W.A.A.F. by his side tried to keep step with him, 'How can I march in step with a woman who waddles like a duck with bow legs?' Horton describes these marching parades as looking like the movements of a centipede afflicted with corns on its toes at irregular intervals! The W.A.A.F.s, in spite of the discipline that the male N.C.O.s endeavoured to drill into them, remained independent and critical of their male 'oppos'. At a station parade in Technical Training Command to which she had been moved Horton describes the scene: 'It was a lovely morning and the Very Senior Officer who passed benignly by the W.A.A.F. company standing respectfully to attention by the roadside was obviously full of a good breakfast and a feeling of charity to all men and women. We hoped, however—we could only hope—that he didn't hear the youngest and pertest W.A.A.F. speak to her neighbour as the V.I.P. rolled majestically past, "Promotion seems to go by weight in this camp." ' In autumn the rains—and consequent puddles—made marching and parading more difficult. Horton was parade-marker one morning when the parade ground consisted more of puddles than hard surface. 'Look here, Smudge,' she protested. 'Do you think I'm a perishing water-spaniel to wade through this?' 'No,' replied the imperturbable Senior Airwoman. 'But neither am I Moses to part the waters for you!' After many months in Technical Training Command Horton achieved the ambition of many airwomen in being posted to a flying-training station at Doncaster. The journey from Reading to

Doncaster was not of the most comfortable, and her reception at her station was hardly engaging. After reporting at the guardroom, she reached her billet, one of a number of huts showing black against the snow. In darkness she fumbled her way to her bed—no hot water, of course, in which to wash after a six-hour journey, and the hut was cold and dirty, with snow water dripping through holes in the roof. Her bed, for the short time she stayed awake, felt like a nest of tennis balls. But what matter! She was at a flying-training station and to-morrow she could see aircraft actually in the air, taking off and landing on her 'own' airfield.

Her great ambition was to become a flight mechanic, but on her own showing she was not a mechanically minded type. Nevertheless, she plugged ahead, doing voluntary work in the hangars and, in her very limited spare time, studying technical books. Horton comments on the breezy informality of the trainees at her operational training unit—mostly Dominion cadets and mere boys—and the rigid discipline that the training staff sought to impose. The W.A.A.F. certainly saw both sides of the picture and could laugh or sympathize as necessary.

From the O.T.U. Horton was posted to Locking for a course in technology—her ambition. This station, according to her, was not a happy one. A trainee who had been there some time epitomized the situation by saying: 'When you've been here a fortnight you start drawing ducks on the walls and throwing bread to them. After a month they quack back at you!' 'Never in my previous service,' comments Horton, 'had I been so yapped at. In the eyes of the permanent staff at Locking we were untouchables, only to be tolerated if kept in subjection by constant insults or petty bullying.' She does admit, however, that the instructors, as apart from the disciplinary staff, were kind, patient and conscientious.

In the end Horton and the rest of her class qualified, though according to her account they had little to show for their course except the catch-phrase, 'If the bastard flew yesterday it will fly again today.'

Now, with many others, she was two-thirds of an air mechanic, and her ambition to work on aircraft that were doing a job, not merely the wrecks used for instruction and which would never fly, was finally fulfilled.

In Flying Training Command, except for the rare occasions when

The death of *Courageous*

W.A.A.F., 1939–45

By Courtesy of the Imperial War Museum

A senior key-puncher

Flight engineers of Coastal Command

its aircraft were called in to augment a raid by Bomber Command, the role of the officers, airmen and airwomen, was 'non-operational'. This did not mean that they ran no risk of enemy attack. Airfields were bombed, night-training aircraft returning from a sortie might be shot down by an 'intruder' as they came in to land and there was the ever present risk of death from disease incurred by the prolonged working hours under bad conditions. Horton found herself posted to Kirton Lindsey as a flight mechanic. The Chief Technical Officer, after some preliminary enquiries, suggested that she had better resume her trade of clerk, G.D. Horton wasn't having any! Flight mechanic she was and F.M. she intended to be. I must admit that I was never called upon to deal with a truculent W.Λ.Λ.F. as was the fate of many junior officers. For this relief much thanks!

At Kirton Lindsey she was in heaven. One day, strapping a pilot into his Spitfire, she was called to pronounce upon the serviceability of the undercarriage which seemed very much on a slant. She comments: 'Helping a pilot to fasten his Sutton harness always reminded me irresistibly of strapping a baby into a pram! Just when you thought you had got him all ready he would set up a roar because he had dropped a glove into the "works" which it was impossible to retrieve without unpacking him!'

The cold winter of 1943 was not an easy routine for anyone on flight duties. After the long trudge from the W.A.A.F. site for those who had no bicycles, work started in the dark of a winter's morning. Pulling the covers off the Spitfires, frozen stiff and most unco-operative, was a bad beginning. Later came the job of lying on the tails in a blast of icy wind as the men fitters ran the engines in the daily test. After this there were the odd jobs to be done with numbed fingers and inadequate tools. Snow clearance from the runways was a periodical 'bind'. But it had to be done and this labour added much to the fatigue of the men and women on flight duties.

Horton took a poor view of the conditions under which the men and women of the R.A.F. had to work. 'Between bad food, cold damp billets and the neglect of minor ailments . . . I felt that I had only a strong constitution to thank for being able to finish my eighteen months on flight duties with only a few rheumatic pains in the result. Few of the W.A.A.F. mechanics I knew lasted more than a year or two at their trade. . . .' Were the women expendable? Could they be thrown into discard the moment their usefulness ended? That they

M

suffered hard times there is no doubt, and, after all, Horton and her sisters were the toads under the harrow. But I have a feeling that, on the whole, the W.A.A.F. had no worse a time, and perhaps a slightly better time, than the men they were called upon to replace. Training Command was, of course, under very great pressure. The operational commands had their slack periods when the enemy eased up, or the weather intervened. But for Training Command it was 'non-stop'. Unless 'birds were walking' flying carried on! Training aircraft were unpicketed at 6.30 a.m. by their sleepy crews who then attended on them till dusk, going to their meals in relays. A never-ending procession of 'kites' took the air, circled round at 'safety' distance, landed, changed pupils and were off again. As dusk fell the aircraft would taxi to their dispersal points and then, by the light of hand-torches, the mechanics would start their last job of the day—the D.I. or daily inspection. At the best they would knock off between 8 and 9 p.m., but if something was wrong it would be very late indeed before, tired, bedraggled and filthy, they could escape to their bunks and welcome sleep.

A.C.W. Horton's description of the men and the women with whom she worked gives a good picture of the personnel of the R.A.F. in war-time. The flight-sergeant fitter, unsmiling to the point of being christened 'Wooden Face'; his 'oppo', the flight-rigger sergeant, ginger moustache, skin wrinkled like a hippopotamus and with an acid tongue; Taffy, the fitter corporal, inclined to be amorous and vicious when his advances were repulsed; Lofty, the rigger, rather weak in the head—'I'm all right with me 'ands, it's the 'ead part I can't master!'; Tom, the middle-aged rigger from Yorkshire, probably the most reliable worker on the flight, as ready with a joke as with a helping hand to anyone in difficulties; Micky—arrogant as well as stupid and lazy; Dicky, the pilferer who never returned a borrowed tool. And the girls! Small, rotund 'Tommy' was a clergyman's daughter. She had been trained in domestic science and wanted to be a cook. So of course she was made flight mechanic and spent her days in cleaning engines and carting oil about the sheds. Blonde 'Dizzy's' day started after work when she stripped and made a transformation rather than a change. 'Dot' was a large, good-tempered, utterly shiftless child, with sprawling limbs and a broad, bland face. She seemed totally insensitive to dirt, so much so that 'Scruffy', a particularly untidy corporal, once said to her, 'It's by no means the people who work hardest who get themselves the dirtiest!' Dot was once seen at work on an aircraft entirely disregarding a vent-pipe that was steadily dripping oil on to her hair, when one step sideways would have put her in safety. Her day of triumph came when she called the male Equipment Officer, who had angered her in some way, a bald-headed old bastard!

By contrast 'Chalky' White was a dainty creature with great grey eyes and a shining golden bob. She too was a flight mechanic, but Horton claims that Chalky was always spotlessly clean and her hands showed no signs of toil. She was a great trial to the N.C.O.s, having definite views on the amount of work required of her.

I have drawn on A.C.W. Horton's descriptions at some length because it is essential that people outside the service who may be interested to read this book should appreciate what went on under the façade of uniform and discipline. On parade everything appeared in order to an inspecting officer. He was not to know of the undercurrents that swayed the lives of the men and women standing smart and clean before him. But sometimes—if very attentive—he might catch the whispered joke, made at his expense, followed swiftly by a furious hiss from an N.C.O. in the serrefile rank, 'Stop talking, you!'

Although these stories are limited to one or two stations in Flying Training Command, they could be repeated from any of the other commands. It is not possible to gather together a complete cross-section of a population, mix it with a small number of aliens—refugees from occupied Europe—and expect to find a completely dedicated service. The miracle is that there was so much good will and excellent teamwork and, on the whole, a high standard of behaviour.

15

Maintenance Command:
Ubendum—Wemendum

I N T H E years between the two wars aircraft maintenance was largely carried out in the squadrons themselves. Obviously this was a system that would not stand the test of modern war, so very early on the Air Ministry began to establish a series of maintenance units that would be competent to carry out major repairs, and also to a limited extent engage in aircraft research and development. The most important of these were Henlow Station in the United Kingdom, Aboukir Depot in Egypt and Karachi Depot in India. To them came not only the regular airmen, but the apprentices trained at Halton.

These stations sufficed for a while, but before long it became clear that in a major war there would have to be a very considerable expansion. In the schemes prepared from 1934 onwards provision was made for a large number of maintenance units in Britain. These were formed or forming when war broke out in August 1939. This development was orderly and followed a traditional pattern. But the pressure of events in 1940 found it hardly adequate. During the Battle of Britain every garage and workshop was called in to carry out repairs. All over the south of England damaged aircraft parts were being rapidly restored by a makeshift organization that paid little attention to normal service procedure. From this improvisation grew an enormous machine that in the event was able to cope with the vast needs of the R.A.F.

Something of the same sort happened overseas. As in 1914–18, so Egypt and its resources were mobilized, under the direction of the forceful Air Marshal Dawson.

Squadron Leader A. Pugh sent me a note on how the organization worked. It must be said that the conditions under which these improvised units laboured were not of the best, and No. 111 Maintenance

Unit was no exception. Its headquarters were on a barren stretch of land near the Tura Caves not far from Cairo, and the unit was composed of seven workshops scattered about the slum quarters of the town. This was done so that all the eggs would not be in one basket should Cairo ever be subjected to concentrated air attack.

The engine-repair section was situated in Sharia Maddares Roki El Marref, or Street of the School, in a rather distasteful slum quarter. The district was at all times out of bounds to British troops when off duty and was only approached by lorry to bring and take away the British other ranks from and to their quarters close to the Nile at Bulac Bridge.

The pungency of the surrounding atmosphere was almost visible, so intense were the odours, but this had to be endured as the men entered into the spirit of the job on hand and appreciated all it entailed.

Our Desert Air Force in 1941–2 were practically cut off from the Mediterranean and equipment so urgently required had of necessity to be brought by the long sea route of some 12,000 miles. It became necessary to make do with our limited local resources and with a small nucleus of R.A.F. tradesmen work was set in motion to overcome our deficiencies.

Advertisements in the local Cairo papers brought astounding results. Each individual was vetted by the police and doctor before being forwarded to the respective branch of 111 M.U. that needed them. The M.U. had been fortunate in the airmen posted from Aboukir Depot for they were the 'king-pins'. The local talent came from all walks of life, but to find such different nationalities as Egyptians, Greeks, Cypriots, Maltese, Arabs, Palestinians, Sudanese, Jews, Copts, Armenians, plus a smattering of others, made one wonder just how the work could ever run efficiently.

Fortunately the technical supervisor of local labour had a working knowledge of seven languages, and owing to the fact that many of the men understood two or more tongues it was possible to get on a working basis.

The work of the engine-repair section was to receive all the Rolls-Royce Merlin and Kestrel engines from the Desert Air Forces, completely strip them to their last nut and bolt, and after an overhaul and bench test get them back to the desert for further useful life.

These engines arrived from as far afield as Aleppo in Syria, Malta, Tobruk, in fact from all over the desert. In many cases they arrived completely covered with a coating of sand at least a quarter of an inch thick. Some had been dragged by tanks on to rocky ground before they could be loaded, and suffered considerably in doing so, yet those engines left No. 1 E.R.S. as jet-black gleaming power units with the guarantee of the R.A.F. behind them.

The staff had received the guidance of a Rolls expert specially flown from England and this gentleman told them that if conditions were the same as at home the output per month should rise to ninety complete overhauls. Luckily he had not seen the effect of the Khamsin. This is a hot sand-laden wind blowing from the desert, and its effect on dissembled engines was substantial, transforming them from gleaming components, viewed and ready for assembly, to gritty, dull, inanimate shapes. The sand was forced into the shops through the wide spaces between roof and walls. In spite of this grave handicap the staff refused to be beaten and a record of some 106 engines were overhauled and sent back to the desert in the month of March 1942.

A general view of the E.R.S. complications and trials can best be exemplified by an account of a typical day. It must be appreciated that the inhabitants surrounding No. 1 E.R.S. objected very strongly to the shop being there at all. Threats had been made to burn the place and precautions were taken to safeguard life, limb and property. This necessitated an armed Egyptian policeman patrolling the place, a 'Gaffieh' or watchman to prevent pilfering, and an armed airman to check the passes of visitors and to use his discretion in case of trouble. These formed the day guard. At night six armed airmen stood by with an N.C.O. with a telephone to use in emergency. In May 1942 this was changed to a guard of ten Indian troops under an N.C.O. to relieve skilled airman from this duty.

Personnel arrived by truck via the Cairo main station, and carried out a number of intricate manœuvres to dodge the hordes of men, women, children, donkeys, camels, taxis, gharrys, all seemingly going to all points of the compass. In time it was possible to judge reasonably accurately where to expect a shower of filth, garbage, chewed sugar-cane and spit, as the truck wended its way towards the shop. Craftily thrown stones and plenty of abuse announced the point of arrival, chiefly because the school inmates took a delight in throwing stones at a moving vehicle, and if one stopped to remonstrate the budding scholars performed works of art on the sides of the truck which were never taught at school.

The local stinks were accentuated by the sprinkling of creosol all over the floor to keep out the Egyptian fly, and as it was effective in doing so no one complained.

The airmen were usually allotted a number of local tradesmen, according to the latters' mentality and capabilities. In Cairo one airman to six locals was found to be advisable.

Usually the requests of the locals to see the C.O. was tackled, primarily to get them back to work as soon as possible. These complaints were composed of anything from hashish being surreptitiously sold in the shop, of insufficient pay, of fighting, theft, immoral wives and workmates, sickness, Coptic Christmas not coinciding with 25th December or praying in working hours, and toilet accommodation (religious feelings governed this). These matters tactfully cleared, the slamming of a window in the face of a camel who had thrust its neck into the office, a hurried waft of a blotting pad to clear the dead flies from the table and then off to the work in hand.

Boilers steamed like mad during the initial wash of engine parts, and paraffin baths had their team of cleaners rubbing and polishing components. View boys with a select band of airmen checked worn parts and worked to the 'permissible worn tolerances'. Cylinder-bore regrinding; pistons, connecting rods, superchargers, carburettors, magnetos, pumps and the heterogeneous mass of the engine parts, all these were checked and words of encouragement passed to the various gangs so employed.

The hours of sixty per week were often exceeded (always voluntarily) and though the shop thermometer which registered to 110 was invariably sitting tight at the top degree, the men worked, perspired profusely and laughed at it all. Street fights (immediately outside the front entrance) were allowed to proceed so long as they did not interfere or obstruct the work; the only precaution taken being to call the airman sentry inside and close the main doors. Hell might be let loose for all the airmen cared, but the flow of engines was not checked.

Night visits were paid between 12 p.m. and 4 a.m., oftener when all-night work was called for, and although this became an eerie task it was soon apparent that the beam of a good torch was by far the most effective 'weapon' in case of attack. One driver had his left eye nearly gouged from its socket at night and on his discovery of the attacker the following day an exciting knife fight took place. A little blood was shed and the assailant, after a beating-up by the policeman with the butt of his rifle, was soon on his way for an enforced rest of a month.

The shop soon became a novelty to visitors, among them Turkish generals, for whose country the R.A.F. also worked, American correspondents anxious to give a story to the U.S.A. and hosts of other interested parties (fourteen in one day). Once in June 1942 the E.R.S. was honoured by a visit from H.R.H. The Duke of Gloucester. The squadron leader could not help wondering during this visit how H.R.H. came to possess such a sound fundamental knowledge of the engines. At one point during the visit the Duke was informed that one of the locals, Sayed, had been fitting piston-rings to R.A.F. engines twenty years ago. H.R.H. laughed loud and long when (after asking what he was doing now) he was informed that he was still fitting piston-rings. In point of fact he saw him at work and each smiled at the other, or, rather, Sayed grinned.

Not only in Northern Egypt but also in the Sudan the work went on. At 139 M.U. Khartoum in 1942 far better conditions prevailed than Cairo ever knew. There were but three items which warranted comparison: local labour, 'Haboobs' or Khamsins and excessive heat.

When employing Sudanese labour for the overhauling of R.A.F. engines it was necessary to have one airman to three Sudanese. Even the best of them had but the experience of being a motor mechanic with probably a vague impression of an internal combustion engine. The language question became a problem, but if one particular phase of work was repeated a sufficient number of times a gleam of interest spread quietly over the face of the Sudanese and so one knew that he had grasped what was meant.

Careful checking of his finished task (and acknowledgement that it had been satisfactorily done) was the first step in speed and the ultimate production of the finished engine. Seven types of Bristol engine, two of Rolls-Royce and an American engine were all safely undertaken and produced in fair numbers. 'Haboobs' (the Egyptian Khamsins) were a possibly greater menace to engine overhaul than anything, even the heat.

Work commenced at 5 a.m., which meant a fairly early call after a hot, restless night. The mirages appeared across the desert by early breakfast which gave a good indication of the rapidly advancing heat rising to 118 degrees in a cool office but jumping neatly to 125 degrees in the hangar used as the E.R.S. At 8.30 in the evening the temperature was 102 degrees. Heat fatigue was frequent, yet the output was seldom checked except by the 'Haboobs'. These terrible sand-storms are preceded by a rapidly increasing temperature and the howl of the wind in the distance.

To see the condition of the exposed engine components when a 'Haboob' died down and normality was reached was enough to make one weep! Sand had to be scooped, shovelled and swept from benches, cupboards, shelves; in fact it was a question of spring-cleaning the whole place before cleaning components and erecting could be considered. Water with a dash of salt was drunk to replace some of the lost perspiration during long periods of work with dripping bodies. This of course was barred from the local Sudanese entirely during Ramadan when no food or drink is taken during all hours of daylight. Naturally they gradually became listless and tired with subsequent loss of output generally. Pressure of a tactful nature was very necessary during this period or they would remain at home and sleep all day.

A number of airmen stationed in Gibraltar during 1942 had a very busy time. Not only was the airfield (carved out of the old sports ground and extended into the bay) a considerable transit centre, but it was here on the borders of neutral Spain that many of the aircraft taking part in the invasion of North Africa were erected. There was also a strange and macabre traffic with the Spanish mainland in dead aircrew recovered from the sea, and in live and escaping prisoners of war who filtered down the escape route from occupied France. One airman, G. H. Smith by name, has told me that the scale of reward for a dead airman was five gallons of petrol, while a live P.O.W. rated at ten gallons. One of the dead may have been the original 'Man Who Never Was' whose strange role has been portrayed in film and story.

On one occasion, while working at his job of erecting Spitfires, Smith saw both British and Spanish frontier guards deliberately turn their backs to the road between Spain and Gibraltar while an aged single-seater bus creaked on to British soil. In it were twenty-six haggard P.O.W.s still with their prison hair crop—à la Yul Brynner. As the bus ground to a stop they leaped out yelling madly, and made off in the direction of the airfield buildings. By next day they had been kitted out and walked around the Rock breathing deeply in Freedom's fresh air. Doubtless also they had several square meals under their belts!

Smith complains of the overcrowding, and of the absence of female society. The 'Scorps' had been evacuated and apart from a few nursing sisters the garrison was nothing but an enormous monastery.

Just before the African landings vast numbers of Spitfires and Hurricanes were standing wing-tip to wing-tip around the perimeter track. The allied pilots, British, Canadian and American, were ordered to pick their own aircraft and then paste the national markings on to the Spits or Hurricanes of their choice. On the evening before the invasion the night air resounded to the cries and shouts of these young men. 'I bagged this one!' 'Say, feller, it's mine.' 'Sugar off, Yank—this is Maple Leaf territory.' It must have been quite a party, thoroughly enjoyed by the airmen whose toil had produced this air armada. Some of them had worked for forty-eight hours without any rest and one warrant officer, utterly exhausted, climbed into a wheelbarrow and went fast asleep.

Smith's final recollection is of a senior officer of the R.A.F. inviting all the members of the erection party into his office where he shook hands, congratulated them and gave them each a glass of sherry and a Churchman cigarette. It was pouring with rain and Smith concludes: 'As I stepped out into the downpour my cigarette went out, but the drink and the handshake left a warm glow inside me that I have never forgotten.'

Elsewhere in the Commonwealth—in India, Malaya, Australia, New Zealand and Canada—similar maintenance units had been established. Their expansion was enormous as the demands of the local air forces and, more especially, of the Empire Air Training Scheme grew to fantastic proportions. From the United Kingdom, as in the Kaiser War, skilled men were drafted to form the nucleus of these new organizations. Were they fortunate? Materially perhaps so, but the higher cost of living and an inadequate compensatory allowance bit deep into their pay packet. At least they could sleep peacefully at night. No bombs, H.E., Buzz or D.A., nor the clamour of our A.A. batteries disturbed their nights. Their days were routine even if they were long. Some missed their families and friends, the companionship of danger shared. There was anxiety, too, for the safety of those at home under the threat of air attack and of the more doubtful possibility of invasion.

During the time when it was my business to give a daily report on the progress of the war to the troops at Candy in Ceylon, it was most noticeable that their greatest interest was in the details of air attack—bomb and buzz bomb—on the homeland. So it was not all honey to be in a safe billet overseas.

Some time in 1942 it was found that the maintenance units would be overloaded if further steps were not taken to facilitate the overhaul of our aircraft.

I have read some conflicting claims as to the authorship of 'Planned Maintenance', but so far as Coastal Command was concerned the idea originated in the mind of a Dr. Gordon, a member of my operational research staff. Gordon had been told to look into the serviceability ratio of the Command aircraft and before long he came to me with his scheme.

Briefly, he suggested that the majority of technicians should be removed from their existing attachment to individual aircraft and grouped in a headquarters unit. The rest of the squadron would consist of a few technicians to carry out the daily inspections and the aircraft hands who pushed and pulled the machines and fed them with petrol and oil.

In the H.Q. unit repairs would be concentrated. As aircraft became serviceable they would be issued to the flights, regardless of who had previously flown them. This scheme knocked for six two of the basic R.F.C. and R.A.F. principles—that of the pilot's personal responsibility for the serviceability of his aircraft, and that of the close relations between the pilot and the technicians who served him. The only people to whom he was closely attached were his crew members. The far-off workshops were no concern of his—it was the Senior Technical Officer's job to look after them. There is no doubt that this scheme, when put into operation throughout the R.A.F., greatly improved the serviceability rate and also enabled a small reduction to be made in the technical trades. Old hands like myself, however, were never very happy, as we felt the change would lead to a reduction in morale. This may have happened, but from the point of view of technical efficiency the scheme worked, and worked well.

Thus, at home and abroad, good organization (largely the result of trial and error), and above all the willingness, enthusiasm and technical skill of the airmen, 'kept them flying'!

16

Air/Sea Rescue

I N THE early days of flying across the sea the organization for rescuing airmen who had the misfortune to fall into the 'Drink' was rudimentary. When the Royal Flying Corps crossed the English Channel in August 1914 each pilot was issued with a motor-car-tyre inner tube, which he was supposed to inflate and loop round his neck and under his arms. I believe some naval craft were supposed to patrol the Channel during our crossing, but personally I observed nothing except a few fishing-boats near the French coast. As the years went by and engines became more reliable it was only for the care of Very Important Persons that the Navy patrolled the line of flight.

But when the coastal air forces were turned over to the R.A.F. in 1918 launches, dinghies, a floating dock and maintenance vessels such as the *Manela* came 'on charge'. Gradually an elementary system of air/sea rescue came into being, and high-speed launches, capable of operating in rough weather, were built and issued to Coastal Command from 1936 onwards. After the outbreak of the Hitler War each aircraft that had cause to operate over the sea was fitted with rubber, inflatable dinghies in proportion to the size of its crew.

But it was the example given by the German Air Force that triggered off a massive development of air/sea rescue, not only in Britain but all over the world wherever aircraft had to fly over the oceans.

During the period of the 'Phoney War' the Luftwaffe suffered losses as a result of its mine-laying operations and its attacks on our shipping. In consequence it established a system of rafts anchored off the Friesian coast and formed one or two squadrons of small flying-boats that were intended to rescue German airmen adrift in the icy North Sea. These boats were painted white and adorned with the Red Cross, in an endeavour to persuade the Allies that they were operating under the Geneva Convention. It was decided, however, that there was too great a risk of these aircraft being used improperly—as photo-reconnaissance planes or in other forms of aerial espionage. In consequence they were attacked whenever they approached our coasts and the enemy soon gave up painting them in Red Cross colours.

Following the German example, flights of Walrus amphibian aircraft were established round our shores, and the number and efficiency of the high-speed launches was increased. Coastal Command held a watching brief over this organization and encouraged the development of better dinghies supplied with rations, water and covers against the weather, with wireless sets, paddles and sails. But the aerial lifeboat was the showpiece! This was a craft that fitted on the underside of a large aeroplane, streamlined into its shape. When the A.S.R. aircraft found airmen adrift in a dinghy the boat would be dropped on the downwind side of the castaways. As the boat left the parent aircraft, parachutes would be ejected and, nose downward, it would fall slowly to the surface. There, automatically, gunwales of rubber would inflate so as to give greater free-board. When the rescued arrive on board they would find food, water and cover. Also a sail, paddles and wireless set. Above all, a petrol engine able to drive the boat 300 miles or more to safety.

But it was while waiting for rescue in their dinghies or in the lifeboat that the aircrew might find trouble. The enemy did not hesitate to fight the rescuers for the bodies of the victims of a ditching. Perhaps the lifeboats had the better chance, as they could keep moving towards safety. But the occupants of the dinghies could only wait helplessly for rescue by naval vessel or high-speed launch.

These craft were directed to the dinghies by several means. Firstly, the reports of aircraft that, fortuitously, had seen the dinghies. Then there was the wireless fix made by shore stations on the lost aircraft's distress signal. Finally, the G.C.I. and C.H.L. radar stations could also help by giving the last position that they had 'seen' of the crash before it hit the sea. During the five years of the Hitler War, Air/Sea Rescue stepped up its operations from ones and twos during the Battle of Britain to hundreds during the Battle for Europe. There were very many gallant actions carried out by the airmen of A.S.R. Here is one story—very typical of the service.

In June 1944 the day and night raids on Germany were in full swing. For the U.S.A.F. attack on Schweinfurt the A.S.R. launches were out in strength cordoning the North Sea at twenty-mile intervals. The day was fine and the visibility good. The sea was slight and, in the most easterly position, High Speed Launch No. 2551, captain Flight Sergeant G. F. Lindsay (ex-merchant marine), and a crew of eleven, bobbed in the summer swell. About noon a signal was received ordering 2551 to a position close to the Dutch coast and Ymuiden. For a while 2551 kept wireless silence, and then, about 1.30 p.m., faint signals were received at base, indicating that a rescue had been effected. As there were no further reports of 'ditchings' all launches were recalled. But H.S.L. 158 had intercepted speech between two U.S.A.F. Thunderbolt fighters which were giving cover to 2551. No. 158 held course for 2551's position as it seemed as though something had gone wrong. At 3.45 p.m. the Thunderbolts reported that there was a small vessel burning off the Dutch coast. No. 158 called the aircraft and asked them to identify the number of this burning vessel. The aircraft replied that it was 2551 and that there were a number of dinghies nearby. No. 158 reached the scene and found several dinghies and a Carley float on which were survivors. Meanwhile the wind had strengthened, and the work of rescue was made much more difficult. Finally nine of 2551's crew and eight aircrew from the crash were recovered alive. Sadly enough, Flight Sergeant Lindsay was amongst the dead, the result of air attack on the launch.

On the launch the number of injured seriously overloaded the two nursing orderlies, so a signal was sent for medical help. Meanwhile H.S.L. 2706 turned up, apparently having turned a deaf ear to the recall signal, and transferred her nursing orderly to No. 158. As darkness fell a Walrus aircraft landed alongside and the two doctors on board jumped on to the plunging launch, no mean feat of taxi-ing on the part of the pilot and of courage by the doctors. Thus several lives were saved.

In the landing and contact with the launch the Walrus punctured a wing-tip float and, unable to take off safely, had to be towed forty miles by No. 2706.

This near-disaster was caused by an attack made by two JU88s on 2551 as she was picking up the aircrew. Her guns jammed and, lying helpless, she was set on fire and several of the crew, including the captain, were killed. Fortunately, before this happened, the dinghies from the crashed aircraft had been collected round the launch, so that the majority of the crew and aircrew were saved.

These launches were very fast—top speed about thirty-five knots. They were driven by three Napier Lion engines of some 500 h.p. The heat in the tiny engine-room was terrific, and most exhausting for the engineers. In addition to the heat, the liveliness of these small craft made it imperative for the E.R.A.s to be strapped to their seats, otherwise they might have been thrown into the engines and suffered grave injury or death.

Many were the long and abortive searches that these craft were called upon to undertake. Sometimes success came, in spite of enemy attack. At others the aircrew would be found—the dead lying in their dinghies or floating in their Mae Wests nearby. The job of hauling them on board was a sad ending to the operation.

An A.S.R. airman has given a vivid description of a late arrival at the scene of the crash:

'Bodies of young men, almost boys, floating in their life-saving jackets, lank hair waving like seaweed, heads fallen back against the inflated collar—eyes half-open, giving them a lazy expression —'Too late, friends—we've had it''. But one young man, pulled alive on board, asked, "Is this the last bus and does it go to London?" His facetiousness was soon abated by a violent attack of sea-sickness.'

There was not always tragedy on these patrols. On some days—not many it is true—the boats and their crews idled the hours away on sunlit seas, fishing, writing, reading and getting an oriental tan on their fair skins. As their work was mostly in the region of our mine-fields from time to time life would resume its warlike tempo when a mine would explode nearby, set off by some defect in its construction.

Occasionally a launch would be attacked by a prowling JU88. Then it was a case of shooting it out with the enemy. Sometimes the fight would end successfully for our side but at others there would be empty chairs in the mess-room ashore. No. 2606 was sunk in this way and only three of the crew were rescued, one of whom died on the way to harbour. This was out of a total of thirteen.

Today there are Air/Sea Rescue organizations all over the world, and they do great work in the saving of life at sea.

17

Fire—fire!

A FINE spring day in 1915. A Maurice Farman 'Long-horn' was doing a circuit of the Farnborough aerodrome. The pupil pilot had done a number of straight flights and this was the first in which he had to turn towards the landing ground. All went well until he shut his engine off to make his landing. I was watching, feeling quite content that he could not fail to 'perch', as it was called at that time. A few seconds later and with growing horror I saw that he had lost control. The aircraft was gliding at a perfectly normal angle but the pilot was making no effort to flatten out. In the resulting crash the petrol flamed and in spite of every effort made by the primitive rescue organization the pilot was burned to death. This tragedy was to repeat itself a thousand times during the Kaiser War, and more often during the Hitler War. Even during the inter-war years many promising pilots and aircrew suffered death in this painful manner. The early flights to Egypt, to South Africa, to the Far East were marred by crashes that ended in a funeral pyre for the aircrew.

The Air Ministry was deeply concerned. Every effort was made to produce counter-measures to the dreadful fire risk. Asbestos suits for the men who manned the tenders that waited on the edge of the airfield; chemical sprays that could damp a petrol fire in a matter of minutes; tackle to drag an aircraft away from the fire it had produced in crashing; and tools to break into the hulls of burning aircraft were all devised and tried out. But a petrol fire is like a shell-burst. I have seen an aircraft crash twenty yards from the rescue tenders. Within seconds the chemical foam was covering the flames and yet one of the crew, even if he had not broken his neck in the crash, would have been so badly burned that he might have died.

Long before the Hitler War broke out, on every R.A.F. airfield while flying was in progress there was a fire tender and an ambulance on the alert. In this way many lives were saved by the courage of the men who manned these vehicles. Naturally, when war broke out and flying operations became intense, their responsibilities increased. The brave actions performed by these airmen had their reward in the lives they saved, but so often all that they could drag out from the flaming wrecks were the dead or the dying. The feelings of the fire crews as they did their job are simply but effectively expressed by an airman, H. M. Oldroyd, who spent two years on Topcliffe airfield:

'I was stationed at this camp, working under a corporal—Robertson by name—who came from Dundee, and about a dozen other men.

Many times, by day and by night, we endeavoured to give of our utmost in trying to save the lives of the aircrew who were doing such a wonderful job. One of our risks was the bombload that might still be on board a crashing aircraft. Sometimes, in a great emergency, these would be jettisoned at safe, or would fall off accidentally—alive! Even at take-off there would be accidents. A bomber, fully loaded, would leave the runway and nose over in the mud. Sometimes it would catch fire and then our job of rescue would be made even more dangerous. Not only the bombs but the ammunition would explode and bullets would fly all over the place. Whatever happened, Corporal Robertson would do his best and help us to help the others in the burning aircraft. He always got us on to the job at the right time.'

In the *London Gazette* can be found the awards for gallantry and citations describing fantastic acts of courage performed by these very ordinary men.

In July 1940 No. 935282 Aircraftsman First Class Vivian Holloway saw an aircraft crash on the airfield and burst into flames. He rushed to the scene and dragged the pilot out of the cockpit, beating out the flames from the burning clothing with his bare hands.

A month later, in similar circumstances, and although ammunition in the aircraft was exploding all the time, he borrowed a gas-mask, wrapped two sacks round his body and plunged into the flames. He succeeded in dragging out two of the crew, but unfortunately not in time to save their lives.

For these acts of courage Hollowday was awarded the George Cross.

N

In September 1940 No. 158305 Leading Aircraftsman John Farley and No. 820067 A.C.1 Thomas Coop were members of a fire-tender party. An aircraft crashed and went up in flames. Coop tried to get the pilot out in spite of exploding ammunition. Farley plunged his arms into the burning cockpit, freed the pilot's legs that were caught in the damaged controls and between them they got him away from the flames. Both men showed the greatest courage and were awarded the George Medal. Sadly enough the pilot died of his injuries.

Sometimes the reward of courage was greater. No. 358920 Acting Sergeant Sidney Boys on three occasions drove his fire tender right up to a burning aircraft and, regardless of the possibility that the bombs might go off, turned the chemical fire extinguisher on to the flames. Thus he saved the lives of three aircrew and for his outstanding courage he was awarded the George Medal.

The stilted phrases of the citations give no picture of these incidents. One has to conjure up the scene from past experience and from the short clipped sentences of the men who took part.

September 1940 brings to life the Battle of Britain and a Hurricane or Spitfire limping back to Biggin Hill with one leg of its undercarriage trailing and the other jammed in the up position. The airfield has been bombed very recently and there are craters everywhere. The pilot does his best, but the damaged undercarriage brings the aircraft to ruin. Petrol runs from the crumpled tanks and a spark from the hot engine starts the fire. This is the kind of story that was repeated a score of times every week as the fight for existence swayed from the coast to London and back again. At night it was the bombers, Wellingtons and Whitleys, engaged on their lawful occasions over Germany, that suffered. The enemy's anti-aircraft fire was accurate and many of our machines returned to their bases in a crippled condition that led to a crash and a fire.

So by day and night the fire tender and ambulance crews were on the alert. There might be times when nothing happened and then suddenly they would be called upon to risk their lives or suffer grave injuries. For those who worked at night it was that type of bravery which is beyond all others. Sitting cold and numbed on their vehicles the hours passed slowly by. Vitality was low as dawn approached and this was just the time when they might be called upon to show their 'guts'. And this was not just for a day or a week, but for six years until in 1945 the shooting war stopped.

It might be thought that the crews manning the barrage balloons round vulnerable points—such as London—would lead a fairly peaceful existence. Crossing St. James's Park one night in November 1940 I saw a shower of incendiaries fall and light up the whole of Westminster. The sentry on the balloon that flew from the Horse Guards Parade was playing football with a number that had fallen round his balloon in an endeavour to get them away from the gas-cylinders stacked round the site. Some of these incendiaries had a high-explosive charge that went off after a short delay and the sentry must have been aware of this fact. Nevertheless he did his job. In the same month No. 852019 L.A.C. William Osborne was on a balloon site that was heavily bombed. The balloon began to sink, having been holed, but Osborne assembled his crew in spite of the continued bombardment and got the balloon safely to the ground. Having nothing to do at the moment he called for volunteers to rescue civilians who were trapped in a damaged house. Two men joined him, but on their way both were killed and Osborne was knocked out by the bomb explosion. He had previously shown gallantry and devotion to duty.

Even on leave airmen sometimes found themselves called upon to act with courage.

During a heavy air raid, presumably during the night blitz, though the citation does not specify, No. 956216 A.C.2 Horace Dews became involved in an incident where a woman and child were pinned by a girder against the basement wall of a damaged building. A.R.P. workers had been unable to free these two, so Dews lay on his stomach and began to burrow with his hands through the rubble. This advance was impeded by another girder, a dead body and a baulk of timber, so he forced his head and shoulders into the hole he had made and wriggled his way forward until he could reach the child. Placing the child in safety he then enlarged the hole and finally got the woman out as well. A few moments later the fire reached the place of rescue.

Dews was justly rewarded with the George Medal.

Another airman rescued a woman from a burning house. He was only able to reach the place where the woman was trapped by having buckets of water poured on him to keep his clothes from catching fire. For this A.C.2 Enos Garrett got a B.E.M.

On 27th August 1941, at 3 p.m., an aircraft crashed through the main hall of Blackpool Central Station. In seconds the whole place was in flames, but Acting Corporal Thomas Hill, R.A.F., dashed into the building and saved one woman. Returning he pulled out another who had been trapped by a fallen girder. With the help of a policeman he extinguished their burning clothing and then, although the whole building was on the verge of collapse, he went in again and dragged out a third woman, whose clothing was blazing. For this extremely gallant conduct Hill was awarded the George Medal. In January 1942 Corporal J. Taylor pulled two aircrew out of an aircraft burning close to a grenade store. He then borrowed another pair of gloves—his own having been burned through—and together with other airmen dragged out two further bodies. He was most severely burned. In recognition of his courage and determination he was awarded the B.E.M.

From Malta come many stories of similar gallant actions. During the bombardment by the Luftwaffe there were more than sufficient opportunities for men to show their devotion to duty. Corporal Hugh Clawson and L.A.C. Edward Mitchison seem to have been outstanding in this work. Altogether the *London Gazette* gives eleven citations to airmen who were stationed in the island at this time. L.A.C. Albert Osbourne got the George Medal for being the first to deal with emergencies in circumstances of the greatest danger. Twice he made torpedoes safe that were in danger of exploding from the heat of burning aircraft. If they had gone off he would have had no known grave. On another occasion he saved a pilot and put out the fires in two burning aircraft. Lastly, he spent six hours, constantly in danger from falling masonry, in endeavouring to free airmen who were trapped in a shelter that had been bombed. During the whole of this time the airfield was being attacked from the air.

Sadly enough he was killed later on by the explosion of an air bottle from an aircraft in flames.

Once more at home, in 1943, as operations grew in intensity there were many fires caused by crashed aircraft, or by bomb accidents.

Corporal Houghton put up a very good show on one occasion. As an armourer he was busy bombing up his own aircraft when he noticed a light in a nearby dispersal point and airmen moving away with some rapidity. He ran across and found that an incendiary bomb-container had dropped off its rack in the aircraft's belly and that some of the incendiaries had fallen out and were alight. Quickly kicking these away, he fetched a steel sheet which he placed on the container, which by now was white-hot. With the help of other airmen he then pushed the aircraft away from the fire and saved it from destruction.

Incidentally, there was a 4000-pound high-explosive bomb on board!

I have read of a case where a W.A.A.F. was foremost in dragging an injured man from a crashed and burning aircraft but unfortunately the reference is lost. In any case it is in keeping with the work of these stout-hearted women, and I hope I may be forgiven for having forgotten her name.

18

In Peril by the Sea

IN BOTH world wars a vast number of airmen were carried thousands of miles by sea in very great discomfort. The lower decks of the *Megantic*, a White Star liner conveying 3000 troops of all sorts to Egypt in 1916, remain vividly in my memory. By day the men who were harboured there could come on deck for a breather. But at night, in a Mediterranean June, all the scuttles were closed and blacked-out for fear of enemy submarines. Fortunately it was only a ten-days' trip and there was no disaster. But the men took some weeks to recover from the purgatory they had suffered.

Casualties among the troops from submarine attack were not severe. In the Hitler War even though the 'Queens', the *Mary* and the *Elizabeth*, and the famous French ship the *Pasteur* carried tens of thousands of troops without loss, there were some tragedies.

The *Ceramic*, an ageing Shaw Savill liner capable of a modest seventeen knots, was, on 3rd December 1942, detached from Convoy O.N. 149 and ordered to proceed independently to South Africa. She had on board, in addition to her crew numbering 278, nearly 400 passengers, of whom some 250 were service men on duty or returning to their homes in South Africa. On the night of 6th December, some 500 miles north-west of the Azores, she was torpedoed by a U-boat in extremely rough weather. The U-boat commander fired four torpedoes in all at the unlucky ship and she broke up, carrying to their death a number of people who had been unable to get into the boats. Those in the boats did not survive for long. In the wind of almost typhoon force rafts and boats were quickly turned over and all were lost—save one man, Sapper E. Munday, Royal Engineers, who was taken prisoner. A few wretched swimmers grasped the projections on the U-boat's deck, but were beaten off by the crew, under orders from the captain, and drowned or were cut to bits by the submarine's propellers. In all some 650 people, including many women and children, went to their death.

Squadron Leader A. Pugh was on board the *Empress of Canada* when she was sunk.

At five minutes to midnight on 13th March 1943 the ship was torpedoed. She had left Durban on 1st March with 'time-expired' men, sick and various ratings, French, Greek, Polish A.T.S. and Army, apart from the crew and 500 Italian P.O.W.s. A speed of some eighteen knots by day and twenty-two by night had been maintained and zig-zag tactics had been employed; in fact everything pointed to an uneventful trip. By 11.30 p.m. on the 13th everyone had 'turned in' except those on duty, including of course the manning of defence stations; and things were much the same as on previous nights.

The explosion of the first torpedo caused the ship to lift and roll as if kicked by some giant boot, and then followed a noticeable quietness for a number of seconds. It was not long before there were numerous sounds of movement (along the corridors and ladders) of passengers making for the boat deck. The lights below decks were still alight and there was no sign of anything in the nature of panic, but it became noticeable that the nearer to the 'boat deck' the crowds became more tensed and hurried. No lights were exposed on the upper deck except the hand-torches of the crew, and one could see that the respective parties were assembling at their 'boat stations'.

The boats which had been left suspended on their falls were being filled methodically, but on reaching the boat station for the R.A.F. officers and men it was found that it had been allotted to Greek ratings. Guessing that there was obviously a reason for it, a glance over the ship's side confirmed the earlier suspicions, for by the light of a torch it was possible to see a lifeboat hanging from the aft falls; it was the Greek seamen's boat. The explosion had unshipped the boat from the forward falls and it was hanging uselessly there.

A ship's officer said that a large raft would be available for the R.A.F. so there was little to do but wait till the raft was unlashed and launched. The ship was still under way to use up the steam in the boilers and the valves wide open to get rid of as much steam as possible and so prevent a boiler explosion. The noise of the escaping steam made talking out of the question for some minutes, but the R.A.F.

had grouped quietly awaiting the launching of the raft. No boats from the promenade deck could be lowered as the electrical releases were not functioning, and the crew appeared to be concentrating on the large rafts. The list which had scarcely been noticed at first now assumed reasonably severe proportions. Without a word of warning one of the rafts screeched down its slips, followed by a shower of sparks. There was a splash and a shout that about 'eight men had been dragged off with it'. No sound came from the sea and it is believed they were all killed immediately.

There was still considerable way on the ship and, realizing the hopelessness of trying to jump and swim for it, it was decided to rely on the small rafts that could be lifted by four men. When the ship slowed almost to a standstill the R.A.F. started to throw the smaller rafts overboard. It was agreed that jumping into the sea and swimming for the rafts was the only chance. Things were now very quiet on board as practically all had left and the airmen put into practice the suggestion to 'move together', and soon most of them had swarmed down ropes to the ship's rail. By now calls were coming from those who had reached the rafts and help was given to the rest to reach and hang on to them.

The list of the ship as seen from sea level was a little unnerving and steps were taken to get as far away as possible. By hanging on to the man-ropes of the raft progress was made (though apparently very slowly) and the crash of falling equipment into the sea spurred everyone to give 'maximum effort'.

Much later a larger naval Carley float was found. Someone had a watch of the water-proof type and it showed that the R.A.F. men had been swimming and dragging the raft for nearly three hours. Suddenly there was a sound of engines running. It was thought to come from the ship's motor-boat, but hopes were soon dashed as a searchlight sought and held the float in its glare. Many of the men slipped back into the sea, fearing that they would be taken prisoner. There was also the possibility of being machine-gunned.

Soon Italian voices were heard and those near enough to the submarine saw that it was numbered J.45. In addition the Italian doctor who had attended to P.O.W.s on the *Empress of Canada* was seen to be taken on board. Three seamen carrying machine-guns ordered off anyone attempting to climb aboard the submarine. This also applied to Italian prisoners who were swimming close by.

The searchlight covered the float for a long time and then suddenly swung round in another direction as someone called to the submarine. A call went out for a 'ship's officer', but although there were two with the Carley float party no one spoke, and after some little time the engines were again heard as the enemy moved off. All night the men hung on. The float was by now so weighed down that the sea levelled with their chests. At various periods during the night there were awful screams. Sharks were taking their toll, but all that was visible were the red lights of the crews' torches attached to their life-jackets. Light of day showed the survivors in a poor state. Their bodies were covered completely in black oil fuel, and all were very sick and weary. Luck again came their way in the nature of a large raft and all but four were able to climb on to it.

The lightening of the float made it buoyant enough to support these four, but sharks menaced them a number of times throughout the day and of course there was nothing to eat or drink. Conversation between the four proved that they were of the R.A.F. (vests and shorts meant nothing) and that they would 'stick it out' together. After twenty-one hours of this swimming and exposure on the float the *Empress'* motor-boat arrived towing a water-logged lifeboat almost filled with Italian P.O.W.s, some injured among them. It was agreed that the four R.A.F. should crowd in and organize things. There was a little muttering when it became evident that the new arrivals were to deal with the food and what little water remained. In the end the R.A.F. rationed everything with particular fairness to all concerned.

A bad night followed with heavy seas running and strong winds. No one could sleep and things did not look too good the next morning. Scarcely ten boats, rafts or floats were in sight.

Although a Catalina flying-boat had been seen during the afternoon, and which had soon left to get help, it was agreed that if it did not return by the following day an attempt should be made to sail some 600-odd miles vaguely in the right direction. By nightfall of the third night a speck was seen, followed soon by a twinkling signal lamp. The *Boreas*, a destroyer, had arrived. Soon the rescued were safely sipping soup and smoking, their troubles over.

The conduct of these airmen, from their patient manner whilst waiting for a raft on the *Empress of Canada*, their efforts on the small raft and their scrupulous fairness in the waterlogged lifeboat, was exemplary. No one was left in doubt that whatever the circumstances might be there was as fine a type of man doing the quiet efficient work of the maintenance, repair and salvage staffs of the R.A.F. as may be found in the history of any service. Amongst the 324 lost out of a total of 1900 were twenty-two officers and men of the R.A.F.

On Wednesday, 7th July 1943, the troopship *Duchess of York* was in convoy some 500 miles west of Cape Finisterre—in the area patrolled by the German Focke-Wulf long-range aircraft based on Bordeaux. In the convoy there were two other ships, the *California* troopship and a cargo vessel, the *Port Ferry*. The escort consisted of a Tribal Class destroyer, the *Iroquois*, and two frigates.

During the evening, about 7.30 p.m., an aircraft was seen, but too far off to be identified. An hour later the alarm went and all the troops except the guncrews were ordered below. About 9 p.m. the guns opened up and about half an hour after that the ship was hit by a bomb just aft of the rear funnel . . . as a result the troops were sent farther into the bowels of the ship.

About half an hour after being hit the order came to abandon ship. The bombing had stopped and there was a large fire burning on the deck which prevented those in the stern from reaching the boat deck and boats.

The *California* was also blazing and her boats were away. . . . Most of the airmen in the stern of the *Duchess* climbed down ropes and rope ladders into the sea and reached rafts being thrown out by crew and airmen farther along the ship.

At the time of the attack some of the airmen were at a film show and being on the other side of the fire were able to get away with most of the crew in the boats.

As darkness fell the men on the rafts felt a long way from safety, but after about two hours a lifeboat from the *Iroquois* stopped beside the raft to which seven or eight airmen were holding and they were hauled on board. The engine of the lifeboat then refused to fire and the *Port Ferry* offered to take the survivors on board. For some reason the offer was refused and after another twenty minutes the *Iroquois* appeared out of the dark and the rescued scrambled up a net into the ship.

After thirty hours' sailing the 400 survivors on the *Iroquois* arrived at Casablanca on 13th July, too late, unfortunately, for breakfast, but I daresay they made up for the deficiency at lunch!

Losses at sea were by no means the end of this story. Ships in harbour, or lying off shore in fancied security, were often bombed and sunk with loss of life. The sinking of the *Lancastria* troopship in Bordeaux Harbour is a case in point.

From Northern and Eastern France in June 1940 thousands of airmen had come to the western ports to be evacuated. The *Lancastria* was crammed to suffocation with these evacuees. Before she could sail she was dive-bombed and destroyed.

Later, on 22nd November 1942, the liner *Scythia* was lying in Algiers Bay, with her complement of airmen waiting to be landed. It was a clear bright night, and the men were leaning over the bulwarks, looking at the dimmed lights of the town and congratulating themselves on a safe passage from England, in spite of all the efforts of the German U-boats to sink them. About 7.30 p.m. one of these men decided to go to bed and, with his friend, went down to their billet on E deck. For some unexplained reason both men were uneasy, and instead of slinging their hammocks in their usual place on the starboard side of the deck they bedded down under the shelter of the companion-way. Soon after the alarm sounded and gunfire was heard. Picking up their emergency rations and water-bottles they put on their lifebelts and as nothing more happened huddled down and tried to sleep. One of them found that sleep in a lifebelt was impossible and took it off. Vaguely he heard aircraft overhead but, tired out, he slept till dawn. Suddenly there was a heavy explosion, and he received a terrific blast which threw him across the deck. All the lights went out and a flood of water surged over him. After a sharp struggle he stood upright, gasping and choking. He groped for the companion-way, but in the dark could not find it. He was in despair when a pinpoint of light appeared and a voice said, 'O.K., lads, make for the light.' Against the rush and surge of the water pouring across the deck this was hard work, but finally he and the others reached the upper deck and safety.

In other disasters, notably the sinking of H.M.S. *Glorious* off the Norwegian coast, S.S. *Lancastria* as already mentioned in Bordeaux Harbour, H.M.S. *Anselm* and the S.S. *Laconia* off the west coast of Africa and L.S.T. 420 off Ostend, some 800 airmen were lost at sea. Compared with the very great numbers successfully and safely carried to their destinations this is not a very large figure. But each one of those drowned airmen represents a family tragedy. In the sum they are of interest only to statisticians.

19

The Odd-Job Men

I N THE Kaiser War airmen travelled to some very remote spots in
which to carry out their work. Flight Sergeant Ford, now living
in Canada, was one of these.

Early in the New Year of 1917 a party of N.C.O.s and other ranks
(twelve all told) set off from Farnborough for Russia. Their mission
was to act as instructors in the flying and maintenance of R.F.C.
equipment which had been sent to Russia from the U.K. Flight
Sergeant 'Ginger' Monk was the senior N.C.O. in charge. The party
sailed from Liverpool and after an adventurous journey dodging submarines arrived at Murmansk on the northern coast of Russia, nearly
150 miles inside the Arctic Circle. At Murmansk they disembarked
and boarded a train of box cars for the journey to St. Petersburg. This
journey took seven to eight days, during the course of which they
lived on the rations (mainly bully beef and jam) which they had
brought from England, supplemented occasionally by a loaf of black
bread which they managed to scrounge from some wayside village,
plus, of course, vast quantities of tea.

At St. Petersburg they left the box cars and boarded a Moscow
train with (when compared with the Murmansk–Petrograd journey)
palatial accommodation. Arrived at Moscow they piled out of the
train with all their paraphernalia, kitbags, blankets, unused rations,
etc., and looked around for the officer who was presumed to be there
to meet them. Nary an officer! What to do? The stupid(!) telephone
operators could not understand English or French and, of course,
none of the British could speak Russian. However, having heard
somewhere that most educated upper-class Russians could speak or
understand French, the two flight sergeants solved the problem by
striding up and down the platform and cursing mildly—but audibly—
in French. This resulted in a lady addressing them in English with

'Can I help you?' (The French must have been that of Stratford-atte-Bowe.) With the help of their benefactor, who could speak Russian, they eventually got in touch with the British authorities, and soon a truck arrived which, after about a thirty-minute journey, deposited them at an aerodrome on the outskirts of Moscow—across the road from what was at that time Petrovski Palace. The C.O., Colonel Jimmy Valentine, and his second-in-command, Major Maund, met them and installed them in a delightful little summer-house affair on the aerodrome (the floor was as hard as floors usually are when slept on, and they could have used an extra blanket) and the next day they got to work.

The first job was the erection of various British aeroplanes. These were still in their shipping crates, which had been deposited at the aerodrome. When they were erected and the engines installed they were flight tested. The aeroplanes were mostly Sopwith 1½ strutters and R.E.8s, though there was one Sopwith triplane. Once the planes had been test-flown classes were set up at which Russian mechanics were instructed, via interpreters, in the care and maintenance of them, while the officers did the flying instruction.

Meanwhile the Czar had abdicated—to the accompaniment of a big 'to-do' in Moscow—and the whole of Russia was in a turmoil. No one knew for sure what was happening—particularly the R.F.C. So, failing orders to do otherwise, they carried on with the instructing job and building the occasional aeroplane.

This went on until about the middle of May, when Jimmy Valentine (as they all spoke and thought of him) decided: 'Enough of this nonsense! We'll go down to the front and do some fighting!' So, in a very short while, about twenty aeroplanes (Sopwith 1½-strutters and R.E.8s) were loaded in their crates on to flat cars and, accompanied by three or four volunteer Russian mechanics, the party set off on its new adventure. Finally they arrived at a place called Denisauf where, with the sometimes over-enthusiastic help of the local inhabitants, they off-loaded and erected the aircraft in a field by the side of the railroad. This field was really too small for operations but, because of its good off-loading facilities and the presence of a railroad siding, it was decided to keep it as a base for future overhaul and repair work. The newly erected planes were flown to a makeshift, but larger, aerodrome at Cheremkoff, near the town of Podgaitza, by the side of one of the main roads leading to the Galician front in Austria. Here the squadron without a name, in liaison with the local Russian commander, General Brusilov, carried out bombing raids (forty-pounders), photographic sorties and so forth. The mechanics, besides doing all the maintenance and repair work, doubled as photographers, gunners and bomb-droppers—no bomb racks, just drop 'em over the side and hope for the best! Amongst other things they set up an engine overhaul shop and this, in conjunction with the base at Denisauf, sufficed to 'keep 'em flying'. Whilst at Cheremkoff they had contact with Lieutenant-Commander Locker Lampson's armoured-car outfit, and were responsible on one occasion for the wrecking and/or ditching of numerous armoured cars, through the surreptitious gift, by one of the airmen, of a gallon of alcohol (used by the photographers for quick-drying film) which the R.N. boys promptly drank—neat!

After a few months of this, luckily with no casualties, and after all kinds of rumours as to the march of events back in Russia, the party woke one morning to discover that the Russian Army had decided to quit and had disappeared back home in all directions, leaving the British, with their twenty or so aeroplanes, and the R.N. armoured-car boys, 'holding the bag'. Nothing to do but get out, quickly! However, they stuck around long enough to fly over to Denisauf and set fire to several aeroplanes under repair or still in crates, as well as the stores, before flying off to Proscurov, just over the Russian-Austrian border, shot at indiscriminately by all and sundry from the ground. Ford flew out with Colonel Valentine in an R.E.8, and when they landed at Proscurov discovered that two longerons had been shot through and only their guardian angels knew why the tailplane didn't fall off in flight.

From Proscurov they made their way by various means of transportation, from bullock cart to train, and eventually arrived at Kiev, where Colonel Valentine died and was buried. From Kiev they went wandering again, but eventually arrived back in Moscow about the middle of October, just in time to be caught in the November Revolution when the Bolsheviks took over, in a bloody and very noisy battle which lasted a week or so. During this time those who could wore 'civvies', and all carried identification *bumaga* (papers) issued by both the Bolsheviks and the Czarists, which Major Maund had mysteriously procured.

The R.F.C. stayed in Moscow pending arrangements being made for their return to the U.K. until the middle of January 1918, meanwhile celebrating two Christmases, one British and the Russian one two weeks later, at both of which, in spite of scarcity, rationing, etc., they managed to do themselves quite well, both as to food and drink.

At last they arrived back in Petrograd where they were billeted at the British Embassy, at the end of Nevsky Prospect on the River Neva. Sir G. Buchanan was the British Ambassador. No food, however, was available at the Embassy for a dozen or so hungry ack emmas. Having by this time become fairly proficient in the Russian language, 'Ginger' Monk and Ford crossed the bridge over the Neva to the Peter and Paul fortress, which was at that time one of the Bolshevik H.Q.s, and arranged, with no trouble at all, that they should be fed until such time as they left Petrograd for Murmansk and home!

After another box-car journey Murmansk was reached, only to discover that there was no ship going home at that time. So the party took advantage of the hospitality of the R.N. and were taken on the strength for accommodation and rations—including rum—of H.M.S. *Glory* which, according to the crew, had been there so long that she was aground on bully beef tins!

After about a week of this H.M.S. *Andes*, a peace-time liner which had been taken over by the Navy, showed up, and from this ship they finally disembarked at Greenock, a little over a year after their departure from Liverpool.

On reporting to the Air Ministry in London they were all sent on leave, and after leave expired reported back to various manning depots. Here Ford and a couple of others, because of their previous experience, were attached to the mysterious and, at that time, highly secret 'Elope' draft, eventually arriving back at Murmansk again about the middle of April 1918.

But this is another story.

During the Hitler War many men engaged for service in the R.A.F. and expecting to be closely associated with aeroplanes found themselves doing some very unusual jobs. In this account there has been no attempt to place these stories in chronological order. Each stands as an isolated incident.

A. L. Shovelton of Birmingham at one period in his service career found himself in a wireless observer post in Eastern India. These posts were set up with the object of reporting enemy aircraft attempting to raid Calcutta or other important centres of production and communication. Since the Indian telephone service was very restricted in scope the observer posts had to make their reports by wireless telegraphy, their only daily link with the outside world. Shovelton's experiences are interesting.

The life of the men on a wireless observer post in India was one of the loneliest possible. The nature of the work demanded that these posts should be situated far from the beaten track, and if the crew that manned them were to find existence endurable they must possess a great sense of team spirit and of humour. These two virtues, coupled with the fact that their wireless equipment did at least enable them to listen to the news bulletins, prevented them from going completely 'dippy'. Some posts had gramophones, but at critical moments the driving spring would shatter, or the appeal of a well-worn record of Joe Loss playing 'In the Mood' become unsatisfying.

Of course there were brighter moments. Once Shovelton's post had the joy of entertaining two nursing sisters to tea at a post far out in the jungle. The sisters were newly arrived from England and 'wanted to see how these poor boys existed'. Heavily escorted by four officers, they presented themselves to see half a dozen ordinary chaps (alerted as to the impending visit) who were very surprised to see each other looking well shaved and wearing freshly washed khaki drill. This was very different from the normal scruffy chin, bare hairy chest and a pair of repellent-looking shorts. Shovelton felt quite sure that the sisters left the post feeling that they were quite happy and keeping well and fit!

On a Sunday afternoon in late June—that is, in the full flush of the monsoon rain—the airmen were all feeling 'browned off'. Business was slack as the Japanese Air Force was not very keen about flying in monsoon weather. Too many turbulent clouds that, in their updraughts, could drag a wing clean off, and the driving rain that made observation almost impossible. There had been no mail for a fortnight, the cigarettes were mildewed and matches would not strike. To cap everything the petrol-electric generator had packed up and the post was 'off the air', something as tragic as the failure by an expert bomber crew to bomb an important target. Even the ministrations of Fred, the catering manager, who was quite an expert in dealing with internal combustion engines, produced no result. Fred was furious—even refusing his 'char' as he brooded over the engine's intransigence. Relief was to come with the arrival of the 'dood wallah'—the milkman. Like all Indians this citizen was working his usual racket—supplying milk that was 50 per cent dirty water—and charging the full price. Fred's eyes lighted up—he forgot the engine in his determination to give the 'dood wallah' hell. But there was the language difficulty. The more Fred shouted at the Indian that he wanted no more of his adulterated milk the more the Indian looked puzzled. The trouble was that Fred's Urdu was strictly limited. He started off with 'Nay dood kal', which in kitchen Urdu can be taken to mean 'No milk tomorrow'. But what Fred meant to say was that he wanted no more milk for several days as he proposed to use the condensed milk from the stores. So he proceeded to shout 'Nay dood kal kal kal', merely repeating the word 'tomorrow' three times. He got more and more furious as the Indian gawped at him, and finally drove him off the camp. By the time he had worked off his speen on the milkman Ted had forgotten his grievance against the engine. Harmony on the post was restored. As night fell and the rain continued its non-stop performance a pacified Fred put on his favourite record, 'I Hear You Calling Me', and climbed under his mosquito curtain to sleep.

It was not only the milkman who was a rogue. Fred and Harry were walking in the neighbouring bazaar when Harry, a North Countryman, spotted some pigeons. Here was something he knew and understood, as at home he had been a fancier. Quickly he paid three rupees (a most exorbitant sum—eight annas would have been ample) for the two birds he selected and took them back to camp. After an initiating period of a week in a home-made loft he released them. They promptly disappeared towards the bazaar and were not seen again. A few days later a 'travelling salesman' in pigeons appeared at the post. Harry bought two more pigeons, but this time for only two rupees. Put under training again the pigeons went off to the village the moment they were released. A few days later another pigeon salesman appeared, but by this time Harry had lost interest and the bottom dropped out of the pigeon market.

There were other animals that lived in the neighbourhood of the post—jackals, of course, but the tigers had to be taken seriously. They were often heard and sometimes seen. One afternoon two of them were spotted moving in a clearing below the post. After a while they settled down and lay basking in the sun. A careless herd-boy allowed his bullocks to wander near the edge of the scrub. This was too much

o

for the tigers, who immediately made a kill. The herd-boy's screams brought the villagers, who succeeded in scaring the tigers from the carcass, but the Indians were far too frightened to pull it into the village. Rather naturally, by the next morning the 'kill' had disappeared.

Shovelton and a friend had a rather more exciting experience when bathing in the local stream. This stream flowed deep and strong in the monsoon with fresh cool water from the hills. Carrying their towels and with cakes of soap in a bucket the airmen walked to the water and settled down to the business of having a real clean-up. Shovelton says:

> 'Midway through the delights of soaping and sluicing we heard a tiger snarl. Benny said: "Did t'ear yon? 'Twas a tiger, wasn't it?" There was another throaty growl and some movement about thirty yards upstream. "It's a tiger alreet, Arthur," said Benny. "Happen he's looking for his dinner—can't make up his mind which of us two'd be t'best. Don't blame him for liking neither, from what I can see on it there's nowt to choose 'tween thee and me!" It was high time to leave and by good luck we got away unharmed.'

From the heat of Bengal to the raw cold of the coast of Holland. As our armies advanced through the Low Countries it was necessary to establish radar stations for their protection against air attack. One of these was the 'Nelly' post in a Walcheren lighthouse named 'Domberg'. The orders relating to the establishment of this post were, as I have seen myself, most carefully drafted. The efficiency of the station and the comfort of the crew were the subject of much practical thought. Even Valor oil-stoves for heating an isolated and ice-cold structure suffering from considerable war damage were allowed for. In addition to the creature comforts there was a welfare pack of a wireless set, books and parlour games! Airmen of the Kaiser War had to make their own entertainment and were none the worse for doing so. Sometimes I think this welfare business is carried altogether too far. But I must admit that a shell-shattered lighthouse in November can hardly have been conducive to gracious living. The crew of the post consisted of a technical officer and eighteen other ranks of various trades. To guard the post one flight of No. 2804 Squadron Royal Air Force Regiment was detailed for the purpose. It is not clear from the records where these men lived. The lighthouse had the barest accommodation for the technical personnel. I have a ghastly vision of a tented camp, the canvas pale blue in colour from the ever-falling rain, and all its approaches hock deep in mud. In the background are a couple of Soyer stoves smoking away drearily and producing occasional jets of steam. Meanwhile the cook, sheltering as best as he can from the North Sea storm under a sheet of corrugated iron propped up on lumps of broken concrete, does his best to produce something warm for the men to eat. This 'station' is commonly reported to have been one of the most isolated ever manned by air force personnel. And yet one of the crew goes on record as saying that after a bad start owing to the difficult conditions a firm spirit of comradeship was built up. When the time came to move on the airmen were almost sorry to leave. Perhaps the thought of once more meeting the disciplinary sergeant-major, of having to shave every day, enduring a periodical haircut and conforming to the discipline of a regular unit, may have had some influence on this view.

Amongst the other airmen doing odd jobs No. 5026 Squadron—an airfield construction unit—certainly had an unusual experience. The squadron sailed from Britain in July 1945 with the intention of building an airstrip on Okinawa Island for the use of Tiger Force—the British contribution to the bombing of Japan. As it was nearing its destination news came of the Japanese surrender. Some days later the squadron was in Hong Kong, disarming Japanese occupation troops, cleaning up the island and generally making itself useful in the maintenance of law and order.

The airman is nothing if not versatile, and one of his virtues is his ability to turn his hand to cooking.

Flight Lieutenant D. H. G. Lyon, flying a Dakota on supply missions to the Burma front, pays tribute to Leading Aircraftsman Hopkins of No. 62 Squadron:

'The scene is the squadron officers' mess. The place Agartala in Eastern Bengal. The Christmas season of 1944 might have passed almost unnoticed by the pilots had it not been for the efforts of our mess cook, L.A.C. Hopkins. Normally he produced a three-course dinner that would have done credit to a West End London restaurant. He determined to make a supreme effort for Christmas. I think he felt he owed something to the aircrew who, almost daily, risked their lives over the Burmese jungle, while he lived in some security behind the lines. I am sure, however, that it was the aircrew who were in his debt. Working under conditions that would have defeated a lesser man, he produced on three successive nights, Christmas Eve, Christmas night and Boxing Day, a dinner for seventy officers of no less than twelve courses. Each of these courses was dished up delicately, as if it were being presented at Claridges Restaurant. He had only wood fires to cook upon and a small staff of Bengalis to help him. The heat was great and flies and mosquitoes were everywhere. Moreover there was little to cheer *him* up. He lived by himself in an annexe of the mess and all that he had to look forward to after this back-breaking labour was a string bed, a canvas basin and a bucket of tepid water.

He received little recognition for his efforts but he was that selfless type of person who seeks no reward.'

Aircraftsman McCarthy of the 14th Wing Headquarters, A.C. Hudson of Egyptian fame and L.A.C. Hopkins will undoubtedly go to that special part of heaven which is reserved for the best people!

There were others who served as humbly but most usefully. G. Shanks, a gardener by trade, enlisted in the hope that he would be able to fight the Germans—possibly hand to hand. Instead of which he found himself in charge of the station farm at Cranfield. Here he worked throughout the war, caring for forty-two acres of land and a piggery eighty strong. He must have had some help but at least he was a planner and a builder of quality. Think of the fresh vegetables, the chitterlings, the sausages and pork that his efforts placed on the aircrew mess tables! Did any of them thank him? I wonder! But at least he reached the rank of sergeant.

One of the other odd jobs that fell to the lot of R.A.F. airmen was that of wireless operator working behind the enemy lines. Corporal R. Jephson has allowed me to make use of this account of his experiences as a wireless operator with a Mission dropped in Croatia to help the Yugoslav Partisans. He was to spend over a year in forests and caves in the Balkan mountains and to learn to live in the hard way.

On the night of 18/19th May 1943 the First British Military Mission to the Yugoslav Partisans was parachuted from a Liberator of 136

Squadron into the heart of the mountainous part of Croatia near the enemy-held town of Ogulin. It consisted of three men, Major Jones and Captain Hunter (Army) and L.A.C. Jephson, W/O/M. (R.A.F.). The containers which were dropped held arms and ammunition, explosives, food, clothing, maps, etc., sufficient to tide the party over for an 'indefinite period', and last but not least a small wireless transmitter/receiver housed in an attaché case, along with a couple of car accumulators and a charging engine.

The circumstances which led up to the dispatch of this Mission are now history, but at the time such an expedition was certainly expected to be a 'one-way' trip, at least until the war was over. The war in the Middle East was almost at an end and the next step in the struggle in the Mediterranean was the assault on Italy itself, or anywhere else on the northern shores of the Mediterranean. In the Balkans it was whispered that Chetniks were waging a ceaseless guerilla war against the occupying Germans and Italians and that their activities might be joined into the Allied plan to facilitate an easier entry into Europe. These were the forces of General Mihailovitch, an anti-communist and pro-Yugoslav leader.

However, the British authorities in the Middle East were beginning to realize that all was not as it seemed in Yugoslavia. The Chetniks were doing little or nothing to justify themselves[1] and news was received of other guerillas farther north, who styled themselves 'Partisans' and who really were actively engaged in fighting the Germans and Italians, as well as numerous other forces such as the Bulgarians and Ustachi who had allied themselves with the Germans. Accordingly it was decided to send a mission into the area to contact the Partisans, survey the potentialities of the situation, and to maintain close contact with the Middle East on everything that happened. After a preliminary drop by Yugoslav 'Nationals', who reported favourably, the above-mentioned trio set out as accredited British representatives, and for them a great adventure began.

After a safe landing and a rest in a nearby burnt-out village they were taken many miles to the foot of the mountain range called Plesivica, where a long climb of several hours brought them to a wooded valley containing several wooden buildings and workshops. This sheltered the Partisan H.Q. Croatia, along with a small hospital, and was the Mission's home for a month until the enemy discovered

---

[1] There are two opinions on this point.

their whereabouts (possibly because of the two wireless transmitters, British and Partisan) and it had to leave. Dive-bombing by Stukas from the nearby aerodrome at Bihač speeded them on their way. However, reliable wireless contact was established although it was extremely difficult to do so because of the high trees in which they were hidden and the immense distance to Cairo. The range of a small one-valve transmitter from a six-volt car battery is a matter of some uncertainty! No doubt the height of the mountain helped considerably. It was there that Jephson realized what he had 'let himself in for'. The amount of information to be transmitted was immense and every word had to be transcribed into a very laborious code which took a considerable amount of time. Hours were spent daily and nightly working the wireless set and every minute in between was needed for coding and decoding. Jephson became lousy in a few days and soon began to long for some fresh vegetables instead of the black bread, beans and meat which was his staple diet. Little did he realize that a full year would pass before he saw any change in the food, and he lost weight steadily as long as he was in the country. The order to move came as a relief, and after telling Cairo he was closing down for a day the gear was packed and he strode down the mountainside happier than for a long time. By then he was beginning to understand the language and felt much less lonely when he could talk with the small band of troops who accompanied the H.Q. By that time Major Jones had left, and Captain Hunter's duties left Jephson a great deal of time on his own or with the Partisan wireless operator.

During the following months they moved frequently, always a few days ahead of the enemy, who discovered their whereabouts a little too late. The poor peasants who had sheltered the Mission had to take the brunt of the bombing intended for it! These peasants with whom they lived were kindness itself, and often shared their only food and drink to honour the 'Englizi'. Their homes were mere hovels, dirty and full of lice and bugs, and it was impossible in the circumstances to keep clean. Nearly every family had an uncle in America but their geographical knowledge was negligible and soon Jephson gave up trying to explain to them the course of the war and the general world situation. Maps meant little or nothing to them.

Welcome diversions were the arrival of fresh Missions who were dropped at places arranged by the early arrivals and after being briefed were sent on their way to other parts of the country. Among one such party was L.A.C. Smale (R.A.F.), who finally set up his wireless station in Dalmatia and Bosnia.

The arrival of aircraft during the early months was sporadic and very uncertain. Few were available (the number was actually four to supply the whole of the Balkans) and many fruitless vigils were spent night after night in the centre of bleak inhospitable valleys waiting in the rain for the hum of an aircraft which never came. Hope forbade packing up yet all knew in their hearts that such nights were hopeless. Sometimes, when the clouds were low, the aircraft would arrive and after searching in vain for the twinkle of the signal fires through the clouds would turn westwards towards the Adriatic and the ground party would be left disconsolate with nothing but the crackle of the fires to listen to. One such night an aircraft hit the top of a mountain and the whole crew perished. It took the Partisans a week to find the wreckage and snow had covered much of what was left. By some stroke of providence the only thing rescued from the crash was a small package stuck high in a tree. It was Jephson's mail! Thus another load of wood was wasted, and the Partisans had the difficulty of collecting enough wood for more fires without attracting unwelcome attention from enemy reconnaissance planes which suspected their purpose only too well but could never catch them red-handed. Often the fires would be lighted on hearing the hum of a plane, only to realize that this played straight into enemy hands and was just asking for a stick of bombs or a good shooting-up. On such occasions the ground party held its breath and prayed that the valley was deep enough for the fires to go unseen. To the staunch little band of firelighters it was heartbreaking to have to put their fires out after they had been carefully coaxed out of rain-soaked logs. Later a system of mutual recognition signals was evolved and the fires were left unlit until the party were sure of a shower of containers instead of bombs. During this period of small results the main worry was that the Partisans would lose heart or decide that it was not worth the expenditure of time and men for such small reward. However, they kept at it, and later were to be hard pressed to clear the dropping-ground of parachute containers before daybreak exposed the rendezvous to prying eyes.

By this time Jephson was an accepted Partisan, the 'Englez' who was as lousy and unwashed as the rest of them and who could talk and sing with them sufficiently well for a stranger to accept him as possibly a country cousin from a far corner of their land whose accent was not quite the same as the Lika accent.

The Italian capitulation was an occasion for great rejoicing throughout the entire countryside. For the Mission it was a period of great activity. Naturally, it was warned before the actual surrender, and Jephson will always remember the night on which he typed, on a captured German typewriter, an ultimatum to the local Italian Commander on the coast to surrender all men, stores, arms, ammunition, water and transport intact to the representatives of the Allied armies, the Partisans. It was a proud moment for them, and many new boots and uniforms appeared on the scene very quickly. Major Hunter (now promoted) met the Italians a little later and was surprised to see on the Commander's tunic amongst all his Italian medals the British ribbons of the 1914–18 War. Jephson joined the Major later and they made a quick tour of the coast from Sent to Fiume, where the Germans had rallied and recaptured most of the town. Fighting was still going on, and after visiting the suburbs of the town they returned inland. The Partisans held the coast for some months, but the expected Allied landing never came, so it was abandoned to the Germans who then had the onus of feeding the coast population.

The winter was fast approaching and the Major left to visit Marshal Tito. There he was given another assignment and Jephson was alone until the arrival of an I.S.L.D. (Inter-Services Liaison Department) Mission consisting of Captain Reed (Army) and a sergeant W/Op., also Army. They quickly settled down and the new faces were very welcome during the winter. The first snow came, and with it a crowd of ragged, starving, filthy British P.O.W.s, who had escaped from camps in Northern Italy. The Partisans were extremely sorry for them and did all they could to help from their slender resources but they were in need of better treatment than could be given after their experiences at the hands of the Italians. They were a big responsibility and it was a good moment when a Partisan boat smuggled them across to Bari under the very noses of the Germans.

As the campaign developed in Italy the movement of German divisions throughout the Balkans increased. Although at the time they were primarily concerned with their own troubles and not with the Partisans, the latter played havoc with their columns on the narrow mountain roads. The town of Otočac was evacuated only a few minutes before the advance column of a German division arrived, and most of a precious hoard of books, maps and papers was lost in the scramble. The wireless set was of paramount importance and was always the first thing to be packed when a hurried move was ordered. Its aerial was a constant worry and on one occasion the rope suspending it was frozen into a solid length of ice. It had to be 'cooked' in an oven to make it suitable for carrying in a pack. As the winter cold increased Jephson developed sores on his ankles which refused to heal and necessitated his wearing rubber slippers instead of the stout boots which were essential. He soon became unable to walk properly and his right leg swelled to nearly uniform thickness throughout its length. The food position steadily grew worse and the mainstay was bacon and beans. The taste of tea had long been forgotten and often on journeys on cold wet nights the Englishmen dreamed of mugs of it steaming hot. During an extremely bad blizzard lasting for several days the Mission was entirely snowbound and it was weeks before it could move freely again. As the spring approached the Allied bomber offensive increased and it was an inspiring sight to everyone to see streams of silver bombers passing high in the sky on their way to Austria and Northern Italy.

The next arrivals were 'shot down' American airmen who were collected from all over the countryside and were assembled in the next village waiting for the snow to clear sufficiently for the journey to the nearest landing strip at Bospetrovac, in Bosnia. At that time a visiting New Zealand doctor, Major Rogers, ordered Jephson out of the country as soon as he saw him, so he attached himself to the Americans and commenced the long journey south. The wireless set was left in the charge of the I.S.L.D. operator and Jephson never knew what happened to it. Throughout the previous twelve months it had never let him down and it had never failed to make contact with Cairo.

The party consisted of about twenty Americans and Jephson. They journeyed for several days through a countryside scarred with burned-out and deserted villages, and arrived after several days at the foot of a mountain range which lay between them and an enemy-held valley. The following night was nearly Jephson's last and only the kindly help of an American saved him. After a scanty meal of mutton soup the column set off at nightfall up the steep slopes at the foot of the mountain and the rubber slippers offered little grip on the icy snow. Walking with a pair of socks over them improved matters consider-ably. Reaching a pass over the top of the mountain the column staggered along the path in single file, bowing their heads to the driving snow and bitter wind. The Partisan company escort on this section of the journey must have been supermen. They zig-zagged along the route guarding the front, sides and rear, carrying machine-guns and mortars, yet never one faltered. It was learned afterwards that they did the trip every night, escorting various parties along this lifeline into Bosnia. One such party was passed going back into Croatia. It consisted of scores of wizened old women each carrying a captured German shell in her shawl and plodding along, surefooted, in her knitted woollen slippers. Towards daybreak the column had crossed the enemy-patrolled road but by then Jephson was almost done for. The Partisans had one thought, to get as far from that road as they could before broad daylight, but his frozen feet wouldn't take him. Every time he fell in the snow the American behind him hauled him up again and on he would totter, only to fall again. Finally he went down for good and wanted only to be left to sleep, which would have been fatal. The morning destination was still over five miles ahead, but that might as well have been five hundred miles. The American, who seemed to be Jephson's Guardian Angel (he never knew his name), gave him three pills and pushed them into his mouth with some snow. Within half an hour he felt new life in his limbs and was able to catch up with the rest of the party. The dose of benzedrine worked wonders, and carried him to the next village, called Martin Brod. There he ate prodigiously and slept for twenty-four hours. They were now safe, but a two-day journey was still ahead of them. It was a slow business but in the end Drvar was reached. There the British Military Mission under Brigadier MacLean welcomed and fed them and introduced everyone to Marshal Tito and a glass of *rakija* (plum brandy). There was no accommodation, however, so they had to continue the journey to Bospetrovac, near the landing strip. Here their troubles were almost ended. The snow was still deep, however, and although they tramped the five miles to the strip every night for a fortnight it wasn't until hope had almost gone that an American Dakota landed and took the party to Italy. After a month's rest in hospital Jephson was well on the road to recovery. A further month in Palestine made him quite well again. In June 1944 he heard that he had been awarded the Soviet Medal for Valour by the Russian Government. In November he was summoned to Rome to receive the award from Major-General Susloparav. By then he was Acting Sergeant and along with Corporal

Smale, who was awarded a similar, though not identical, decoration, went to the Embassy, where they were lavishly entertained by the Russians who were celebrating the twenty-seventh anniversary of the October Revolution.

This is a good story of duty carried out in the face of very considerable hardships. When he enlisted Jephson could hardly have imagined he would ever have to cope with snow, ice, lack of food, lack of elementary cleansing facilities and a diet as monotonous as it was disagreeable. None of his early training in Britain would have helped him to meet trials of this nature. Yet his British guts pulled him through where many another nationality would have failed. But credit is due to the unknown American and his benzedrine pills!

Leaving the Balkans for Bengal, but maintaining the bug and lice theme, here are some facts about the airmen's life in that salubrious region. Henry Franks has the following observations to make:

'The men suffered severely from prickly heat, and the medical orderly, either to show off his artistic ability or to keep up their spirits, applied the gentian violet to the rashes in designs, according to what the shape of the eruption suggested to his fancy. Thus, walking across the dispersal, it was possible to distinguish which aircraft you were passing according to whether the back of the nearest mechanic was decorated with Mickey Mouse, Churchill, or Betty Grable!'

The hutments were of course alive with insects of all kinds. The airmen used to stand the feet of their beds in tins of 100-octane petrol to discourage the bugs from climbing up them. This worked very well till one night an absent-minded airman dropped a cigarette end in one of the cans, and the whole hut was only saved from conflagration by throwing bed and bedding straight out of the nearest window. The airman responsible had a narrow escape from following his bedding out into the night.

On one occasion the grass of the dispersal caught fire, endangering the aircraft. The airmen snatched off their shorts and with them beat out the flames. 'Fortunately they were still wearing their hats, so could not be charged with being improperly dressed!'

The work of the wireless interception service, generally called the 'Y' service for short, would need a whole book to itself—and then could not be made public for security reasons. This was another of the odd jobs, though a most important one. It was by no means the sole prerogative of the R.A.F. It covered all three fighting services and many other government departments as well. But for certain purposes particular to itself the R.A.F. made great use of its experts.

Walter Schwartz was one of these. In June of 1942 he was a civilian in Egypt. Being a German scholar he was invited to join some indeterminate organization connected with the R.A.F. He was first introduced to a very smart sergeant-major who 'gave him the once-over' and then handed him over to an officer. This individual was not very helpful. He told Schwartz that he knew nothing of what was expected of him, and finally told him to go and find out.

Schwartz joined a small detachment whose main interest seemed to be in wireless reception. He was put on to taking down messages transmitted by the German Air Force, apparently referring to weather conditions, but nobody could break the code in which they were sent. Shortly afterwards he was sent to an advanced field unit at Gambut where less brains and more guts were needed. There, as a German scholar, Schwartz could read the enemy airmen's plain language radiotelephony signals and so follow their movements. Unfortunately nobody had thought to provide his unit with good communications to the British fighter-control centre, so the information he gathered was wasted.

When the retreat to Alamein began he was one of the last to leave, with German tanks on the near horizon. In his account of this period he speaks feelingly of 'that giant, sullen column moving eastwards, composed of Britishers, South Africans, Australians, New Zealanders, French and Poles'.

On reaching his base he says he found a scene of vast confusion —but very shortly was ordered westwards again. General Montgomery had taken charge! His re-formed unit consisted of half a dozen linguists, one W/T mechanic, two wireless operators for communication purposes, a cook, an aircraft hand and Dukie the dog.

The unit soon began to 'crack' the German codes. In particular the German system of aircraft control was solved by plotting the position of the enemy ground observers, and so establishing the grid references in the R/T signals. The preliminaries to enemy bomb raids were also established as the bombers formed up over their airfields. This information was passed on, but nobody seemed interested until

Headquarters awoke to its significance. Direct communications were at once established with fighter control and the success story began! As well as plotting the enemy for the benefit of our fighters the position of our own shot-down aircraft was established and the Air/Sea Rescue Service alerted. In this way many of our aircrew were saved. After Alamein the Germans became stricter in their R/T discipline and also began to 'fox' our 'Y' service. The reference grid was frequently changed—ultimately every three days. Under the pressure of Allied successes things became slacker. Young pilots, new to the front, betrayed themselves by their screeching, nervous speech, very different from the quiet controlled words of their leaders. These young ones would tell each other long stories about their operations, giving away their positions, their losses and the location of their bases.

Very high-frequency radio transmissions sometimes caused confusion. On occasion transmissions from German squadrons in South Russia were heard 'loud and clear'!

Schwartz sums up the unit's success by saying: 'We were fortunate that our group was homogeneous. We were almost all Jewish volunteers from Palestine, born in Germany and our mother tongue was German. We mastered every intricacy of the language, including dialects and slang.'

Wireless interception, established by the British Admiralty in the Kaiser War to our great advantage, has been developed through the years. In the Hitler War it gave each side, but more particularly the British, advanced information of enemy operations. Our advantage in both wars was almost entirely due to our better wireless discipline. In this work thousands of men and women in the ranks served their country laboriously but magnificently. Their work still goes on— without rest and without haste—but always a jump ahead of our adversaries.

One of the very odd and dangerous jobs carried out by a group of airmen was the establishment of a landing area on the frozen surface of Lake Lezjascog during the short-lived Norwegian campaign of 1940.

After the British occupation of the harbour of Andalsnaes, a party of men belonging to No. 263 Gladiator Squadron was rushed up-country to the lake where reconnaissance had indicated that it was possible to establish a 'landing ground' on the ice. Petrol and oil were ferried to the lake in the few vehicles available and about a dozen Gladiators flew in from the aircraft-carrier that had brought them to the coast. From the lake the Gladiators endeavoured to give air-cover to our troops who were advancing inland with the intention of capturing Trondhjem Harbour. Soon, however, the Luftwaffe found them, and without any early warning system, and in a semi-hostile area, aircrew and airmen were fighting for their lives. Refuelling the aircraft out of four-gallon tins in a freezing temperature, swinging the airscrews to start the engines as their predecessors had done in the Kaiser War, since electric starters were in short supply, and all the while wallowing knee-deep in snow, No. 263's men put up a very fine show. There were some weaklings, but not the fitter who went round scrounging batteries from disabled vehicles and so kept the electric starters going for a while. But the task was beyond human endurance. Even the courage and leadership of the C.O., Squadron Leader Donaldson, could not avail. Abandoning the wreckage of their aircraft which had been destroyed on the ice—but not in the air—the tattered remnants of the squadron found their way back to Andalsnaes.

If before the war airmen had been asked if one of their duties from 1939 onwards would have been the disposal of unexploded bombs they would either have ridiculed the suggestion or expressed grave concern at being called upon to perform such dangerous duties. And yet Bomb Disposal was one of the more important activities of the R.A.F. It was a 'cold-blooded job' and has been well described in a book with that title.

Squadron Leader A. E. Haarer, who wrote this story, pays tribute to Wing Commander Harrison, George Cross. Harrison may be re-garded as the leader of the gallant company who, at home and abroad, kept airfields operational after they had been attacked from the air with delayed-action bombs and also removed the apparent 'duds' that might indeed be 'duds' but equally well might be D.A. This work was shared with the Royal Engineers, the airmen being respon-sible for clearing airfields and the Sappers for everything outside them. Sometimes the B.D. squads were summoned on a false alarm. A hole in the middle of one of our bomb dumps proved to have been dug by a rabbit. With his tongue in his cheek Haarer made his men dig deep, thus gaining practice in shoring up the sides of an excavation made in sliding sand. At other times the job was beyond them, as when a 1000-pounder worked its way down into the watery gravel lying below Poling Radar Station. An attempt to dig down to it would have been ineffective as the bomb would have continued to slip deeper and deeper into the watery mess. The time-delay bombs and those with an anti-disturbance booby trap were really fiendish devices. To deal with them successfully required a very high standard of training, the strictest discipline, care of a magistral kind and cold-blooded and calculating courage. The principle upon which the Bomb Disposal organization worked was that the enemy, with their booby-trap devices, were out to kill skilled men and so hamper our war effort. Any B.D. man who got himself killed was playing into enemy hands. So—he must not get himself killed; otherwise he was failing in his duty to the nation.

Of course the B.D. men received help from our intelligence service. Possibly the slave labour working in the German armament factories formed the source of the information that filtered through to England. In one case a large number of German bomb fuses were obtained by our intelligence service, either by capture or other means, and tampered with by our armament people. These fuses were then shipped across to France by other devious means and placed in the hands of the Resistance Movements, so carefully re-packed in their German containers that they were inspection-proof. It was then the business of the 'Resistance' to get the boxes back into German munition stores. Issued from here to enemy squadrons and placed on their aircraft, when the bomb-aimers armed the bombs preparatory to launching them— well! A very loud bang and 'one more German aircraft less'! Think then of the courage of our agents, or of the resisters who succeeded in planting these boxes of doctored fuses in a well-guarded enemy ammunition store. Think too of the ingenuity of the individuals who conceived of such a scheme and carried it out with the help of a thousand others, pilots flying at night over France and dropping the boxes, men who collected and stored them, other men who, with even greater ingenuity, added them to the store of enemy explosives.

Probably the area attacked by aircraft bombs that was most concentrated in time and space was the island of Malta. There indeed Bomb Disposal found full scope for its activities. To me, living in the comparative security of England at this time, the manner in which the Royal Air Force kept going during the height of the enemy blitz is one of the most remarkable examples of endurance on the part of the airmen. On short rations, with no amenities even of the limited Home standard, and with their normal airfield organization in ruins around them, they kept the Spitfires, Hurricanes, Wellingtons and Beauforts alive and operational. The exploding bombs did harm enough, but the U.X.B.s were almost a greater bugbear. Names crop up in the citations in the *London Gazette*, of which there are at least eleven. Flight Sergeant Hanford, Corporals Aitken, Mason and O'Brien seem to have been particularly to the fore in dealing with 'the terror underground'. Indeed, in the most difficult circumstances they helped to keep the airfields serviceable and so contributed to our success in the Mediterranean.

Another very gallant airman, Warrant Officer E. G. Hunt, was at an airfield that suffered six attacks. He dealt with the U.X.B.s, one of which went off and knocked him over with its blast. Regardless of his injuries, which fortunately were not too serious, he continued with his work. The citation supporting the grant of the George Medal says, 'he showed a complete disregard for his own safety, and his gallant actions kept the airfield serviceable'. Excitement can keep men in a frame of mind where they can perform acts of outstanding courage. But this cold-blooded business of sterilizing bombs that at any moment might bring death and destruction calls for bravery of a much higher order.

Of all the bombs dropped by the enemy the 'Butterfly' seems to have presented the disposal squads with their most difficult problem. The 'Butterfly' was a small object, quite unlike the conventional bomb and obviously the product of a sadistic and distorted mind, only vaguely resembling its namesake. When dropped in large numbers on an airfield it put a stop to all operations until each one had been destroyed. After a first lucky experience when an airman, greatly daring, succeeded in disarming eight of them, orders were given that they should be destroyed where they lay. This meant putting a slab of gun-cotton, duly primed, as close as possible to the bomb and then blowing it up. In fact, in B.D.S. parlance, 'popping it off'!

By Courtesy of the Imperial War Museum

A.A. gunner of R.A.F. Regiment

'Blimey! Who cross-threaded this nut?'

By Courtesy of the Imperial War Museum

'Is that our kite?'

20

Fatigues

HUNDREDS and thousands of airmen past and present may well feel that the subject of 'fatigues' is entitled to a chapter to itself, if only because it was and is the most hated aspect of military service.

In the story of the early days of the R.F.C. and of the apprentice school at Halton, there have already been glancing references to this burning subject. Some airmen suffered fatigues more hardly than others. I remember one man named White who, when invited by Sergeant-Major Street to dig a hole for the disposal of refuse, retorted that he hadn't joined the Flying Service to dig holes. After expiating his crime of 'refusing to obey an order' by passing fourteen days in detention, White remained a convinced dissenter and so spent some unhappy periods during his military service. Most men, reasonably enough, realized that someone had to do the less-skilled jobs, and while grumbling furiously, got on with the business. These tasks sometimes produced unusual associations. One airman with a taste for writing makes the following contribution:

'Various "fatigues" were performed by the men, and although many of these were of light type, consisting of helping in the cookhouse for a short time, followed by "skating" off on a bike to the town for buns and coffee at the best restaurant, there was a category of jobs which were not so welcome. The weekly collection of rubbish from the billets scattered in the village was one of these chores. It consisted of taking a R.A.F. covered truck round the various houses commandeered by the R.A.F. for W.A.A.F. and R.A.F. billets, and emptying their dustbins, as this job was not undertaken by the local Council who were fighting another War! I well remember being in the company of three other airmen, one being a barrister in Civvy Street, another a chartered accountant, and the third a publican. We four sweated and swore at the heavy dustbins and eventually returned to camp on top of a load of motley rubbish, not too sweet-smelling at that.'

The other 'heavy' operation was the most hated of all. In the winter, from time to time, the Station H.Q. would receive an ultimatum from the local railway office that a truckload of coke had better be moved from their premises, or else! The Disciplinary Flight Sergeant, told by the C.O. to get cracking, passed the order on by detailing a party to take a lorry and repair to the station yard pronto! These men put on the most disgraceful clothes they possessed and climbed into the truck full of coke. Shovelling heavy lumps of coke from a truck into a lorry is not pleasant work and after an hour or so of this procedure the men had about enough and thought of a visit to the canteen! The coke dust got everywhere into the clothes and through them and especially on to the scalp, where it felt as though the hair was being cut off at the roots. A solution to this problem was to wear a 'cap comforter', that service-issue woollen hat which most recruits start by putting round their necks under the impression that it is a sort of scarf. Of course, no one imagined that they were martyrs, knowing what the lads were undergoing overseas, especially as one or two of the fatigue party had returned from North Africa where, they said, the 'ration run' consisted of about two hundred miles in the scorching sun to fetch the necessary goods. 'Coking' then took on almost the aura of a luxury!

A more enjoyable fatigue involved a visit to the officers' mess, a private house on the main road, and there helping the W.A.A.F. orderlies generally, which included 'spells' off to drink tea, and to be entertained by the girls' artless chatter about the officers. One lass was a real dyed-in-the-wool Cockney from the East End, her impromptu humour was typical, and her yarns abounded in malapropisms. On one occasion the officers held a party at the mess, and it ended as usual rather roughly, the climax apparently being a fight with fire extinguishers, which did the walls no good at all. The W.A.A.F. retailed all this with great contempt of such conduct, and finished with the comment that 'But what can you expect from such an illiterate lot!'

Coal fatigues, cookhouse fatigues, chores of every kind, these all fell to the lot of the airman, whether skilled or unskilled, at one time or another. It was and is a 'levelling' experience and certainly does no harm to the individual, apart from blistered hands and an aching back. Most of us carry out these same duties in our own homes today—so why not in the services too!

But I will admit that two airmen, who in the early part of the Kaiser War had managed an over-all wash in considerable comfort, suffered very badly when, in their clean and scented condition (Life-buoy soap!), they were ordered by the sergeant-major to dig new latrines for the officers' mess. And in the pouring rain as well!

21

Airmen as Infantry and Gunners

I N THE Kaiser War the airfields of the R.F.C. and R.A.F. lay secure
under the cover provided by the Army.

But in the Hitler War the tactics of infiltration, of outflanking,
indeed of landing parachute troops well behind the battle front, as
practised by our enemies produced a very different situation.

Even before the evacuation from Dunkirk the Air Ministry, reading the lessons of the German invasion of Holland, had decided to
establish a Directorate of Ground Defence, to organize what had
become so obviously necessary. This directorate came into being on
27th May 1940, and with the prospect of invasion immediately before
it concentrated in the first instance on obtaining resources for ground
defence. Small-arms were, however, at a premium. At this time the
Prime Minister wrote:

> 'Every man in Air Force uniform ought to be armed with
> something, a rifle, a tommy-gun, a pistol, a pike, or a mace. . . .
> Every airman should have a place in the defence scheme. . . . It
> must be understood by all ranks that they are expected to fight
> and die in defence of their airfields. The enormous mass of non-
> combatant personnel who look after the very few heroic pilots
> who alone in ordinary circumstances do all the fighting is an
> inherent difficulty in the organization of the Air Force. Here is a
> chance for this great mass to add a fighting quality to the necessary
> services they perform. Every airfield should be a stronghold of
> airgroundmen, and not the abode of uniformed civilians in the
> prime of life protected by detachments of soldiers.'

No time was lost in organizing and training station personnel for
ground combat. Every effort was made to obtain the necessary weapons

and, incredible though it may now seem, pikes were ordered and issued where other weapons could not be provided.

The War Office was asked to allot troops for the defence of airfields but, faced with the task of rebuilding the Army, it is not surprising that only 'garrison troops' and almost untrained 'young soldier battalions' could be spared. The R.A.F. personnel were to 'back up' the Army troops, and to augment them an element of R.A.F. personnel for full-time ground-defence duties was established. The officers were drawn from the Administrative and Special Duties Branch, and labelled 'A. and S.D./Defence', and the airmen were in a subdivision of the Aircrafthand trade as 'A.C.H./Ground Gunner'. Army officers of the category that could be spared were lent for 'Local Defence Adviser' duties at airfields.

There was also a call at this time for airmen to man anti-aircraft weapons on merchant ships and the trawlers and drifters that the Admiralty were using to escort the coastal convoys. For example Corporal Thomas Mould, who was one of the earliest airmen to be detailed for this work, spent over two years as a gun's crew on a drifter. During this time he shot down two JU88s that were attacking a convoy and damaged three others. As a reward he was given the Distinguished Service Medal. In February 1942 A.C.1 George Cottrill was machine-gunner on a ship which was subjected to a series of dive-bomb attacks during a period of four hours. He used his gun with great skill and his courageous and determined conduct inspired his fellow gunners so that, after the first attack, the E.A. kept at a respectful distance. Cottrill brought one down and the ship reached port safely. For his courageous action he got the Military Medal. There were many others like these two acting as gunners up and down the world and their story will be told later.

At first the ground defence of our airfields did not work very well.

Divided control, short-notice withdrawal of troops from airfields to meet emergencies elsewhere, and the diversion of technicians from their primary tasks were factors that took their toll. The Air Ministry asked the War Office to appoint a senior officer to watch over the development of ground-defence arrangements at airfields and other installations, and Major-General (later Sir) Claude Liardet, who had been commanding an anti-invasion Division on the south coast, was appointed to the staff of the G.O.C.-in-C. Home Forces as 'Inspector of Aerodrome Defences'.

In July 1941 the Defence Committee (Operations) set up a sub-committee to examine and report on the defence of airfields. Their salient recommendations were that the Army should be responsible for 'area' defence, but that the R.A.F. should be responsible for its local defence, and to this end there should be an 'Aerodrome Defence Corps' to form the 'core' of the defence at the more vulnerable stations. If the War Office did not wish to form the corps under the conditions suggested, the Air Ministry should do so with War Office assistance in the initial stages.

In due course it was agreed that the Air Ministry should form and sponsor this Corps, and in January 1942 a submission was made to His Late Majesty King George VI. To avoid the uninspiring word 'defence' the title 'Royal Air Force Regiment' was proposed, and a Royal Warrant was promulgated.

Little time was lost in implementing this high-level decision. The R.A.F. Regiment was formally established in the following month, and in it were incorporated all officers of the A. and S.D./Defence Branch and all A.C.H./ground gunners. Major-General Liardet, who, at the request of the Air Ministry, had been lent to the Royal Air Force, was appointed Director-General of Ground Defence, Air Ministry, and Commandant R.A.F. Regiment. The War Office also agreed to the transfer of a number of army officers, and even more were lent to the new Regiment for the period of its initial development.

A depot was opened at a requisitioned holiday camp at Filey in Yorkshire, and staffed in the early stages by instructors generously lent by the Brigade of Guards. The Royal Marines at Deal also contributed by training warrant officers and senior N.C.O.s. A few months later the depot moved to Belton Park near Grantham, and Filey became the school of anti-aircraft gunnery. At this time all weapon supplies were earmarked for long-established claimants, and the R.A.F. Regiment had to train and fight with the weapons it could get. For the most part these were arms discarded by re-equipped army units, but many strange items—such as ex-French '75' field guns and Smith guns—were acquired. The supply position in some measure influenced the organization of units, which was almost as varied as their equipment. Nevertheless, they were formed with the rapidity so urgently necessary.

The first task of the Regiment was to relieve army garrisons at airfields and R.A.F. installations in the United Kingdom, and this was completed in a few months.

While Regiment units were finding their feet in the United Kingdom, senior officers were sent to the Middle East to organize the Corps in that theatre. There were already some armoured-car companies and the Iraq Levies (from 'air control' days), and A. & S.D./defence officers and A.C.H./ground gunners, giving valuable service in that area.

So rapid was the development of the Regiment that it was possible in November 1942 to send five infantry-type squadrons and five machine-gun A.A. flights with the North African expedition. In these operations they gave a very good account of themselves. During 1943, the first full year of the Regiment's existence, its squadrons and flights, from Alamein to Tripoli, and from Algiers to Cape Bon, protected airfields from ground and low-flying air attack and cleared up minefields and booby-traps. In some cases they seized airfields in advance of the Army, and captured 3000 prisoners in the process. Meanwhile in India further squadrons of the Regiment were being formed as part of the defence against the Japanese advance on Delhi. Fortunately these units found greater scope when the 14th Army not only halted the Japanese attack but finally drove the enemy out of Burma and accepted his surrender at Singapore.

Throughout the battle of Imphal, the prelude to our advance, the Regiment guarded our airfields, and on occasion fought the Japanese infiltrators at close quarters. Later, it distinguished itself during the battle of Meiktila. Some hundreds of the Regiment had been flown in to guard the airfield which, precariously enough, the R.A.F. were attempting to operate. This airfield was behind the main Japanese battle front, and was from time to time the scene of fierce hand-to-hand fighting. The only recorded occasion of an airfield controller leaning out of the control tower and shooting an enemy graces the story of the battle for Meiktila.

By day the terrain would be cleared and the Dakotas would dive in to land, throw out their supplies and take off again with the minimum of delay. By night the enemy would filter back and next morning the Regiment squadrons would have to carry out the cleansing operation once again. Casualties had reduced their numbers, their gallant Wing Commander was killed early on, but seventy of them annihilated a Japanese force estimated at well over a hundred strong.

I landed at Meiktila shortly after the fighting was over and before the dead had been buried. It was a fantastic scene. Along every ditch, by every bit of cover, Japanese bodies lay in rows. They had been mown down, beaten down by equal or even lesser numbers of British troops, not least among whom were the men of the R.A.F. Regiment.

By the time the 'Second Front' was due to be opened the Regiment had grown to 85,000 officers and airmen.

Preparations for the invasion of North-West Europe were accelerated and about 40,000 R.A.F. Regiment personnel were transferred to the Army to augment the forces available for the land assault. Air attack on the United Kingdom was not, however, immediately to stop. The German pilotless aircraft—the 'buzz bomb'—made its appearance, and the majority of light anti-aircraft squadrons of the Regiment were deployed between the coast and London, and added to the considerable bag of these weapons brought down by fighter aircraft.

On 6th June the first L.A.A. squadrons moved with the assault forces to protect bridgehead airfields across the Channel. At first the Regiment was primarily committed to A.A. defence, but as the Luftwaffe weakened the L.A.A. role became a secondary consideration. Forward airfields were given protection against snipers, raiders and saboteurs, and R.A.F. technical units following closely upon the advancing armies were escorted. By-passed pockets of enemy forces were mopped up.

In December, during the counter-offensive launched in the Ardennes by Field Marshal von Runstedt, R.A.F. radar units found themselves directly in the path of his attack. These were in serious danger of losing their secret technical equipment to the enemy, but in the face of many difficulties they were extricated by Regiment units.

1945 began with sharp proof that the German Air Force was not yet finished with. On 1st January the Luftwaffe launched a concerted attack on airfields in Belgium and Holland. Formations of up to fifty fighters and fighter-bombers delivered tree-top assaults on eleven airfields. The action lasted an hour and a half, and in that time the Regiment shot down twenty-seven aircraft and damaged fifty-four others.

In May, as a fitting climax to this campaign, the Regiment received orders to occupy all airfields in Schleswig-Holstein up to the Danish frontier. In nine columns they moved ahead of the spearheads of the

2nd Army and completed their tasks. They took the surrender of some 20,000 German troops, 1000 aircraft and enormous quantities of stores.

In the post-war period the Regiment has maintained its war-time traditions. R.A.F. Regiment officers took over completely from army officers in the re-titled R.A.F. Levies (Iraq) and the Aden Protectorate Levies. A new 'levy' force was formed to take over from Regiment squadrons disbanding in South-East Asia, and this was by Royal Warrant entitled 'The Royal Air Force Regiment (Malaya)'. The R.A.F. Armoured Car Companies were incorporated in the Regiment, and the R.A.F. Regiment Depot was moved to its permanent home at Catterick.

On 1st April 1949, the thirty-first anniversary of the formation of the Royal Air Force, the R.A.F. Regiment was accorded the honour of Mounting the Guard at Buckingham Palace, and on her accession Her Majesty Queen Elizabeth II honoured the Regiment by assuming the appointment of Air Commodore-in-Chief. On 17th March 1953, in the ballroom of Buckingham Palace, the Queen presented The Queen's Colour for the Royal Air Force Regiment to a representative detachment.

The Regiment has been chosen to provide numerous displays at the S.S.A.F.A. searchlight tattoo and at the Royal Tournament, the Edinburgh Festival, and in France and Portugal. On each occasion when a Regiment detachment appeared at one of these displays it showed its efficiency and 'cocky' pride. As it marched out of the arena, with arms at the slope, it fired a crashing volley. As the French would say, '*Ils sont partis comme un pêt.*'

The life of the post-war Regiment has, however, by no means been confined to ceremonial. It has served actively in Malaya, Iraq, Egypt, Jordan, Kenya, Aden, the Persian Gulf, Gan and Cyprus, and the nature of its contribution in times of so-called peace is reflected in the honours and awards conferred upon its members in the years between the end of the war and up to April 1960: C.B.s 3, C.B.E.s 3, O.B.E.s 9, M.B.E.s 25, M.C.s 5, M.M.s 7, B.E.M.s 14 and Mentions in Dispatches 56.

Changes in policy have been followed by changes in organization. 'Levies' have passed from R.A.F. Regiment control. The Corps now consists of Field Squadrons, L.A.A. Squadrons, Helicopter Squadron Detachments and Crash Fire and Rescue Detachments.

The R.A.F. Regiment's proudest boast is that—albeit a Corps and not a Branch—it has the honour to be an integral part of the Royal Air Force, one and indivisible.

But the Regiment was and is composed of men trained in infantry and anti-aircraft duties. Backing them up were the ordinary airmen whose education in these military matters was, to say the least, elementary. In spite of this limitation many of them were to prove themselves as fighting men. The story follows.

In Iraq, the isolated R.A.F. stations ran some risk if the Iraqis decided that the German star was in the ascendant and in consequence hopped on our enemy's band-wagon. There was no army to defend these stations, only the levies and the airmen, the latter unskilled in using weapons.

The defence of Habbaniyeh Air Station—a successful defence—is therefore something of which the R.A.F. is justly proud.

The cantonment and the airfield lie on flat land overlooked by a ridge which is well within gunshot. Thus, when the recreant Iraqis occupied the ridge their artillery was in a position to deny the use of the airfield to our aircraft—mainly training types—and also to bombard the barracks.

Under the leadership of their commanding officer the airmen organized themselves for war. On 2nd May 1941 they suffered their first casualty. A man bombing up an aircraft with which to attack the Iraqis was hit by a shell—one of those fluke shots that are sometimes achieved by the worst of artillery men—as indeed the enemy were to prove themselves. As a protection against further bombardment beds were piled with kit-boxes and men slept underneath—only to be devoured by mosquitoes. A leading aircraftsman, in charge of tea-making, had so powerful a voice that when he shouted 'Char up' a panic started. For this he received fourteen days' confinement to camp—a somewhat superfluous punishment, in view of the siege that was being conducted by the enemy. He would of course lose fourteen days' pay—but if he had drawn it where could he spend it?

Another airman was running across the parade ground during an alert, anxious only to get to the nearest dug-out. A disciplinary sergeant-major, himself half underground, popped out to tick the airman off for having his stockings round his ankles! And, lastly, there was the native cook, probably an Indian, who was found hiding from the bombardment in a refrigerator!

There was serious work in the air. All manner of training aircraft were equipped with lethal devices with which to dishearten the Iraqis. In spite of a favourable tactical position, of the possession of artillery which usually is superior in close quarters to air bombardment, the enemy were first discouraged, and then, when regular British troops became available, most soundly trounced. Habbaniyeh Air Station remained inviolate.

In two wars I have observed the Arab. I have also read about his past triumphs in the days of Salah-ed-din. Then the best mathematicians, writers, scientists and astronomers were Arabs. What are they today? The Arab myth propagated by Lawrence of Arabia has been debunked many times, and there are few Europeans who have much respect for the Egyptian or the Iraqi Arab. Is it that disease, venereal or malarial, has sapped the quality and character of this ancient people? Whatever the cause there is no doubt that the glory has departed. No Nasser, no Kassim, no other trumpery dictator can restore the Arabs' situation.

Now to Greece, Crete, Cos and Simi—all in the Eastern Mediterranean.

Courage in defeat has usually been an attribute of the British 'troop'. During the débâcle in Greece and Crete when the Germans drove the ill-armed and outnumbered Greeks and British forces either into prison camps or in draggle-tailed rout to Egypt, there were many instances where the greatest courage and determination were shown by our men. Here is a story of what R.A.F. ground crews could achieve in their own field. The story-teller is L. Robinson, an L.A.C. electrician in No. 11 Squadron during 1940–1. At the date of this account the Greek Army had capitulated, and the two airfields near Athens were being evacuated under almost constant air attack:

'Evacuation started on Tuesday 22nd April 1941 from Menidi. The 23rd dawned with Fred Archer, Corporal Dickenson, Porky Blyth, a small Flight-Sergeant Fitter (I can't remember his name) and myself left as a sort of Demolition party. The Jerries completed the job for us and left only a very-much-shot-up short-nose Blenheim, port cowling missing, oil leaking out, and some cockpit instruments missing. As well as a very flat tyre it was full of holes. Also the cockpit hood would not slide shut.

As time went on in between ME109 raids we seriously considered trying to get this kite into the air. During a lull in the proceedings a pilot appeared who had previously been shot down and said that if we could service the Blenheim up to a point, he would get it and us into the air.

One thing I remember very clearly is a great hoarding carrying a poster of 'Vote for General Metaxas' slap bang in the line of take-off and it presented a problem. Late in the afternoon we all scrambled into the Blenheim, now capable of flight. Porky Blyth was in the turret, Fred Archer in the bomb-well, and Corporal Dickenson somewhere in the nether regions. Myself, in the nose complete with instructions as to the course and colours of the day (which I made a complete balls of).

We ran up the engines that grunted and groaned, the wing flapped and we charged at the image of the General on the hoarding. I swear to this day that we passed through his left ear-hole (if you remember he died shortly afterwards). We took off during a raid on the port of Athens but they were too busy to bother with us.

We wallowed along at sea level partly from choice and partly from circumstances, and as the shipping was pretty active I fired the colours of the day at a destroyer and was greeted by a very fine burst of naval ack-ack and some unprintable abuse from the pilot (I had got the colours mixed up).

We steered by visual map-reading, by spotting the islands en route and by the sun (the compass was U/S), and finally we located Crete with a very much overheated engine owing no doubt to the oil leak.

After cruising around for a little time we spotted Heraklion strip and prepared to come in (downwind, I think) only to see a perishing clot in a steam-roller systematically rolling the surface. When he saw us he nipped away smartly, leaving us and the roller to fight it out.

We got down after a fashion, churned off the runway and came to an ungraceful stop in the grass and shrubs at the end of the runway.

After getting out gingerly we dashed off into the rocks as some flipping Huns decided to have a look more closely at the strip.

The pilot and I some time later set fire to the A/C as it was U/S and the Jerry was now very obviously in charge of the situation.

One thing I always think about: not one of us had the faintest idea whether we had enough petrol for the trip. It wasn't even checked as far as I know.'

Crete was not exactly a health resort when the airmen evacuated from Greece eventually got there. The main airfield was at Maleme and it was here that most of the fighting took place. Here, too, Flight Sergeant Salmon and his men struggled to maintain the serviceability of the few Hurricanes of No. 33 Squadron that had escaped from Greece. On 13th May Maleme was continuously under attack by a large force of enemy fighters. In spite of these attacks the work went on, and in the few quiet intervals Salmon kept up morale by organizing games! He was one of that magnificent body of regular N.C.O.s who were the backbone of the ground services.

On 19th May the last surviving Hurricane left for Egypt and on the 20th the invasion of Crete began. The airmen fought as infantry. Upon them descended the parachutists and gliders. In one slit trench eight airmen held off thirty of the enemy and killed thirteen. When their ammunition ran out Aircraftsmen Eaton and Jones volunteered to fetch some more. As they left the trench Eaton was killed, but Jones collected a bandolier of fifty rounds he had seen hanging on a tree. When these fifty rounds had been fired the four survivors withdrew and joined the main body that was composed of a mixture of New Zealanders and R.A.F. While the battle was on Corporal George Banfield, the telephone lines destroyed, kept up communications by W/T with Headquarters at Heraklion. For three days he worked in a tent without any protection, getting his food and drink as best he could. When our airmen withdrew from the airfield Banfield was with them. In the hills round Maleme a defensive position was formed and on the 23rd the Germans attacked. The survivors of No. 33 Squadron, with the New Zealanders, carried out a bayonet charge that almost recaptured the airfield. Casualties were heavy. A further withdrawal then became necessary and Banfield found himself in command of fifty airmen. His party was cut off from the main body at Heraklion, and had to fight its way through the encircling Germans. In this operation Banfield displayed not only bravery but a very good knowledge of tactics. Enemy posts were outflanked, destroyed and prisoners were captured. When his party was halted by the Heraklion defences he led a small group up to the wire and identified himself and his gallant fifty.

In this fighting No. 33, in addition to casualties in the air, lost half its ground crews! On 1st June in Egypt, where the tattered remnants of the squadron had been evacuated by the Royal Navy, the roll-call showed seven pilots and some fifty airmen as survivors.

From Crete to the islands of Cos and Simi in the Aegean. Of the wisdom of sending an unsupported fighter squadron to operate from an island only a short distance from an undefeated enemy air force, and without any early warning system, history will speak at a later date. Suffice to say that No. 74 Squadron was ordered to occupy the island of Cos and from there to harry the enemy.

Any highly organized landing on Cos was out of the question. There was need for speed and surprise. The ground crews were to be infiltrated on to the island in ships and transport aircraft. On 28th September 1943 four aircraft flew from Nicosia in Cyprus and landed in Cos. An airstrip had been fashioned by the ground crews, using bullocks towing a length of railway line as a scraper and then rough-rolling it. By that afternoon JU88s were already bombing the island. The German intelligence system was good! The bombing continued, the airstrip became unserviceable and the airmen withdrew into what shelter they could find. On 3rd October Cos was attacked and after some loss the survivors were evacuated, having achieved exactly nothing. Meanwhile, at Simi, another detachment of No. 74 Squadron destined for Cos had been halted by a 'Special Boat Squadron' unit under the command of a remarkable character called Captain La Praik. He had discovered by reconnaissance that Cos was in enemy hands and hence that the R.A.F. could do no good by proceeding. This was on 3rd October. The R.A.F. party disembarked on Simi Island and here Captain La Praik issued the most remarkable order of the day that it has been my good fortune to read.

After painting the tactical picture in almost official language and then explaining the gravity of the situation he suffered a lapse into barrack-room language. . . . 'We can understand the gravity of our situation so for Chrisake let's get our fingers out and get weaving and we'll show these sods what we are capable of.' La Praik then went on to give some very sensible advice about the manner in which the fighting should be conducted and then lapsed again. 'Lastly, when you hear yourselves referred to as "the bloody R.A.F." it is no more derogatory than No. 1 Patrol being referred to as "a lot of flickering Bimoses" or No. 4 Patrol being "those bastard bloody gunners".

So far you have worked hard and well without moaning so keep it up, but remember—be bloody quick on the job and keep on your toes because if you don't you've flickering well had it.'

This remarkable adjuration, fully justified in the circumstances, produced excellent results. The German invasion came at first light on 6th October. A Commando party nearly a hundred strong arrived in a caique from Rhodes. They were fired upon but landed at Pedi Bay and made their way up to a ridge overlooking Simi town. Some penetrated to the upper town and sniped from the houses. These troops had only rifles, machine-guns and hand-grenades, so the Breda-and Bren-guns available to the defenders were of great value. One of these Bredas was manned by Flight Sergeant Schofield, who wore spectacles on account of short sight. Schofield continued to use his gun even when his spectacles were broken by vibration, the flash eliminator burned off, and the sights had fallen off from the over-heated weapon. All the time he was exposed to ground and air attack. Not satisfied with what he had achieved, he managed to capture a prisoner single-handed and only went to the dressing station when a wound he had suffered earlier on turned septic. His Military Medal was very well earned.

Meanwhile, the dive-bombers had been at work. The temporary Headquarters was hit and a sergeant and sixteen airmen were killed. The squadron doctor, Flight Lieutenant Ferris, behaved with the utmost gallantry. His medical equipment was destroyed so he worked with a hand saw and a pair of scissors. A man trapped under fallen masonry had his leg amputated with these tools. To reach him Ferris had to hang head downwards in the hole, his ankles being held by two airmen. Hardly the best position to carry out such an operation, but nevertheless he succeeded. Ferris also attended Greek casualties, injured when the local hospital was bombed.

In the end the land battle turned in our favour. Sixteen Germans were killed and six prisoners taken. The remainder of the enemy took to their caique and escaped.

Out of the original party of No. 74 Squadron airmen that landed at Simi—some forty to fifty strong—thirty-seven made their way back to Cyprus. There the remains of No. 74 were reunited at Peristerona. Their welcome was hardly calculated to raise their spirits: 'The rain began and continued until everything was swamped out. Most of the tents leaked and so all clothes and bedding were soaked.'

It is worth considering that fewer than fifty airmen, untrained in land warfare, had beaten off the attack of double the number of German Commando troops, and driven them back into their ship. Jolly good show, chaps!

A year later fighting still went on in the Eastern Mediterranean. Though the German Army had been ousted from the Balkans there were still a number of trouble-makers in this theatre who were using the Greek Communists, the ELAS insurgents, for their own purposes. Sergeant J. G. McEvoy tells a story of these difficult times. He was a codes and ciphers man, attached to Air Headquarters at Kiphissia near Athens.

'On 19th December 1944 the H.Q. was attacked by ELAS. During the first attack a humorous incident occurred. The main ELAS force was drawn up in a fairly straight line at the back of the hotel we were defending. The noise of gunfire was deafening when suddenly a whistle blew and both sides ceased fire. A figure in khaki battledress appeared from behind the ELAS lines, jumped the barbed-wire fence and walked up the slope towards us. As he came nearer he stopped and spoke to some of our men, and then, when he passed me, he said in very good English: "Good morning, Sergeant. How are you?" Thinking that he was one of the Greek officers attached to our H.Q., I replied, "Very well, thank you, sir." As it turned out he was one of the enemy and, after a talk with our officers, he went back to his own lines. A day later we were taken prisoners, and although a local chieftain addressed us as his brothers, we were stripped of everything of value that we possessed. A week later, marching through the mountains we stopped at a village and were herded into a barn. Two Germans came in to see us, obviously hand in glove with ELAS, and one of them said, "Well, the positions are very much reversed now, aren't they?"'

This is an ugly story, but illustrative of the confusion that existed at the time. According to the canons of conventional warfare this headquarters should not have been under threat of attack, much less overrun. But Greece was in a turmoil. Left-wing elements found the going easy when starvation and disease preyed upon the population. Banditry was the most profitable form of employment, arms and ammunition abandoned by the Germans or provided by us to the dissidents were in plentiful supply. Who cared for the British? They had failed the Greeks once before; they might fail them again and in any case they were trusting and friendly and so easily dealt with.

From Greece to Ceylon. W. G. Comeau, who had a bellyful of fighting on the ground in Greece and Crete, found his way by devious means (he admits they were almost desertions) with No. 11 Squadron to the Scented Island.

No. 11 had served well and faithfully in North Africa, and had considerable experience of advancing and retreating across the sands of Libya. Ceylon was a big change!

On arrival, the airmen soon became aware of the unpreparedness of Ceylon's defences. In such a paradise most of the troops were content to live for the day, taking full advantage of the many amenities the island had to offer; on the other hand, evacuees from Singapore were spreading depressing stories about the invincible Jap. Yellow-robed, pro-Japanese, Buddhist priests wandered through the flights at will, unmolested and making notes openly. There was a rift between the Desert and the Far East personnel difficult to bridge. Free fights were commonplace.

Defensive weapons were few and most of the available armament was locked up in army stores. The island could have been captured before the troops had time to arm themselves. No. 11 Squadron's airmen deplored this state of affairs. Fed up with running away they decided that, come what may, they intended to stand firm. Two projects stemmed from this decision: to form guerilla bands capable of independent action and to put up adequate aerodrome defences.

Meanwhile groups of blackened-faced erks exercised every night around and about Colombo. Airmen took turns to plan the nightly manœuvre, setting up road blocks and invading civilian gardens and houses. Although it was all very serious there were plenty of amusing episodes. One airman hung for two hours in a tree swarming with white ants. His colleague across the road sat on a civilian verandah, tommy-gun on his lap, sipping iced drinks and being entertained by his host's two attractive daughters. A Sinhalese family was terrified when an L.A.C. fell through their roof into a water tank, and one friendly civilian aided an 'escaping' airman with a ladder with which the erk climbed a high wall; he flatly refused to allow the pursuers to borrow it.

Q

Given a free hand with the aerodrome defences, soon stakes, barbed wire, thirty tommy-guns, and numerous boxes of hand-grenades were assembled, material painstakingly stolen from army dumps. Obtaining it had been a test of the airmen's ingenuity.

Soon the defences took shape. The ground-gunners, proud of their Middle East record, reacted so sharply at night that even the Station Adjutant would make a detour rather than cross the aerodrome and receive the inevitable machine-gun burst above his head.

Now armed with tommy-guns, the guerilla bands were beginning to make the army sit up, especially after two airmen entered an army camp and mock-sabotaged it. The camp chosen had been guarded by keen-as-mustard Sinhalese recruits.

No. 11 Squadron claimed that the example it had shown caused Higher Authority to sit up. In any case the squadron's activities had an immediate impact upon the complacent army camps who afterwards brought out a series of arms and jungle-training courses. Their respect was great enough for them to pit a Company of beefy Dutch Commandos against No. 11's defences at a later date.

On the eve of the Jap attacks Wing Commander Smythe, the C.O., assembled the whole squadron. In an electric atmosphere and without mincing words he told the men what to expect and he knew at that moment that the whole squadron was behind him. The C.O. was respected because, while encouraging the fighting spirit of his airmen, he had allowed them a free hand in carrying out their training. With officers and N.C.O.s detailed to see that the job was done, the enthusiasm would have disappeared.

Afterwards, willing hands fused the grenades, slinging them back in their boxes and dispersing them by rickshaw to strategic points. Ignorant of his cargo, each coolie received an additional 15 cents 'Danger Money'.

The following day became the blackest in the squadron's history when all the available Blenheims, sent to bomb the Jap fleet, were shot down. The pick of the aircrews were lost; men who had served in the squadron for years, looked upon as personal friends by ground crews and aircrews alike. And the laboriously created defences were never tested! So much for human endeavour.

While the airmen of No. 11 Squadron were preparing for battle in Ceylon, the R.A.F. in India was growing new wings. The battering it had received during the retreat from Burma and in the disastrous

Indonesian campaign had been grievous, but time, new equipment and fresh personnel were restoring the air situation. Soon the 14th Army, under the cover of the 'Air Command South-East Asia', was to go over to the offensive and drive the enemy to defeat. Through the Chin Hills and down the Irrawaddy the airmen ploughed their way in jeeps and trucks until the victory parade in Rangoon gave them their reward. A squadron leader comments, 'The air operations which played so important a part in the advance of the 14th Army could not have been possible but for the devotion, the endurance and the magnificent work of the ground crews! . . .' I met some of these men in Calcutta, in Comilla (R.A.F. H.Q. in Assam), at Cox's Bazaar, a fighter station on the Arakan coast, and at Meiktila after the battle, and they made me feel very proud of my service. Mostly wearing nothing but shorts, shoes and a bush hat, brown as berries and tough as old boots, living on a bare ration and exposed to a number of unpleasant tropical diseases, they worked cheerfully and diligently so that 'kites' could take the air when needed. At times they had to act as infantry, as at Imphal when Japanese patrols got inside our lines. In the dark there might be a quite lively encounter between L.A.C. Jones, wielding a rifle and bayonet as skilfully as he used a spanner by day, and a determined and resourceful enemy with an unpronounceable name. Jones usually emerged unscathed from the contest and entitled to cut one more notch on his rifle butt. Meanwhile, there was the matter of the daily inspection of his aircraft to be carried out and as dawn came up the midnight hero, yawning mightily, would turn over to routine duties.

It seems to me that the adaptability of the airman was one of his greatest virtues. He may have been a bit of a nuisance in other respects, but give him a strange new job to do and he would make a very good fist at it.

22

The Round-up

IN OCTOBER 1945 there were 1,250,000 men and women in air-force blue. In ten years the service, from a figure of 30,000, had grown to this great number, and still, most remarkably, had retained its cohesion. This is not to say that the general level of efficiency, discipline and skill reached that of the experts of the earlier days. Having regard, however, to the greater complexity of the equipment they had to handle they were very close on the heels of their predecessors. In my opinion, if there was one highly developed virtue they possessed it was that of teamwork. In times of difficulty man turns to his neighbour for comfort, and the R.A.F. was no exception to this rule. In the dark days of 1940 the squadrons worked as one man and the spirit built up at this time informed the entire service.

There is little doubt of course that the hard core of regulars and in particular the ex-apprentices were a stabilizing influence. Nevertheless, a 40 to 1 dilution must have placed an immense strain on the loyalty of the 'old sweats'. But the strain was taken successfully! This then was the nature, broadly speaking, of the vast force that was demobilized in 1945–6 with little trouble. There was no recurrence, at any rate on an important scale, of the mutinies that took place in 1919. The machinery of discharge worked reasonably efficiently and with basic fairness. In this connection the issue of a suit of plain clothes to each departing airman had an odd and nefarious consequence. The civilian population were still rationed as to clothes and a new suit had a very high value on the Black Market. Spivs attended at every demobilization centre and offered large sums for the parcel of civvies that the airmen carried. The early mugs were taken for a ride, but soon our 'wide boys' were on the job. The trade continued, but in the official parcel bought by the spivs there was nothing but crumpled newspaper! The lessons on scrounging and other sharp practices that the airmen had been taught during their period of service had not been wasted!

In the plans made during the latter part of the war the Air Ministry had made certain decisions in regard to the size and character of the post-war Air Force. Unfortunately, Russia's behaviour and the need to remain strong in the face of her threats did nothing to help these plans, which had to be recast. National Service continued and with some justice it can be said that in the immediate post-war years the discipline and efficiency of the R.A.F. was at a low ebb. It was therefore very refreshing to meet one of the peace-time airmen who had sound views on both these subjects. Travelling from Buntingford in Hertfordshire to London, sometime in 1949, I entered a carriage in which a young aircraftsman was in deep conversation with a grey-haired man who sported a R.F.C. tie. The gist of the boy's conversation was this. For two years he had been at a station where discipline was strict and efficiency at a premium. Every airman was happy because he knew exactly what was expected of him. A move to a new station had produced a very different result. There discipline was very slack; the work was carried out in a slovenly manner; and the airmen did not salute their officers. The boy had no doubts whatsoever that firstly discipline, and then efficiency, made for a happy station.

Starry-eyed liberals are always tilting against discipline. Enlisted men are encouraged by these people to voice complaints to their M.P.s or to write to the Press. There is a fanciful idea now that all Britons are so intelligent they can judge for themselves whether an order is reasonable or unreasonable and act according to their own views. History has shown a thousand times and will continue to exemplify the principle that discipline is the basis of success, whether in the life of an individual, in the Armed Forces, or within a nation. The discipline of the R.A.F. has been restored by the methods found applicable in recent years, and it is my impression that it is a happy service. There is so much to interest—so much to which the men can look forward. Not only will they service supersonic aircraft of great range and hitting power, but before them lies the whole field of missile development. As things are progressing today the modern highbrow airman may find himself in a position where he may actually press the button that launches the 'weapon'. Such a position of authority is something to look forward to and work for. But as one of those who believe that conventional weapons as we know them now will be with us for many years, I feel there will still be a need in the R.A.F. for the type of individual I have tried to describe in this story. Bless 'em all, boys and girls together! They are (most of them) of the salt of the earth!

Principal Events 1871-1947

1871   Formation of a committee of Royal Engineer officers to study the employment of balloons in a reconnaissance role.

1878   Establishment of Balloon Equipment Store at Woolwich.

1882   Balloon Equipment Store moved to Chatham, where it was renamed the School of Ballooning.

1890   Balloon Section Royal Engineers formed and moved to Aldershot in 1891.

1897   Balloon Factory under a Superintendent (Major Templer) established at Farnborough, Hants.

1911   Air Battalion Royal Engineers formed at Farnborough.

1912   Royal Flying Corps (Naval and Military Wings) formed, absorbing the Air Battalion and the Naval Air Service.

1914   The Naval Air Arm breaks away and forms the Royal Naval Air Service.

1914-18   The Kaiser War. Expansion of Royal Flying Corps from some 100 officers and 3000 men to 30,000 officers and 300,000 men and women (W.R.A.F. formed 1918). R.N.A.S. final expansion reached 50,000 of all ranks.

1918   Formation of Royal Air Force. R.N.A.S. joined the R.F.C. in this new organization.

1919   Almost complete demobilization of the R.A.F.

1922   The start of reorganization. Trenchard's policy of a sound base before expansion and rearmament.

1937   Part of the naval side of the R.A.F. breaks away to form the Fleet Air Arm (decision of the Inskip Committee).

1939   Outbreak of Hitler War, and subsequent expansion of Royal Air Force to a total strength of one million and a quarter men and women.

1946   Partial demobilization, but retention of some 300,000 men and women in the post-war Air Force. Continuance of National Service.

The arrival of jet aircraft in service squadrons.

The V. bomber project commenced.

Six aircraft firms given contracts for missile development.

1947 onwards.   The strength of the R.A.F. maintained at about 200,000. The squadrons equipped with jet aircraft of very modern design —the fighters armed with the Aden gun and missiles and the bombers with the 'deterrent'.

Index